CLIMBERS' CLUB GUIDES
Edited by Bob Moulton

Southern Sandstone

by Dave Turner

Chalk Sea Cliffs section by Mick Fowler

Outcrop Drawings by Ben Bevan-Pritchard

Maps by Don Sargeant

Published by the CLIMBERS' CLUB

First Edition (South East England) 1956, Reprinted 1960
by E.C.Pyatt.

Second Edition (South East England) 1963
by E.C.Pyatt with Appendix by D.G. Fagan, J.V. Smoker and E.C.Pyatt

Third Edition (South East England) 1969, Reprinted 1974
by E.C.Pyatt and L.R.Holliwell

Fourth Edition (Southern Sandstone) 1981
by T.J.H.Daniells

Fifth Edition (Southern Sandstone) 1989
by D.B.Turner

© The Climbers Club 1989

British Library Cataloguing in Publication Data
Turner, Dave
  Southern Sandstone. — 5th ed./by Dave Turner/Chalk sea cliffs by Mick Fowler/outcrop drawings by Ben Bevan-Pritchard/maps by Don Sargeant
  1. South-east England. Sandstone regions. Rock climbing. Manuals
  I. Title II. Fowler, Mike III. Daniells, Tim
  796.5'223'09422

  ISBN 0-901601-46-2

front cover:	Slab Boulder, High Rocks *Climber: Guy Mclelland* Photo: Dave Jones
back cover:	Henry the Ninth, 5b, High Rocks. *Climber: Dave Turner* Photo: Ben Pritchard
frontispiece:	Fandango Right Hand, 6a, Bowles Rocks *Climber: Dave Jones* Photo: Gordon Staniforth
reverse of frontispiece	Bludnock Wall, 5c, High Rocks. *Climber: Paul Hayes* Photo: Steve Gordon

Data conversion by Transprint Communications and Acorn Printing and Typesetting, Bath

Produced by The Ernest Press, Glasgow

Printed by Martins of Berwick

CONTENTS

Acknowledgements	page 7
Introduction	9
Historical	17
Bassett's Farm Rocks	24
Bowles Rocks	29
Bulls Hollow Rocks	52
Eridge Green Rocks	58
Harrison's Rocks	72
High Rocks	113
High Rocks Annexe	144
Stone Farm Rocks	149
Under Rockes	158
Minor Outcrops	162
Chiddinglye Wood Rocks	162
Penns Rocks	166
Ramslye Farm Rocks	169
Other Outcrops (listed alphabetically)	171
Other Rock	181
The Sea Cliffs of South East England	183
Margate Area	186
Dover	186
Hastings	194
Beachy Head	197
Cuckmere Haven	200
Brighton	201
Commandments	203
Graded List of Selected Climbs	204
Rescue - Sandstone Area	208

MAPS AND PLANS

The Sandstone Area - map	front end leaf
The Central Sandstone Area - map	8
Bassett's Farm Area - map	24
Bassett's Farm	27
Bowles Rocks - Western Half	30/31
Bowles Rocks - Eastern Half	40/41
Bulls Hollow Rocks	53
Eridge Green Rocks - Southern Half	60/61
Eridge Green Rocks - Northern Half	68/69
Harrison's Rocks - general map	73
Harrison's Rocks - Northern End	76/77
Harrison's Rocks - North Central Section	78/79
Harrison's Rocks - South Central Section	88/89
Harrison's Rocks - Southern Wing	102/103
High Rocks - general map	115
High Rocks - Eastern End (Continuation Wall)	116/117
High Rocks - Central Section	120/121
High Rocks - Western end	127
High Rocks Annexe	146/147
Stone Farm/East Grinstead Area - map	149
Stone Farm Rocks - Western half	152/153
Stone Farm Rocks - Eastern half	154/155
Under Rockes Area - map	158
Under Rockes - plan	161
Chiddinglye Wood Rocks	165
Penns Rocks	167
South East England Map	rear end leaf

DRAWINGS

Bassett's Farm - Main Wall	page 25
Bowles Rocks - Fandango Wall	35
Digitalis Wall	37
Sapper Area	39
Range Wall	43
Hate Buttress	45
Funnel Wall	47
Finale Area	51
Eridge Green Rocks - Sandstorm	63
Romulus Area	67
Portcullis Block	71
Harrison's Rocks - West Face of North Boulder	75
Slab Bay/Luncheon Shelf	83
Luncheon Shelf/The Flakes Area	85
Slimfinger Wall	87
Circle Climb Area	91
Necklace Block	93
Wellington Block	95
Two-Toed Sloth Area	99
The Isolated Buttress	101
Muscle Crack Area	107
Unclimbed Wall	111
High Rocks - Warning Rock	125
Grand Canyon - Left Side	131
Coronation Crack	133
Tilley Lamp Wall	135
Honeycomb Area	139
The Isolated Boulder	141

PHOTOGRAPHS

Slab Boulder, High Rock	Front Cover
Bludnock Wall, High Rocks	Reverse of Frontispiece
Fandango Right Hand, Bowles Rocks	Frontispiece
Sugar Plum, Bowles Rocks	Opposite Page 16
Temptation, Bowles Rocks	17
Digitalis, Bowles Rocks	32
Inspiration, Bowles Rocks	33
Devaluation, Bowles Rocks	48
Hate, Bowles Rocks	49
Long Layback, Harrisons Rocks	80
What Crisis?	81
The Republic, Harrisons Rocks	96
Wooly Bear, Harrisons Rocks	97
Philippa, Harrisons Rocks	112
New Route, High Rocks	113
Krait Arête, High Rocks	128
Dyno Sore, High Rocks	129
Honeycombe, High Rocks	176
Primative Corner, Stone Farm Rocks	177
Great White Fright, Dover	192
Fisherman's Friend, Dover	193
Henry the Ninth, High Rocks	Back Cover

ACKNOWLEDGEMENTS

My thanks are due: to Tim Daniells whose guide provided the basis for this book; to the writers of all the earlier guides for similar reasons; to Trevor Panther and his Harrison's guides, from which some useful historical and route information was gleaned; to Don Sargeant for his crag maps; and to all those whose efforts have contributed to a better guide, in particular Gary "Gazzer" Wickham and Gordon Staniforth.

The photographs were kindly supplied by Ben Pritchard, Mick Fowler, Steve Gorton, Dave Jones, Geoff Pearson, Gordon Staniforth and Ed Stone. I would also like to thank those who offered photos which were ultimately not used.

The historical section is based on that written by Bob Moulton in the 1981 guide.

Mick Fowler kindly wrote the greatly enlarged Chalk Sea Cliffs Section, based in part on a manuscript written by Gordon Jenkin.

My main thanks must go to Ben Pritchard - "The Boy Whimper" - for the excellent line drawings of the outcrops, for a number of the photographs, for checking through much of the text and perhaps most of all for co-driving under circumstances which were, to say the least, stressful.

Dave Turner 1989.

DISCLAIMER

Should any differences or discrepancies in description or grade of the ensuant contents thereof hereafter to be known as the same arise the same shall be referred to arbitration in accordance with the statutory provisions for the time being in force applicable thereto but for which herewithallwithout or perhaps not the writer accomplices and contributive malefactors herein involved completely deny any liability or indeed culpability as they do for all attempts through or in connection with the text at witticism humour sarcasm or blatant character assassination whilst at the same time all aforementioned grades were correct at the time of writing and the same which are not quite the same same as the same mentioned previously maybe and probably perhaps henceforward are fully inclusive of Various Alien Techniques henceforth to be known as VAT however all liable parties reserve the right to deny his her or its identity when confronted by or with any such irate enquiries pertinent to the subject matter hereafter stated in fact the aforesaid same while the above is in totality underwritten by the overseer who undertook an obligation to uphold the downbeat though highly idyllic undertones encompassed in the ascendant narrative laid down upon these hallowed pages hereafter or thereafter if you are somewhere else.

Also available on CD.

With special thanks to the legal profession.

8 INTRODUCTION

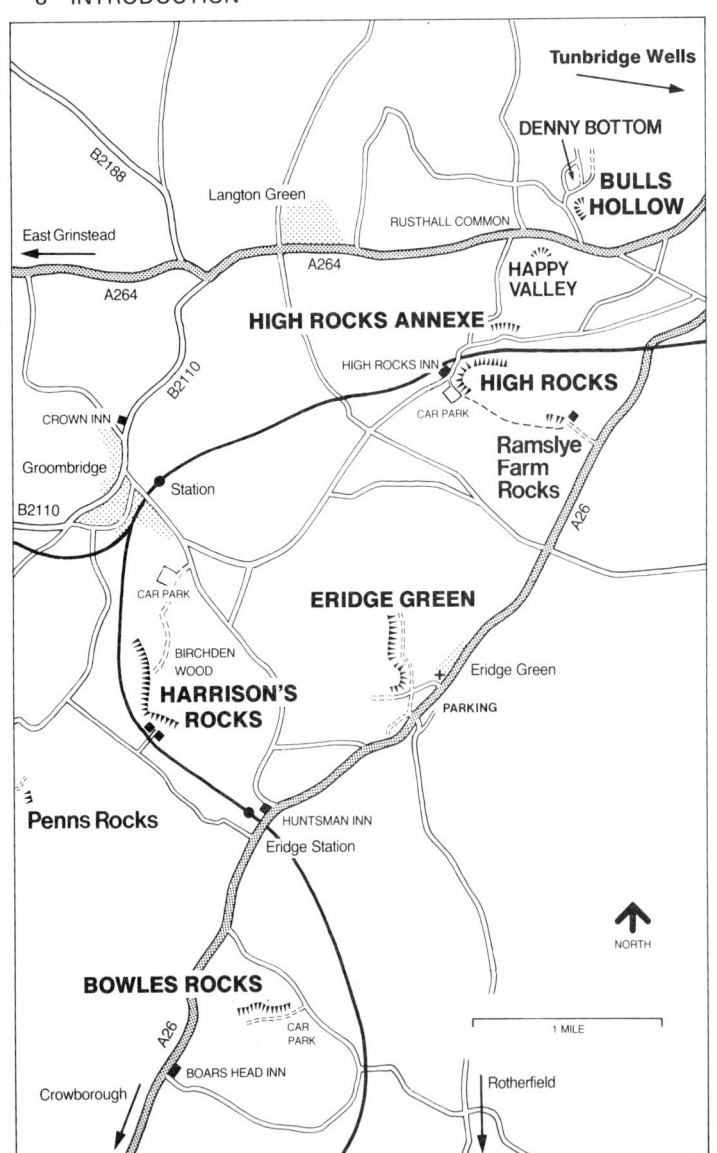

Introduction

This book is a thorough revision of Tim Daniells' 1981 Southern Sandstone guide. A number of innovations have been introduced largely in terms of "modernisation" so as to align this guide where appropriate with standards elsewhere. The major changes that will be noticed are the inclusion of line drawings of the outcrops and the adoption of a star rating system. The drawings will hopefully not only make route finding easier but also enhance the general appearance of the book. There have been a surprisingly large number of new routes to document mostly and necessarily in the highest grades, the easier lines having long since been climbed. Furthermore, the softness of the rock means that holds are constantly changing so that the grades of many long-standing routes need revision.

The three most popular outcrops, Bowles, Harrison's and Stone Farm, seem to be attracting more climbers than ever whilst many other outcrops are still relatively neglected. With the use of the star rating system it is hoped to encourage climbers to explore more widely and thus spread the load away from the Big Three. High Rocks certainly deserves more attention particularly by those climbing at 5b and more, whilst Bulls Hollow, Under Rockes and Bassett's Farm are all well worth a look.

The book remains largely devoted to the Wealden sandstone but with a much enlarged coverage of chalk sea cliff climbing, reflecting the commendable and increasing activity of assorted loonies there. This section is written by Mick Fowler. It goes without saying that climbing chalk is extremely serious and it should be treated with a great deal of trepidation.

GENERAL RAVE

The sandstone outcrops of the Central Weald provide a relaxed and popular playground for climbers in the South East, as well as for visitors perhaps travelling to or from the continent. The very pleasant woodland settings and comparatively laid-back attitude in the area contrasts strongly with the generally more serious climbing to be found elsewhere. This is not least exemplified by the local top-roping ethic, itself wholly justified by the friable nature of the rock. There are "no mind blowing runouts on impending headwalls" to be had here, unless of course you head for the chalk sea cliffs.

The visitor may be surprised by the number of rules and guidelines but after a short acquaintance with the area the need for these will be apparent. Sandstone is a very soft rock and thus requires much care to keep it intact as a climbing venue. Please read the section on Erosion below.

The area is well endowed with good Pubs, many of them Free Houses. The Crown Inn, Groombridge, and The Boars Head, near Bowles, are both indicated on the maps but there are many others of equal worth. The location of the new routes book tends to vary; currently it is to be found in The Crown Inn. From time to time over the last two decades a 'climbers cafe' has been open in Groombridge. Unfortunately, this has recently closed down, leaving only a more up-market cafe outside High Rocks though there are plenty more in Tunbridge Wells.

THE ROCK
Geologically the outcrops occur within the Tunbridge Wells Sand formation which is itself part of the Hastings Beds group of sandstones, silts and clays. These are the oldest rocks that crop out in the south-east and they occur within the core of the Wealden Dome where, because of their generally resistant nature, they form the broad deeply-dissected ridge known as the High Weald. Sandstones occur at several stratigraphical levels in the Hastings Beds, but only those in the Tunbridge Wells Sand are sufficiently thick and resistant to form natural crags solid enough for climbing. The sandstone is a sedimentary deposit formed in the Wealden lake in the Cretaceous period, about 100 million years ago. It is a young deposit, in geological terms, and is little more than a compacted sand with some surface hardening caused by secondary sedimentation. All the detailed features result from wind and water erosion and none from the shattering which provides the lines of weakness on the older volcanic rocks of the mountain districts.

Where the surface is case-hardened and the rock dry the frictional qualities can be very good. The main features are deep cracks and chimneys separated by rounded bulging buttresses. Slabs are infrequent, though there are many good easier-angled climbs at Bowles Rocks. The holds tend to be rounded and sloping with few (natural) incuts and therefore need or eventually develop good arm strength, not least because one often cannot trust ones feet. In places the wind has eroded pockets in the rock, often deep enough to provide good holds. The softness of the rock is well illustrated by these pockets, the edges of which break off easily under stress. Further weathering can produce jug-handle type holds which eventually break leaving projecting knobs that are much poorer holds.

Those outcrops which are shaded by trees can get into bad condition after rain and may revert only slowly to a climbable state. This is often exacerbated by the fact that the rock is porous and can become saturated with water. As surface moisture evaporates it draws further water to the surface by capillary action, greatly prolonging the drying time. Lichens can then grow on the faces making the holds slimy and difficult to use. Vegetation flourishes in places and can be a hindrance in areas that have been neglected for a time.

ACCESS AND THE ENVIRONMENT
All the outcrops in this guide form part of the inhabited countryside and as such are on private or Forestry Commision land. Climbing is allowed only through the cooperation of the landowners (or perhaps blissful ignorance in the case of some minor crags). At two of the major outcrops there is a payment for access which will be

unacceptable to many climbers, particularly the excessive charge at High Rocks. Some efforts are being made by the BMC and others to change this latter situation.

As in previous editions information is given of outcrops where climbing is not permitted; full details of known access restrictions being noted. This is not intended to encourage climbing on such outcrops but in order to maintain a record of what has been done so as to provide information should a given access situation ever change.

THE INCLUSION OF AN OUTCROP OR ROUTES UPON IT IN THIS GUIDE-BOOK DOES NOT MEAN THAT ANY MEMBER OF THE PUBLIC HAS THE RIGHT OF ACCESS TO THE OUTCROP OR THE RIGHT TO CLIMB UPON IT.

The sandstone outcrops of Kent and Essex provide a moist and sheltered environment much akin to that of the west coast of Britain. As a result many of the rock plants here are similar to those of that coast. It is believed that such plants have persisted in these specialised habitats, well outside their normal distribution range, since about 5,600 years ago when the whole country experienced a warmer and wetter climate than now. As a result there are a number of very rare species of Mosses and Liverworts associated with the rock, for the protection of which (and other features) certain outcrops are designated as Sites of Special Scientific Interest (SSSI). These are pointed out in the text. In addition, polygonal markings in the rock face itself can be found at High Rocks which are very rare in the south east and thus of some geological interest. In the interests of science (and to keep such areas open to climbers) it is important that great care be taken to avoid unnecessary damage to the rock and associated flora.

EROSION

As mentioned above the major well known outcrops continue to bear the brunt of the increasing popularity of sandstone as a climbing ground. Indeed, it has surprised many long term habitues, particularly at Harrisons, how well the somewhat fragile sandstone has stood up to the abuse it receives. This is not to be complacent however.

The intensive use of Bowles, Harrison's and Stone Farm in particular has led to a great deal of largely avoidable erosion, particularly at the tops of climbs. The rock is relatively soft and friable and is suffering appalling damage in some areas. In places deep unsightly rope grooves have appeared, sometimes over a foot deep, which eventually break off leaving a sandy scar. Once the case hardened surface is removed and the sandy interior exposed further erosion by the elements is greatly accelerated. At Bowles and Harrison's the respective Managements (and a number of commendable volunteers in the latter case) now tend to fill in the rope grooves with concrete before the damage becomes irrevocable. However, this should not be necessary - prevention rather than cure should be the operative word.

IT IS ABSOLUTELY ESSENTIAL WHEN TOP-ROPING TO USE A

LONG BELAY SLING AND POSITION THE KARABINER JUST OVER THE EDGE OF THE CRAG SO AS TO MINIMISE DAMAGE TO THE ROCK BY MOVING ROPES.

IF YOU SEE THIS BEING IGNORED PLEASE MAKE POLITE OR STRONGER SUGGESTIONS AS TO THE CORRECT PROCEDURE.

CHIPPING
UNDER NO CIRCUMSTANCES SHOULD HOLDS BE CUT OR CHIPPED. This practice is still going on, particularly at Stone Farm and those involved are pathetic. If you catch anyone doing this please stop them. There is no one here to repair damage and if unchecked the situation will eventually be irretrievable. Many of the routes chipped in the past have now been climbed without using the cut holds and the same will eventually happen to today's chipadeedoo-dahs (to plagiarise a word from the slate scene) care of a future generation. Sandstone crags are not slate quarries. Please leave problems you can't do to someone better (or with stickier boot rubber) rather than vandalizing the rock.

ETHICS AND THINGS
Southern Sandstone is unusual in that top-roping is the normal and accepted style of ascent. This ethic has evolved and is maintained because the soft and friable nature of the rock does not lend itself to leading. Conventional protection devices badly damage the rock and the sandstone will often fail anyway in the event of a fall. It has been suggested that bolts be placed on Sandstone to enable leading but this seems pointless given the ease with which top-ropes can be placed and because of the damage such bolting would inevitably bring about. The choice lies between soloing or top-roping, with the exception of Temptation at Bowles which can be led clipping the in situ bolts. A few other routes have been led with normal protection but this practice is not to be encouraged. Soloing is recognized as ultimately the best style of ascent. Soloists should obviously treat all but the best holds with extreme caution. Clearly top-roping enables one to push oneself to the limit in complete safety (depending on who is belaying!) and rapid improvement in ability is thus possible for beginners. Nearly all the hard climbs were sieged on their first ascents, an approach which predates the current trend on bolt-protected limestone routes - hard climbing under safe conditions.

The use of chalk as an aid to climbing has been the cause of some bitter argument in this area, despite its widespread acceptance (or at least widespread use) elsewhere. However, at the crags where the use of chalk was once banned it is now tolerated. In general it is suggested that its use be kept to a minimum; that is, use it but don't throw it everywhere. Powdered resin in the form of a poff (as used by Fontainebleau climbers) is becoming more popular as an aid to friction and it also seems to be less visually offensive than chalk. A poff typically consists of a handful of resin crystals placed in a piece of cloth and tied off into a ball with string; it is then hit against footholds (or handholds) to release a fine sticky dust.

The softness of the rock raises an ethical problem in that cleaning out a hold is often indistinguishable from enlarging it - brushing the sandstone even just a little too hard can create or remove holds, so please take care.

EQUIPMENT

It is recommended that an old rope be used for top-roping since the abrasive nature of the rock can quickly ruin a new one. The ideal rope is the hawser laid nylon type, not least because of cost. New kernmantel leading ropes are pretty much a waste on sandstone, though tougher non-stretchy caving ropes can be recommended. To avoid causing or enlarging rope grooves the top-rope should be arranged with a belay sling long enough to allow the (screw gate) karabiner to hang over the edge of the face. Ropes should not be run directly around trees or through in situ bolts because the former will be killed and the latter simply worn through, thus requiring costly replacement. The rock is suffering a great deal from such abuse so please follow this advice and help preserve the rock for as long as possible.

Soft rock boots only should be worn, such as E.B.'s, Firés etc or training shoes, plimsolls and so on. Heavy duty climbing or walking boots should NOT be worn. Some local climbers favour barefoot climbing which, though uncomfortable initially, can be very useful for cramming toes into small pockets if you like that sort of thing.

The use of a mat or cloth to clean boots is recommended while the practice of blowing sand off holds before using them is well worth adopting.

AID CLIMBING

The few artificial routes described are rarely ascended and have very little in the way of in situ aid points. Their inclusion is purely for the record and should not be taken as encouragement to aid climb. Many past aid routes have since been free climbed (for example, Patella, Kinnard, Temptation, Sossblitz, The King etc). At Harrison's and High Rocks there are TOTAL BANS ON AID CLIMBING largely to prevent the damage that inevitably results. However, the use of jammed sling knots etc is of course no problem, though even here care should be exercised.

ABSEILING

Abseiling down climbs is best avoided at all times because of the ease with which holds can be broken off. There is a TOTAL BAN ON ABSEILING AT HARRISON'S. If one has to abseil please do not do so down existing routes and in other places bear in mind that what appears unclimbable may well not be so. The *only* major crag with any really blank faces is High Rocks; there are virtually no faces untouched by free routes at any of the other major outcrops.

It is appreciated that abseiling can form an important part of many introductory courses but please choose your site carefully. A possible alternative is to find a suitable building, which would almost certainly give a longer and thus more exciting descent. Climbing walls are also good venues - see the list below. Suggested sites at High Rocks are:-(1) a metre right (facing the crag) of Coronation Crack (no.136) but certainly not the pocketed wall just left of Krait Arête; (2) the large concave wall left of Chockstone Chimney (no.82) which is holdless; (3) the wall up the slope to the left of Salad Days (no.88); (4) there are many big blank walls in the Continuation area left of Sorrow (no.79); (5) any of the numerous bridges at High Rocks (owner permitting).

THE GRADINGS

A numerical grade is given for each route ranging from the easiest, 1a, rising through 2a, 2b, 3a, 3b, 4a, 4b, 4c, 5a, 5b, 5c, 6a, 6b, to the current top grade of 6c. Wherever possible the grade given is the collated opinion of many climbers. The letters NS in brackets after the grade mean that at the time of writing the climb has not been soloed; it has of course been climbed totally free (one hopes) whilst top-roping. The grades given are for good conditions while those climbs that seem to be in a permanently poor state are often indicated in the text.

The 6c grade has now been introduced for a few climbs and it may be that some of these warrant 7a or indeed are over-graded - only time will tell. The use of this new grade obviously reflects rising standards but also enables some of the wide disparities within the grades below to be relieved. In this vein a general policy of upgrading where reasonable has been followed despite the tendency to downgrade by locals. It should be borne in mind that repeated top-roping of familiar climbs does tend to reduce their difficulty to the purely physical. Visitors shouldn't be put off by locals who know where all the holds are and have done the routes three million times before. Some can climb 6a or more on sandstone but drop down to about VS when leading elsewhere, so take heart sandstone bumblies.

STARS AND DAGGERS

No, not a section on bitching and back-stabbing by budding superheroes though it might be more fun......... However, stars have been allocated to some routes to pick them out as better climbs than their neighbours and to help indicate those crags or parts of crags worth a look. Clearly, the stars only apply when the routes are in condition, which in some cases is not very often. Three stars have been reserved for the best, two for the very good and one for recommended routes at each grade. The absence of stars does not necessarily mean that a route is unworthwhile, merely that others on the *same* crag are better. This applies particularly to Bowles which has so many good climbs. A certain bias in favour of higher grade routes may be noticed. This is not to put down lower grade climbs but reflects the simple fact that many of the best lines are in the higher grades. The dagger signs have been used to indicate unrepeated routes, for which the grade is more uncertain than most.

NEW CLIMBS

There is a new routes book in the The Crown Inn, Groombridge, though its location tends to change quite regularly. It should not only be used to record new routes but also to record changes to existing routes, repeat ascents, comments, wit(?) etc.

CLIMBING WALLS

There are a number of climbing walls in the south-east, some of which are included here for those interested. The list is a guide and is not intended to be comprehensive.

(1) The Michael Sobell Sports Centre, 7, Hornsey Rd., Islington. Tel. 01 607 1632.
Open at most times. The prefabricated section may be closed for instruction at times whilst the corridor provides strenuous traversing on very polished holds or brick edges and is best used for stamina training. There are however some desperate boulder problems and there is even a small guide book detailing most of them.

(2) The Brixton Sports Centre, Brixton, London.
Good for beginners, top-rope required. Not good for casual bouldering or traversing.

(3) The Brunel University Climbing Wall, Kingston Lane, Hillingdon, Uxbridge. Tel. Uxbridge 74000.
Open at most times. The best wall in the area with excellent walls, a roof and an adjustable-angle slab. The numerous crash mats make it an excellent place for bouldering. Overcrowding can be a problem.

(4) North London Rescue Commando Wall, Cordova Road, London E3. Tel. 01 980 0289.
A very good new wall in an old warehouse, consisting of prefabricated panels. A good alternative to the now horrendously popular and polished Sobell Wall, particularly in view of the planned expansion of the wall. Limited opening times - so ring first.

(4) Harrison's Car-park Toilet Block
Offers some good and quite difficult traversing possibilities; useful if it is raining to justify the pub visit, if you need to. On sight the Gents is 6b, and the Ladies perhaps a little easier.

(5) The Whitgift School Wall, Haling Park Rd, South Croydon. Tel. 01 688 9222.
Not open to the public at the time of writing but included in case the situation should ever change. If enough people make enquiries then it might. Outdoors.

(6) Monks Hill School, Selsdon, Surrey.
Not open to the public and not worthwhile anyway - it consists largely of a slab with jugs on it. Outdoors.

(7) Warlingham County Secondary School, Tithe Pit Shaw Lane, Warlingham, Surrey.
Not open to the public but would be of minor interest to locals if ever it were. Outdoors.

16 INTRODUCTION

(8) City University Climbing Wall, The Saddlers Sports Centre, Goswell Road, London EC1. Tel. 01 253 9285.
Open at most times, though it is best to check beforehand. Outdoors. A very early wall and thus most of the harder climbing is on brick edges and is therefore repetitive, but a nice (and cheaper) summer alternative to the Sobell.

All the following walls are 'natural' brick walls and as such are generally limited to brick-edge type holds. Nonetheless, they offer an interesting (and cheap) alternative for those who seek them out. Repointing or redevelopment may of course render these walls useless or non-existent at any time. An A-Z mapbook is useful (essential) for locating these esoteric diversions. For further information see articles in High, April and July 1985.

(9) Cottage Grove Wall, Cottage Grove, London SW9.
Close to Clapham North Tube Station. Apparently, offering good sustained traversing and some good boulder problems.

(10) Emmanuel Road Railway Arches, London SW12.
Large railway arches, often wet.

(11) Regents Canal Area, Islington, London N1.
A number of venues all very close or adjacent to the Canal including:

  (a) Magician Area - near the junction of Noel Road and Wharf Road. A big corner line and some other nearby problems.

  (b) The Playground by Packington Street bridge - a number of thin finger cracks.

  (c) George's Columns, Baring Street - a series of narrow pillars and a nearby bridge.

  (d) De Beauvoir Walls, on Whitmore Road bridge and abutting retaining walls right next to the canal.

(12) Hornsey Wall, between Hornsey Rise, Crouch End Hill and Haslemere Roads, Islington - just over a mile from the Sobell Centre; a series of rising arches, some requiring a top-rope, in quite pleasant surroundings.

---

1. Sugar Plum, 6a, Bowles Rocks. *Climber: Ben Pritchard*. Photo Ed Stone.

Historical

The earliest known reference by a mountaineer to the sandstone outcrops in the Tunbridge Wells area is in the book 'A Tramp to Brighton' by E.J.Kennedy, president of The Alpine Club from 1860 to 1862. He refers to searching for a specimen of the Tunbridge Filmy Fern (*Hymenophyllum Tunbridgense*) in 1857, "...through woods across meadows towards some crevices in the rocks that I had known some years earlier". However, he only mentions "the Tunbridge Wells Rocks", giving no further detail.

The next recorded mention of a sandstone outcrop in South East England by a mountaineer seems to have taken place around 1908, when Charles Nettleton noticed Harrison's Rocks while passing along the valley below with the Eridge Hunt. He afterwards returned with Claude Wilson but it is not known whether they actually did any climbing.

The first recorded climbing began in 1926, when the possibilities of Harrison's were realised by Nea Morin (née Barnard), who had climbed on similar outcrops at Fontainebleau near Paris; a family connection which subsequently led to the introduction of the EB (Eric Bourdonneau) rockboot (then the PA or Pierre Alain) to British rock. The early explorers also included Jean Morin, Eric Shipton, Gilbert Peaker, Osbert Barnard, E.H. Marriot and Miss Marples. Among the routes climbed in this period were such classics as *Long Layback, Long Crack, The Sewer, The Isolated Buttress* and the excellent *Unclimbed Wall*, which retains the 5b grade to this day. Most of these routes originally had different names. In the late 1920's the same group was active at High Rocks, climbing *Steps Crack* (another "modern" 5b) and some of the main chimneys. High Rocks has a long history as a pleasure ground, being first popularised in 1670 by James II, when Duke of York.

In 1934 H Courtney Bryson and M O Sheffield, members of the Mountaineering Section of the Camping Club, produced the first guide-book to Harrison's, listing about thirty climbs. Knowing little of the previous explorations they renamed most of the routes although many of their climbs were in fact new, including the ever-popular *Hell Wall* and *Zig-Zag*. In 1936 Courtney Bryson went on to produce a new guide, which covered additions at Harrison's such as *Set Square Arête* and *Slab Crack* but which also drew attention to several other known outcrops in the area. This was to be an inspiration to the next generation of sandstone climbers, many of whom had known little or nothing of outcrops other than Harrison's - though this still applies in some quarters even today.

Oxford University climbers climbed at High Rocks in 1936-37 and routes described in their journal included the classic *Simian Progress*,

---

2. Temptation, 6b, Bowles Rocks. *Climber: Matt Saunders.* Photo Ed Stone.

North Wall (the first recorded routes on the Isolated Boulder) and *Crack Route* on Hut Boulder.

In the early stages of a long and notable career on sandstone, Ted Pyatt visited High Rocks just before the Second World War with members of the Polaris Mountaineering Club, of whom B N Simmons was particularly active. They knew nothing of the previous work and the outcrop was in effect developed from scratch; *Anaconda Chimney*, *Boa Constrictor Chimney and Cobra* (originally A, B and C Chimneys) were among their climbs. Exploration at High Rocks was continued after 1942 by members of the Junior Mountaineering Club of Scotland; Frank Elliot, who had already established a reputation on gritstone was a prominent figure. New climbs during this period included Shelter Slabs, Swing Face, Python Crack and Helix.

Little new development took place at Harrison's after the early 1930's until 1941, when Edward Zenthon (of the JMCS) put together a girdle traverse of the outcrop. This was over 300 metres long and, though somewhat broken in continuity and quality in places, was an outstanding achievement. Many of the gaps continued to be filled at Harrison's through the war years, mainly through the efforts of Elliot.

At Eridge Green little climbing had been done until 1941, when visits were made by parties from the JMCS, of which Pyatt had now become a member. The rope grooves at the top of the Rocks, particularly Eridge Tower, bear witness to their early popularity. Elliot again was the outstanding contributor with fine routes such as *Battlement Crack*, *Barbican Buttress* and *Amphitheatre Crack*. The ascent of the latter was achieved by combined tactics using a chockstone specially imported for the occasion from Dow Crag.

In 1945, a new wave of exploration began at Harrison's under the inspiration of Clifford Fenner, a forester by profession, so giving rise to *Forester's Wall*. Standards were raised considerably by the addition of the fine and elegant *Slimfinger Crack*, which is the first record of a route still retaining the 5c grade. Classics such as *The Niblick*, *Monkey's Necklace* and routes of similar calibre were also done at this time.

By 1947, JMCS members had added the majority of the climbs at High Rocks Annexe and Continuation Wall. In addition, by this time most of the Stone Farm routes had been done, by either JMCS or PMC members.

After Pyatt's 1947 guide, Harrison's continued to be the most popular outcrop and standards continued to rise as is indicated by the fact that two climbs from this period, *Monkey's Bow* (by Mike Ball) and *Baboon*, are now graded 6a, perhaps the first climbs in Britain to merit this grade. Other notable additions included *Piecemeal Wall* by the Lakeland pioneer, Arthur Dolphin, and *North West Corner*. Nea Morin was very much involved in this activity and, among many contributors, Johnnie Lees and Pete Warland were outstanding. The former led many of the NS's of the 1947 guide, including *Crowborough* and *Birchden Corners*, and contributed many routes of his own. Notable ascents by visiting climbers included Menlove

Edwards's eponymous *Effort*. This was done as an unroped solo, an extremely impressive feat, and perhaps a reflection of the ability required to ascend his Welsh routes of the time without modern equipment. Also in this period Tony Moulam did the first solo of *Slimfinger Crack*, another major achievement.

In the early 1950's, a forceful new group emerged in the form of the Sandstone Climbing Club. The Club was formed in 1951 by Ned Cordery, Salt Sullivan, Mic O'Connor, Doug Stone and Des Entwhistle. They soon moved their attention from Harrison's, where they "often felt outclassed by the earlier inhabitants", to High Rocks (where they had use of the hut that used to exist behind Hut Boulder) so as to work up their standards. The success of this exercise was soon evident and the first generation of SCC climbers were responsible for most of the harder routes at High Rocks in the 1956 guide including *Advertisement Wall, Henry the Ninth* and *Simian Mistake*.

Between 1956 and 1963 the SCC monopolised development at High Rocks, adding over seventy new routes; many of these were of the highest standards including four with the new 6a grade in the 1963 guide. John and Paul Smoker, Phil Gordon, Billy Maxwell and Martin Boysen were industrious performers during this period. Among the SCC's routes were *Mulligan's Wall, The Lobster, Engagement Wall, Sphinx, Tilley Lamp Crack* and *Effie*. Boysen was one of the first exclusively sandstone-bred climbers to make a real breakthrough onto high standard mountain rock, and subsequently the Alps and further afield. It has been written that he climbed so much on occasions, that afterwards he couldn't use a knife and fork to cut up his dinner. Although there were other notable exceptions, many other sandstone experts failed to adapt their high standards to other types of rock. Indeed John Smoker, one of the most effective SCC members, was once described by Joe Brown, on seeing him climb, as "the cycling window-cleaner".

During this period the SCC were also steadily adding routes at Harrison's and here they were later joined by members of the North London MC, whose routes included *Bonanza* and *Baskerville*. One of their number, Max Smart, was responsible for *Elementary* and *Far Left* on the Unclimbed Wall, two fine additions.

Bowles Rocks was the only major outcrop to have been ommited from Bryson's 1936 guide. Nea Morin is known to have climbed at Bowles shortly after the war and the SCC to have been there in the early 1950's, but it was left to Pyatt to rediscover the Rocks when working on the 1956 guide. In it he made the tantalising comment, "if conditions should change at some future date the outcrop would be an excellent prospect". In 1959/60 the SCC (initially as prospective purchasers of the Rocks) started an intense period of cleaning and they pioneered the large majority of climbs, including some of the very hardest such as the aptly named *The Thing, Hate,* and *Digitalis*; Boysen and John Smoker featured prominently. The Thing is probably the first route to now be given the 6b grade. The Bowles Mountaineering Trust purchased the Rocks in 1963, outbidding the

20 HISTORICAL

initial asking price of £400. One of the initial purchasers involved was the father of the popstar Mick Jagger. Terry Tullis, currently the Harrison's Rocks Warden, and Julie Tullis were both involved with the extensive gardening and cleaning required to make this the excellent climbing area it is today, as well as contributing some new routes. It was at this time that the unfortunate hold-chipping and rock engineering occured on, among others, *Drosophila* (which had already been climbed by the SCC), *Sapper* (admittedly now a fine climb) and the well named *Devaluation*.

Bowles in fact served a wide range of purposes prior to its present role. There is evidence of prehistoric habitation and later smugglers (trading cannons and other iron products for French brandy and cigars) are thought to have used the outcrop as a hiding place. During the 19th century the rocks provided a backcloth to an avenue of trees and a carriageway leading to the house of John Bowles, a Dutchman. Subsequently the Rocks provided the site for a gypsy camp and a rubbish tip. During the Second World War, Bowles was used as a firing range, hence the numerous pockmarks on the Range Wall. In the late 1950s and early 1960s notoriously ferocious pigs had their sties at the base of the Rocks. This seems to be the reason for the large square-cut holes under the base overhangs in the region of Carbide Finger.

One of the most active climbers during the latter half of the 1960's at Harrison's was Trevor Panther, who remains an active sandstone climber to this day. Among his climbs were the fine *Sossblitz* (with Peter "Soss" Sorrell), albeit with an aid point, *Knam, Glendale Crack* free, *Crucifix* and *Grant's Wall*. One of Panther's young protégés, Ben Wintringham, climbed the classic *Flakes* and *Celestial's Reach*, and was also responsible for *The Limpet* and *West Wall Eliminate* (now *Woolly Bear*), though these two climbs are almost certainly much harder now due to the loss of holds. Martin Boysen, on leave from High Rocks, did *Coronation Crack* in 1967, whilst Greg Morgan climbed *Orangutang* in the same period.

Another active group during this period were Les and Laurie Holliwell, and Robin Harper. They laid strong emphasis on soloing and on using sandstone as training for bigger things. Laurie Holliwell was to follow Boysen by becoming one of the top Welsh climbers; among his best achievements on sandstone were to solo *South-West Corner* and *Vulture Crack* - the former remains as one of the hardest propositions to have been soloed. It is now even harder since a crucial large hold fell off at the top!

Little history is known about Bulls Hollow; the 1947 guide-book described twenty routes and little else was added up to 1963. Between then and 1968 the number of routes was doubled by Les Holliwell when working on the 1969 guide, though many of the routes may have been climbed before. Some of the hardest and most worthwhile routes were among the additions including *The Wall*, an atypical route for sandstone and one of the best at Bulls Hollow.

During relaxations in the access restrictions, a considerable number of routes were quietly added at Eridge Green by the Holliwell group, though once again much of this was probably a question of formalising previous unrecorded SCC activity.

A lull in development followed the 1969 guide until a wave of new route activity commenced in late 1971. Between 1971 and 1975 by far the most active pioneers were Nigel Head and Gordon DeLacy. They can probably be credited with around half of the 150 odd new routes contained in the 1981 guide; particularly notable among their routes were *Nightmare* and *Fandango Right Hand* at Bowles, and *Adder* (free) and *Dysentry* at High Rocks. In the late 1970s Mick Fowler, another climber who established his reputation in North Wales and elsewhere (including the chalk climbing described later in this book), was responsible for advancing the standards of sandstone climbing by adding many high grade, good quality climbs. With routes such as *The First Crack* (free), *Honeycomb* and *Infidel* at High Rocks, and *Sandstorm* and *The Crunch* at Eridge Green these included some of the earlier 6b's on Southern Sandstone. During the 1970s Boysen on periodic visits climbed *Sandman* (on which his reach was a great asset) at Bowles and *Boysen's Crack* at High Rocks.

Adder and The First Crack were two of a number of old aid climbs to have been climbed free, giving some of the most impressive lines on Southern Sandstone and some of the hardest climbing of the time. Important solo ascents in the 1970s and early 1980s included the Harrison's *Coronation Crack* by Stevie Haston and *Hate* by Fowler. *The Thing* was led by Andy Meyers, with a Friend and a nut for protection, and after a number of falls, apparently coming dangerously close to the slab beneath at times. *Digitalis* and *Serenade Arête* were soloed by Ron Fawcett, on a rare visit to Southern Sandstone when he soloed "all but two or three of the routes at Bowles on sight" - despite this quote there were 16 NSs in the subsequent guide to Bowles!

Since Tim Daniells' 1981 guide a number of very good but necessarily hard routes have been done at the major outcrops. Most of the smaller less frequented crags have also been further developed. One of the major and most able contributors particularly in the early eighties was Guy Mclelland. Of his numerous ascents a number are outstanding. At High Rocks he climbed two major additions with the hugely overhanging and impressive *Judy* and subsequently the less imposing but equally fine *Salad Days*. David Jones was also active during this period and, often climbing with Mclelland, put up a number of important new routes as well as numerous fillers-in. His most difficult contribution was *Time Waits For No One* at Bulls Hollow which, though very short, provides some sustained technical climbing. Of his other routes, *Harlequin* (Chiddinglye Wood), *Meridian* (Under Rockes) and *Kathmandhu* (Stone Farm) stand out. Together with Mclelland he accounted for most of the new additions recorded at Penns Rocks and Ramslye Farm. Furthermore, he soloed extensively, removing the NS suffix from numerous 5b and 5c routes. Other climbers active in this period and subsequently include Barry "Rambo" Knight, Chris Arnold, Dan Wajzner, Martin Crocker,

Martyn Lewis, and Frank Shannon - all of whom have contributed to the development of the area in various ways.

There are few lines remaining at Harrison's but one of its last great problems was picked off by Mclelland with very little effort. This was a free version of Crisis - *What Crisis?* - which retained an aura of difficulty (of the 7a type) for a number of years, though it has now seen a number of ascents. In the same period Dan Lewis climbed *The Republic*, another fine addition to the Harrison's repertoire, while his talented brother Martyn created *Karen's Kondom*, named after a (strange?) sculpture he had done.

In addition to Mclelland a number of other climbers were active at High Rocks in the mid-eighties. In particular, Martin Boysen caught out the regulars with his ascent of the superb *Krait Arête* (pronounced Krite), which had repelled the efforts of many strong climbers; he himself had been trying it on and off for twenty-five years. Subsequently, Boysen managed another major line with *Moving Staircase*, the name reflecting the sloping nature of the crux footholds. A year or two later Gary Wickham found some motivation and picked some plum routes here, including the highly problematic *Kinda Lingers* and the excellent *Nemesis*; the latter perhaps stimulated by Matt Saunders' ascent of the adjacent *A Touch Too Much* - a good route with a name appropriate to its first ascentionist.

Perhaps surprisingly, Bowles Rocks continues to give some excellent new routes. The impressive wall of *Temptation* was climbed by Dave Turner who subsequently led the route, sticking his neck out and clipping all the many bolts on the way. On the same wall the old aid climb *Kinnard* was turned into a very sustained free climb by Paul Hayes, thus creating one of the longest roped climbs on sandstone.

There continues to be some discreet activity at Eridge Green, the best of which was once again the work of Mclelland. *The Beguiled* is a tendon-ripping problem on a steep wall, while in contrast *Diagonal* is a delicate, technical proposition. At Stone Farm a few surprisingly good new routes were climbed in the mid-eighties. Ed Stone put up the very tricky *Birdie-Num-Nums*, Mclelland powered up the extremely strenuous *Guy's Route* - which is dangerous even on a top-rope - while Barry Franklin created the technical *Illusion*. Sadly, a large number of chipped holds have appeared here, a reprehensible practice which can only be condemned.

Bassett's Farm, a small but fine outcrop omitted from Daniells's guide because he couldn't find it, was "rediscovered" by Ian Mailer and friends. Between them all the worthwhile lines were climbed before its location was revealed, including the fine *Karate Liz* and *Dislocator* by Mailer, and *Dan's Wall* courtesy of Dan Lewis.

In 1987, while working on this guide-book, Dave Turner set to work on some of the more obvious remaining lines. At Bowles the Patella-Digitalis wall provided yet another fine climb - *Nutella* - while the much-eyed line on the Engagement Wall at High Rocks gave the highly gymnastic *Dyno-Sore*. An altogether different proposition was a wall in The Grand Canyon which required a protracted effort before

HISTORICAL

it finally yielded *Cool Bananas* - perhaps the hardest route on sandstone to date. At Harrison's Turner later climbed *Lager Frenzy* -"the last great problem" of the crag. Trevor Panther's 1986 Harrison's guide provided the incentive, claiming it would require a "superman...rocknast" to free climb it.

The early and mid-eighties saw a number of notable solo performances. Dan Lewis managed some of Harrison's harder routes, including *Celestial's Reach, Forester's Wall Direct*, and *The Mank*. At Bowles he made a frightening unroped ascent of *Sandman*, with a somewhat worried person below to divert his 13 stone frame from the boulder should he have come unstuck. Again at Bowles Paul Hayes soloed *Patella*, a highly insecure proposition. Returning to Harrison's, *Right Unclimbed* received a solo ascent from Gary Wickham -impressive because the crux is very easy to fluff - while *Grant's Wall* and the precarious *Grant's Groove* received similar treatment from Ian Mailer. Furthermore, Mick Fowler returned once again to sandstone and made a very impressive ropeless ascent of his own route, *Infidel*.

In 1987 Matt Saunders risked a lot with his solos of firstly *Temptation* and then to top that *Carbide Finger* - without doubt the most impressive solos on sandstone to date. Indeed, his first attempt on the former ended with a broken ankle. Carbide Finger, undergraded and certainly the most difficult climb in the last guide, has now seen a number of ascents. It seems that it is harder to top-rope than lead as it is extremely difficult to avoid helpful tension from the rope in the latter case.

On the face of it the future of sandstone climbing is somewhat limited. However, there are still a number of obvious good lines, at High Rocks and Eridge Green in particular, awaiting an extended period of good weather and an enthusiast armed with time, patience, and perhaps even a blow-torch to dry holds. A glance at the graded list is sufficient to see that a considerable number of routes in the 6a and above categories have yet to be soloed. Some of these are clearly out of the question while at the same time routes such as Krait Arete, Salad Days, Judy, The Beguiled, Nightmare, Lady In Mink and so on are all reasonable propositions. So, get to it ....

Finally, and perhaps most important of all, a great deal of extra care is needed to minimise erosion, otherwise Southern Sandstone will cease to be.

Bassett's Farm   OS Ref 491 414

Bassett's Farm, described in the 1964 guide but overlooked subsequently, has been recently 're-discovered' and nearly all the worthwhile possibilities climbed. It consists of a steep smooth main wall and some lesser buttresses to either side. The central wall provides some good sustained climbs and the crag is certainly worth a visit to do these.

The outcrop is located near Cowden to the north of the main climbing area - see the map below. Approaching from the B2026 there is a bend in the road just before Bassett's Farm itself is reached. There are two iron gates here and room for one or two cars to park. Climb over the first gate and follow the public footpath for two hundred and fifty or so metres toward some trees, which initially conceal the crag from view.

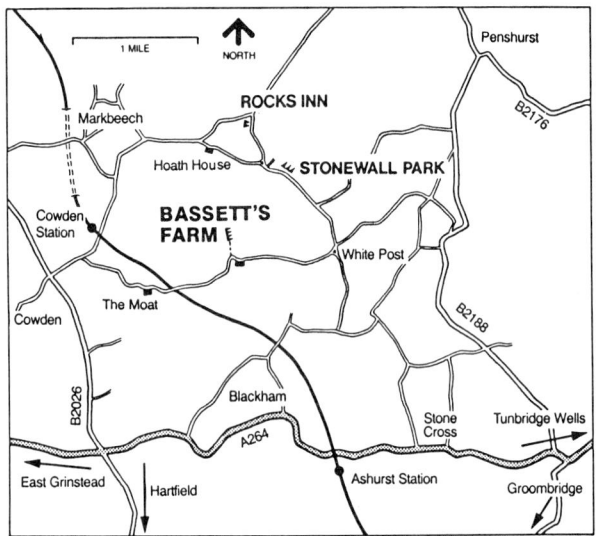

Access is at present uncertain although no problems have yet been encountered. Nonetheless, discretion would seem to be the best option.

AS WITH ALL SANDSTONE CRAGS PLEASE USE A LONG BELAY SLING AND POSITION THE KARABINER OVER THE EDGE OF THE CRAG SO AS TO MINIMISE DAMAGE TO THE ROCK BY MOVING ROPES.

BASSETT'S FARM ROCKS 25

To the left of the main wall the crag is lower and broken, offering some further scope for routes but a lot of cleaning will be required. The climbs are described starting on the wall facing the main wall:

1 Chossy Arête 5c(NS)
The greasy left arête of the wall.

2 Tree Route 4c
Climb out of the cave to finish by the tree.

3 Silly Arête 5a(NS)
The right arête bears little resemblance to its Welsh namesake.

There is a descent gully with tree roots to the right, then another larger gully right again. The main wall starts with a small buttress:

*4 Ken's Wall 5b(NS)
Start below an obvious flake on the left of the wall and follow this until it peters out. Traverse right until it is possible to reach the break above via an undercut in the niche; move back left then go straight up to an awkward mantelshelf finish.

5 Kenian Crack 4b
The obvious crack before the start of the central wall is still a little chossy but would improve if it saw more traffic.

**6 Dislocator 6a(NS)
Well named. Climb straight up using the painful old bolt-holes to an obvious peg (not an aid-point) in the upper wall. Then, either layaway right to reach the tree root, or traverse off left more easily. The start is now obstructed by a large fallen tree.

Further right there is a scoop in the upper wall right of the big tree; this used to be at the top of the crag and provided an ideal belay point but was toppled in the October 1987 storms.

**7 Karate Liz 6b(NS)
Climb straight up to the left side of the scoop with a very long reach or lunge to reach the top. Very strenuous at the top and quite technical throughout.

*8 Dan's Wall 6a(NS)
Go straight up to the right side of the scoop starting two metres left of Excavator.

*9 Excavator 5c
The left-hand side of the arête left of the chimney.

10 Foam Dome 5a
Sounds a bit rude. The wall right of the chimney to finish in the obvious scoop.

The next three routes are now obstructed to various degrees by a large fallen tree.

11 Solution 5b(NS)
Start a metre right of the chimney and go straight up.

12 Hypothesis 5b
Start as for Solution and go up to and follow the left to right diagonal line to finish past the stalactite on the next route.

BASSETT'S FARM ROCKS 27

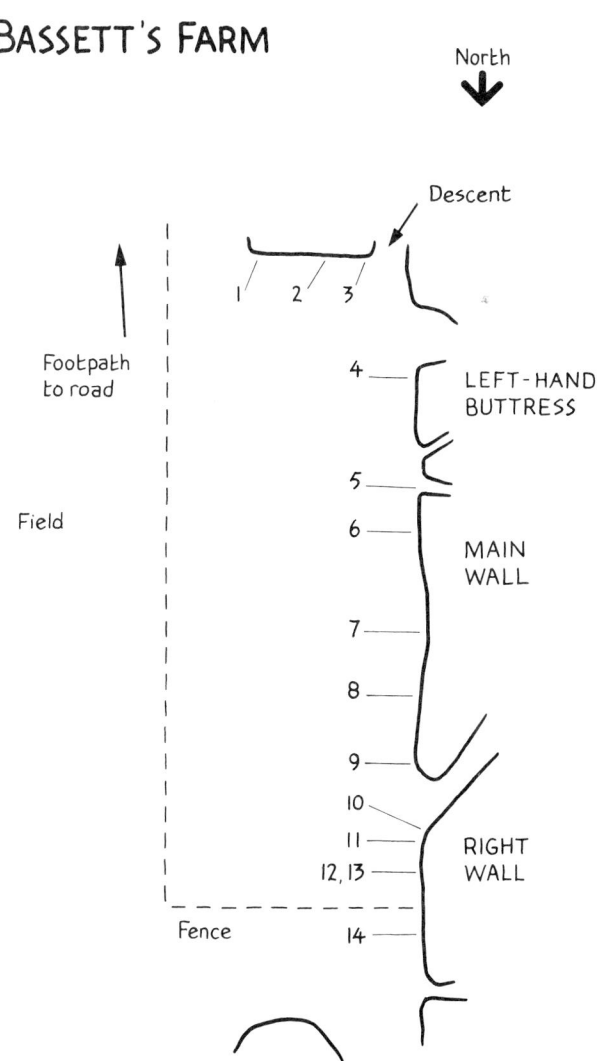

28 BASSETT'S FARM ROCKS

13 Ian's Answer 5c(NS)
Start in the middle of the wall below a large break right of the fence. Go straight up to finish at a stalactite.

Bowles Rocks   OS Ref 543 330

The rocks are situated about one and a half km south of Eridge station and are marked 'Outdoor Pursuits Centre' on the Landranger O.S. map. The usual approach is from the A26 between Tunbridge Wells and Crowborough - see map on page 8 (also on 158). The turn off to Bowles is about one km toward Crowborough from Eridge station - signposted 'Bowles Outdoor Centre'. The entrance to the rocks is on the right about half a km along this road.

The Bowles Outdoor Pursuits Centre is administered by a Trust and is primarily concerned with courses of instruction, of which climbing is a major part. There is a dry ski slope here which can be used by the public. If interested in these aspects contact The Director, Bowles Outdoor Pursuits Centre, Sandhill Lane, Eridge, Sussex - telephone Crowborough 4127.

A scheme known as 'Open Climbing' operates, meaning you can climb anywhere not required by Centre instructional courses. It is occasionally necessary to close the rocks completely but this is extremely rare. To find out if 'Open Climbing' is in operation telephone the number given above.

There is an entry fee of 80 pence a day, or 50 pence after 2pm, at the time of writing which may put some people off. However, the outcrop is in excellent condition due to the work of the staff and the fee goes toward this. Season tickets are available at £12 for a year - these no longer include use of the pool. There is a bar in one of the chalet buildings by the ski slope which opens on Sunday lunchtimes; it also serves some snack foods.

The main part of the crag provides perhaps the best sandstone rock wall in the region. The rock here is generally harder and consequently less sandy than at other outcrops whilst its open nature, southerly aspect and the upkeep by the Centre mean it is frequently the only dry crag. As a result Bowles is very popular and can become unpleasantly crowded at times though the route quality somewhat compensates for this.

There are a number of routes with cut holds and it is hoped that no more of these will appear, as has been the case for sometime. Indeed, most of these vandalized routes can be climbed on natural features only. The use of chalk has been banned in the past by the Centre. Recently a compromise was reached whereby it is allowed on hard routes only. This quite obviously cannot be upheld since it is elitist. If one group can use chalk then why not others? It is suggested that chalk be used conservatively, with respect for the views of others.

AS WITH ALL SANDSTONE CRAGS PLEASE USE A LONG BELAY SLING AND POSITION THE KARABINER OVER THE EDGE OF THE CRAG SO AS TO MINIMISE DAMAGE TO THE ROCK BY MOVING ROPES.

30 BOWLES ROCKS

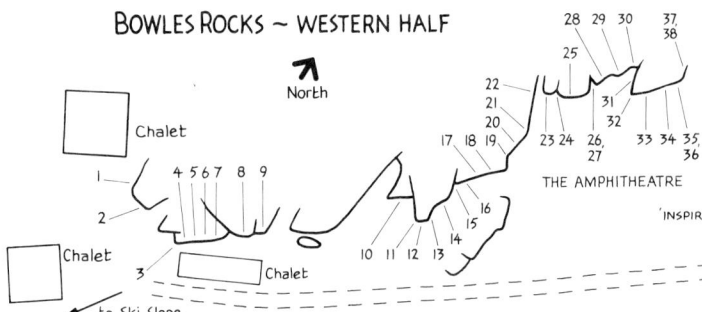

The climbs are described starting at the far end from the public car-park, beginning with a low boulder just right of the staff car-park in front of the toilets. This has a slab running from bottom left to top right and has two little problems:

1 **Bull's Nose** 4b
The arête below the top of the slab. Pull up on good holds, with a mantelshelf over the nose to finish.

2 **Badger's Head** 4c
Use the protruding ironstone knobs about a metre right of the last route.

Past several low boulders, and immediately behind the left-hand end of the chalet is:

3 **Hibiscus** 3b
Two mantelshelves on the blunt, now overgrown arête.

4 **Helter Skelter** 5a
A diagonal gash is climbed to a horizontal break and a thin finish.

The next feature is an easy descent chimney. The slab on the right gives some pleasant little routes.

5 **Chalet Slab Left** 3b
Go straight up the left side of the slab on the obvious ironstone protrusions. The slab to the left leading into the chimney is 3a.

*6 **Chalet Slab Direct** 4c
Climb the centre of the slab past an obvious ironstone knob which provides an excellent hold. At the top move left a little and surmount the overhang.

7 **Chalet Slab Right** 5a
Climb the right-hand side of the slab to an awkward mantelshelf onto the ramp. Finish straight over the steep wall above. The wide crack on the left is an easier alternative finish, making the climb 4c.

8 **Mohrenkop** 5b
The front of the tall block right of the slab. Strenuous but good holds.

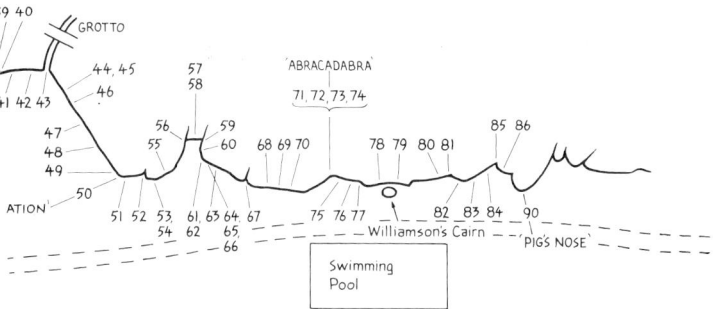

9 Two Step 5b
Unsatisfactory. Mantelshelf onto a ledge on the right of the block; move right on this until good holds on top can be reached and mantelshelf again.

Away to the right past a gully and a few boulders is Problem Slab, *providing a number of short problems. Beyond this is:*

10 Roman Nose 4b
Better than an Egyptian one? A couple of moves up the very short wall just right of a short thick flake.

*11 Umbilicus 5c
Start on the left side of a long ironstone edge; stand up on this then climb the left arête of the impending wall above and mantelshelf to finish.

12 Geoff's Route 6b
A severe problem. The wall a metre right of Umbilicus with very hard moves to reach good holds on the slab. Move onto the slab to a prickly finish up the short wall. There is a 6a boulder problem just right of the start.

13 Blue Moon 5c
A strenuous mantelshelf is made onto the nose. Finish direct to the holly tree. There is a 6a problem on the little wall immediately to the right of the start.

14 Court's Climb 4b
Move left from the corner and mantelshelf onto a large ledge. Move back right to finish. Often greasy.

15 Grotty Groove 2a
Climb the grotty groove.

16 Running Jump 2b
Immediately right of the corner. A leap and two mantelshelves - beat 2.3 seconds. This can be climbed less energetically but is less fun that way.

17 Scirocco Slab 5a
The steep slab two metres right of the previous route. Technical moves. A number of variations are possible between this and the next route at 5a or so.

*18 Netwall 4a
Start right of the last route just before the slab changes direction. Follow the cut holds trending rightwards almost to the tree. Pleasant and devious. A number of variations are possible, including a more direct finish and a harder direct start.

19 Corner Layback 4c
Layback (take it easy), move right and jam to finish. The wall to the right is 4b.

The original route of the next piece of rock, **Aphrodite** *6a, takes the vague nose just right of Corner Layback to the break followed by a swing right to join:*

20 Zoom 6b
A powerful dynamic move on undercuts about three metres right of Corner Layback leads to the break; continue straight up.

21 Santa's Claws 4c
Follow the artificial line of granite holds grouted in the rock. Tricky start.

22 Chelsea Chimney 2a
This is straightforward when climbed inside but is much harder when laybacked using the outside edge.

The easy way up and down this area of the rocks is **Reclamation Gully** *1a, which bounds the left side of Reclamation Slab. The slab features four routes.*

*23 Reclamation Slab Left 3b
Climb straight up the left edge, using this as required. The further right you keep the harder it gets.

There is an eliminate line up the centre of the slab which avoids all cut (that is big) holds on the upper half - **Reclamation Slap** *5c(NS).*

**24 Reclamation Slab Right 2b
A very popular route with beginners. Follow the line of cut holds up the right side of the slab.

25 Mental Balance 5b
The right side of Reclamation Slab avoiding all cut holds. Very delicate.

The next steep wall features three good routes.

**26 High Traverse 4c
Start easily up the rib left of the banana-shaped depression and traverse right along the high level break to finish up the corner of Babylon.

27 Slyme Cryme 5c
Start as for the previous route but take the square-cut overhang on its

---

3. Digitalis, 6a, Bowles Rocks. *Climber: James Mace.* Photo Steve Gordon.

right side. A boulder problem direct start is possible using small ironstone holds.

28 Banana 5c
Surprisingly, this takes the banana-shaped depression to the break -don't slip; continue up the difficult crack above with a long reach to finish.

An eliminate line directly between Banana and Drosophila, **Proboscis** *6a(NS), is worthwhile but independent only for the finishing moves over the bulge.*

29 Drosophila 5b
Go straight up the fine wall on good but, unfortunately, chipped holds. At the top trend right to finish. Be careful with rope positioning to avoid taking a flyer into the right wall.

*30 Babylon** 4b
The main corner crack taken direct gives a good climb that is unfortunately often wet.

31 T.N.T. 5c
A delicate climb. The centre of the smooth and often greasy wall on small holds.

*32 Coathanger 5c
The overhanging arête. Start on the left side, step up and swing onto the arête. Finish carefully up the edge on its left side. A direct start is a long reach and is 6a.

Just to the right is the overhanging Fandango Wall, a favourite place to get pumped and with some frustratingly hard boulder problems - see route descriptions. There are a number of short but worthwhile low level traverses - see also Icarus below. On the very lowest break is **Tobacco Road** *6b, which starts in Skiffle and finishes up the Right Hand, or continues across to TNT as* **Nicotine Alley**, *more 6b. At mid-height is* **Sugarplum** *6a, which also starts in Skiffle and goes all the way across to Coathanger. Otherwise, use your imagination. It is possible to climb on every square inch of this wall and routes have been claimed thus. Only the original and best are described here.*

***33 Fandango 5c
Spectacular. Start with difficulty up the centre of the wall. At the first break move left and go up to the top overhang. Swing right to an awkward mantelshelf finish. A direct start is 6a. One can also go straight up from the start, taking the overhang at its widest point - 6a.

***34 Fandango Right Hand 6a
Start as for Fandango to the break but move right and go up to the overhang (crux). Move right then back left round the overhang and finish straight up. Somewhat strenuous. A direct start up to the curved flake just to the right is 6c.

*35 Pastry 5c
Climb Skiffle for two metres, move left a metre or so under the bulge and then pull over it to the next break; from here trend right to finish

---

4. Inspiration, 5c, Bowles Rocks. *Climber: Geoff Pearson.* Photo Dave Turner.

just right of the nose without moving into the chimney. A direct start is possible just left of the chimney at 6c.

An alternative line is **Poff Pastry** 6a. *Follow Pastry over the bulge then trend left almost to Fandango Right Hand to a thin finish on the left side of the nose.*

36 Icarus 6a
Climb Skiffle for two metres and traverse left under the first bulge; pull over this and make a rising traverse leftwards onto Fandango Right Hand. Move left to gain a standing positon on the Fandango foot ledge and then go on round across Coathanger and T.N.T. Descend Babylon (30) for two metres and then traverse on a line of handholds across Banana to easy ground.

**37 Skiffle 3a
The obvious twisting crack is easier than it looks.

38 Orr Traverse 5c
A good traverse. Start at Skiffle and traverse right, generally about two metres from the ground, to the Digitalis pedestal. Step down and then across to Inspiration (50). Either move right onto and over the bulge (crux), Orr (5b) go up Inspiration then step across. Step down again after this and carry on to Meager's Slab (56). Continue across to Pegasus (66) etc.

*39 Mick's Wall Arête 5c
Straight up the blunt arête immediately right of Skiffle. Finish left of the crack above.

40 Mick's Wall 5b
Somewhat eliminate moves just left of centre of the wall lead to the overhang. Move left to the nose and up the awkward crack to finish. A direct finish seems possible over the roof but has not yet been done.

**41 Kemp's Delight 4b
An enjoyable route up the centre of the wall about a metre right of the last route. Follow good but chipped holds up to the overhang then traverse right into the chimney to finish.

42 Mick's Wall Variation 6a(NS)
Awkward moves up the wall immediately left of the chimney lead to a bulge. Finish direct. There used to be a large oak tree to grab at the top but the climb still goes without it.

43 Grotto Chimney 2b
Climb the obvious chimney to the small cave and an easier but dirty finish; this can be avoided by a pleasant ramp leading out right.

The next sweep of rock features some of the best and most impressive climbs at Bowles.

*44 Patella 6b
Just right of Grotto Chimney. Climb directly past the small old bolts (crux), surmount the overhang and layback up the crack above. The more popular and original approach is to use the bolts as holds thus giving a good 6a climb.

**45 Kinnard 6b(NS)
A totally free version of the mysterious aid route and now even more

BOWLES ROCKS 35

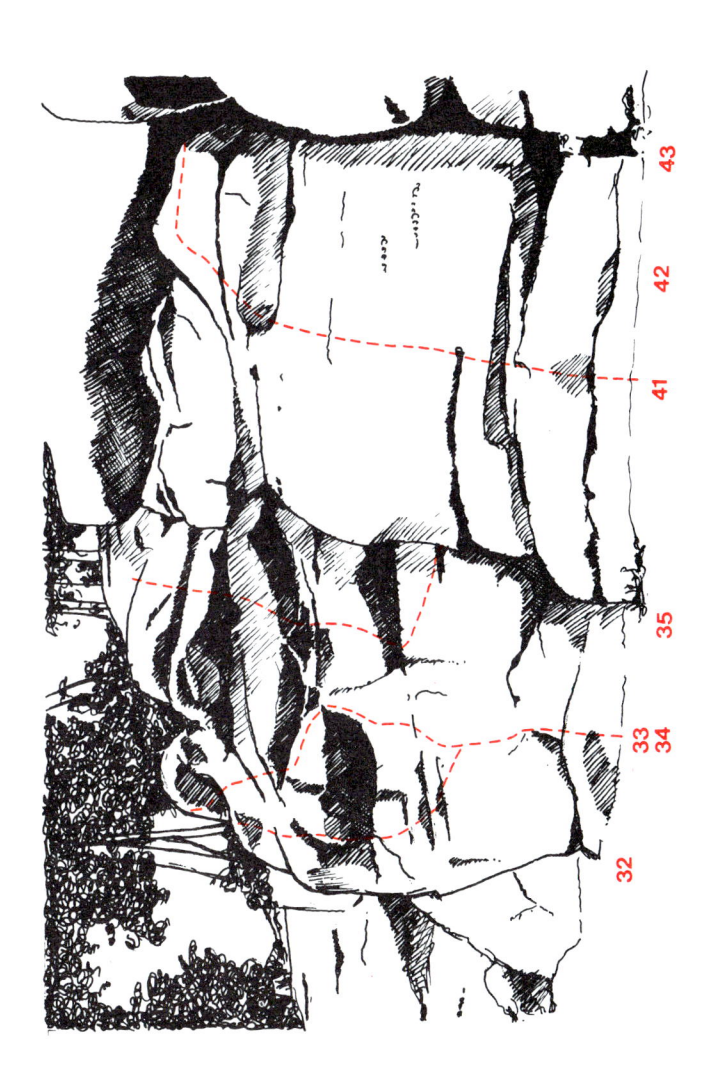

Kinnard. Start as for Patella to the bulge then hand-traverse the high level break all the way to Inspiration and finish up this. Very sustained but not technically hard.

*46 Nutella 6b(NS)
A wicked move on tiny finger pockets two metres right of Patella leads to the high-level break; hand-traverse strenuously right to a vague corner and finish past the ring bolts with a second cruciality.

The next feature is an obvious line of large ring bolts on the wall above a rock pedestal. This gives an A1 aid route or arm over arm thuggery using the bolts as holds - 5b. Please take care not to damage natural holds because:

***47 Temptation 6b
Free climbs the line of bolts directly to the top starting from the pedestal - the Temptation is to grab the bolts. An impressive and technical climb, which can be led.

***48 Digitalis 6a
An airy and heart-quickening route. From the pedestal go up and right on good holds until a finger tip layback is reached (crux). Move right and mantelshelf over the nose as for Inspiration. An undercut direct start is possible to the right.

A direct finish to Digitalis on the left side of the nose is rumoured but not confirmed.

**49 Serenade Arête 6a
The impressive arête gives a fine sustained climb marred only by its proximity to Inspiration. Start up the left side, moving onto the arête on the good breaks. The crux follows on the steepest part, followed by a step right and then back left onto the wide ledge to finish as for Inspiration.

**50 Inspiration 5c
A varied climb with a spectacular (frightening?) finish. Climb the awkward wide crack just right of the arête and the easy staircase to the roof. Move left to the airy sloping ledge on the arête and finish with a difficult mantelshelf.

*51 The Thing 6b(NS)
A sticky tape job but no fetishists please. Follow Inspiration to the top overhang then use a horizontal flake to gain an obvious jam at the lip. Vaguely strenuous thugging follows. Swinging off is more fun than the climbing.

**52 Juanita 5c
The hand width crack in the roof right of The Thing. Start with a hard pull onto the slab directly beneath the crack. Climb straight up the wall to the roof then with a surge of adrenalin go out over the outside.

53 One Nighter 6c(NS) †
Get it? The roof two metres right of Juanita. Climb up to the roof any way you like and use pockets as undercuts to gain the horizontal break -interesting if you face outwards to do so. Finish with a skin-ripping grovel onto the top.

**54 Sapper 4c
A popular and unusual trip. Start by stepping onto the arête from Yoyo

BOWLES ROCKS 37

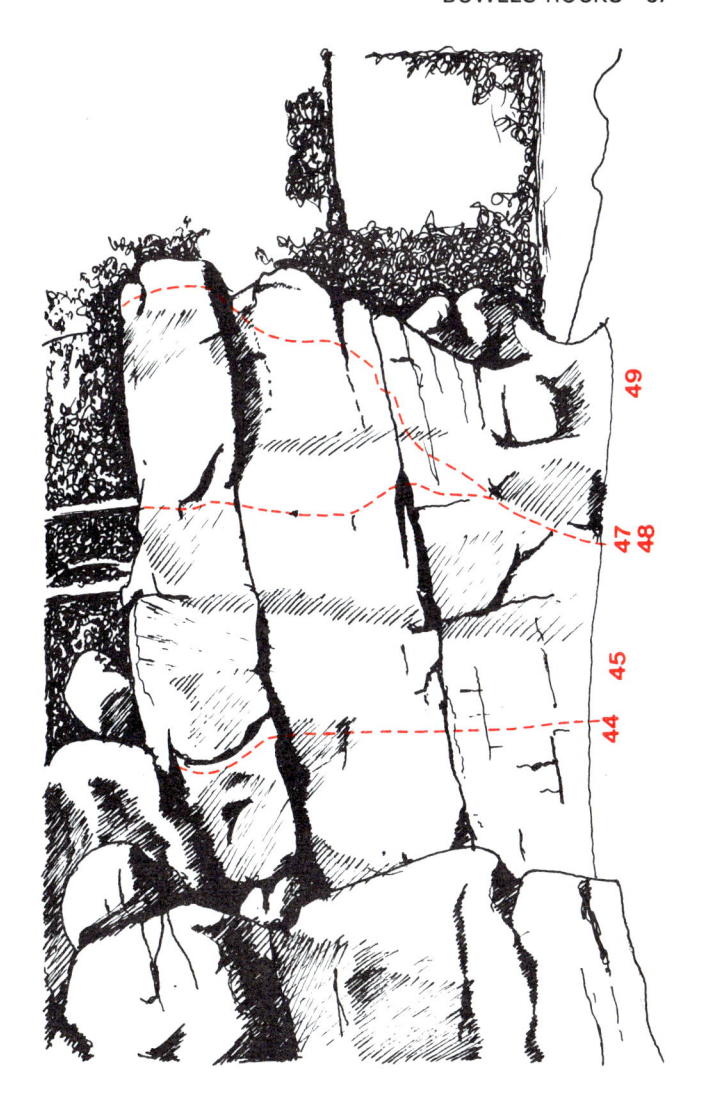

38 BOWLES ROCKS

and traverse all the way left to the staircase of Inspiration and go up this to the roof. Move right beneath the crack of Juanita and squeeze up the body-sized hole at the back of this. Alternative starts include a hard pull over the overhang two metres left of the arête 5b or the initial crack of Inspiration, also 5b.

*55 Burlap 5b
Climb the square-cut arête straight up to the overhang and finish delicately up the wall to the right of this.

The next feature is a steep recessed slab, known as Meager's Slab.

**56 Yoyo 4a
The crack bounding the left side of the slab. Take care not to jam your feet in too well.

57 White Verdict/The Ly'in 6b(NS)
Two overlapping eliminates up the centre of the slab, slightly to the left and slightly to the right respectively. Both inflict pain on the finger joints. Use of the arêtes is forbidden.

58 Meager's Right Hand 5b
The right side of the slab is climbed using the right edge until it is possible to move left to the centre at the large break. Finish straight up the middle.

59 Sing Sing 3a
The crack crack bounding the right side of the slab slab. This is a thrutch when climbed by body jamming, but is very much harder though more pleasant when bridged on the outside - take your pick.

60 Manita 5c
Like Joan Collins? The leaning wall immediately right of Sing Sing is climbed using small pockets, with a long reach in the middle. Pull onto the ledge and finish as for Jackie.

*61 Jackie 5b
An enjoyable technical climb up the rounded arête right of the recessed slab. From the wide ledge climb the steep little slab round to the left. Alternatively, grovel over the left end of the steep wall at about 5c.

**62 Murph's Mount 4b
Start in Sing Sing and traverse right past Jackie onto the slab; climb this in the middle to the big ledge then traverse left and finish up Sing Sing. Starting as for Jackie makes the climb 5a.

63 Nero 5c
Pull onto the slab as for Jackie or start two metres right with a jump for the break. Climb the middle of the slab to the ledge and the centre of the steep wall above.

64 Salamander Slab 5c
Start as for Nero but trend further right and make long reaches up the impending wall to gain the birch tree.

A direct start to Salamander Slab has been climbed — **Cheese Sandwich** 6a(NS). *Start one metre left of Perspiration; gain the first break with the hands, move left a bit and pull with difficulty onto the slab.*

BOWLES ROCKS 39

40 BOWLES ROCKS

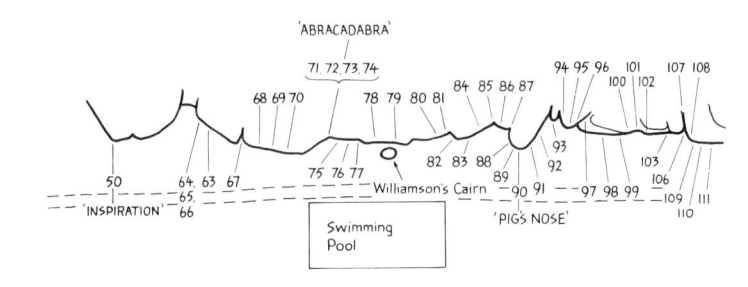

The next wall is undercut by large overhangs and is interlaced with routes upon which numerous variations are possible. A number of ring bolts are present, enabling some routes to be led - use only the in situ bolts and chockstones because conventional protective devices will badly damage the rock.

***65 Peter's Perseverance** 4b

A fine outing. Start as for Murph's Mount (62) and traverse right to the crack (bolt belay). Continue the traverse and then go straight up the face by a large pocket (bolt runner), to finish up the wide crack by the tree stump.

***66 Pegasus** 4b

A very worthwhile extension to Peter's Perseverance. Follow that route to the large pocket but continue traversing (bolt runner) to a delicate step down; move across Abracadabra (74) and go up to a broad ledge past a limestone chock to a block and bolt belay. The traverse may be continued at two levels to Charlie's Chimney (85). It can then be extended, 5b, across Hate (87) as a hand-traverse, round Pig's Nose (90) and into Birch Crack (93). This section is less well protected than the earlier parts.

A number of variations can be made on the extension to Pegasus. The first, 5a, is an easier finish across Hate. Descend Charlie's Chimney and cross Hate at the level of the first horizontal break to eventually join Chelsea Traverse (104). The second variation is at a lower level but is 5c. Traverse right from Abracadabra just above the overhangs, following Target into the cave; cross Devaluation (83) by the obvious difficult hand-traverse to eventually join the low level traverse of Hate.

*****67 Perspiration** 5c

Is the word. Start beneath the overhanging crack; up-thrutch it and continue more easily to the overhangs. Either traverse right to exit at the wide crack by the tree stump, or make the route more sustained by continuing direct.

*There is an eliminate, **Boiling Point** 6b(NS), taking the roof immediately right of Perspiration.*

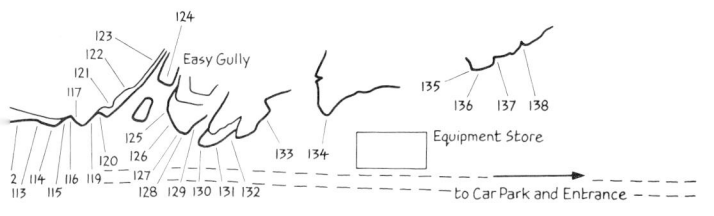

BOWLES ROCKS ~ EASTERN HALF

68 Them Monkey Things 6c(NS) †
A powerful and rarely climbed route. Climb the sandy roof two metres right of Perspiration to the short vertical crack; gain and somehow use a good but small layaway hold at the top of this to reach the good breaks above and easy ground.

**69 Carbide Finger 6c
A tasty climb with unusual but interesting positions - knowing the numbers is all important. The thin crack in the widest part of the roof with two peg runners gives a powerful and sequency series of moves on side pulls and undercuts.

The next roof crack right with a slate wedge in it has been aided but is rarely ascended. However, just right there is:

*70 Cardboard Box 6b
Gain the thin horizontal flake under the roof. A technical leap for a right handhold then usually follows with more hard but less pleasant moves to stand up. Finish up (Recurring) Nightmare.

The next three routes are described as starting up Abracadabra but many prefer to start from Williamson's Cairn and traverse in above the bulge.

**71 Swastika 5b
A fine exposed route. Start up Abracadabra to the first big break then traverse left and go up a shallow groove in the centre of the front face. Exit via the wide crack by the tree stump.

*72 Nightmare 6a(NS)
Start up Abracadabra to the ledge then traverse nearly three metres left and climb the steep wall on the left side of the blunt nose to a difficult mantelshelf. Finish as for Swastika.

73 Recurring Nightmare 6b(NS)
A logical finish to Carboard Box. The bulging wall two metres right of the blunt nose on Nightmare, with a long reach for a flat ironstone hold, is harder - 6c - for those less than tall. Finish direct.

74 Abracadabra 5a
Straight up the despicably awkward wide crack. Some find this harder

than Cardboard Box! Continue much more easily to the top or, better, step right into Ricochet.

To the right is Range Wall, which is undercut and rotten at the base. It is also marked by Williamson's Cairn.

75 Conjuror 6a
Levitate up the sandy bulges just right of Abracadabra and follow a direct line to the top avoiding both Abracadabra and Ricochet. Perhaps a wandering line would be more appropriate?

The next four routes start from Williamson's Cairn but were originally climbed direct or by traversing in from Abracadabra.

**76 Ricochet 4b
Start on the cairn and go up to the first foot ledges. Traverse left for about three metres and climb the pock-marked wall directly to the top.

**77 Four-by-Two 5a
Start as for Ricochet but traverse nearly two metres left and go straight up from there.

**78 Pullthrough 5b
From the cairn go straight up the wall on cut holds to finish up a groove on the right. An unpleasant direct start just right of, and without touching, the cairn is 6a - mind your back.

***79 Lee Enfield 4b
A Stirling route. Go up to the first break from the cairn, then climb the wall diagonally rightwards to a hard pull into a niche. The climb is 5a if the sapling is not used.

**80 Target 5c
Start up the left wall of the cave, then swing round onto the front face. Climb directly up the wall above just right of Lee Enfield to finish awkwardly to the right of the niche. A sandy direct start is 6b.

81 Cave Crack 5a
Start in the back of the cave. Go up to the roof and follow the crack rightwards round this and then to the top.

*82 E.S. Cadet Nose 5a
Climb the rounded arête to the right of the cave, avoiding the previous route by keeping to the right side of the arête after the start. Go straight up to finish. A direct start on the front face is 5c.

**83 Devaluation 5b
A pleasant route up the centre of the wall but unfortunately mostly on cut holds.

The final hard move of Devaluation can be done by a figure-of-four move - that is, put both hands on the jug then put the left leg up between them and over the right hand. Udge your weight upwards until eventually a sitting position on the right hand is reached. Reach the next break with the left hand thus entirely avoiding intermediate holds. The left-handed will find it easier to put the right leg over the left hand. Either way this requires some practise but can be very elegant when perfected.

*84 Sandman 6b
The blunt right arête of the wall is easier for the tall and utterly

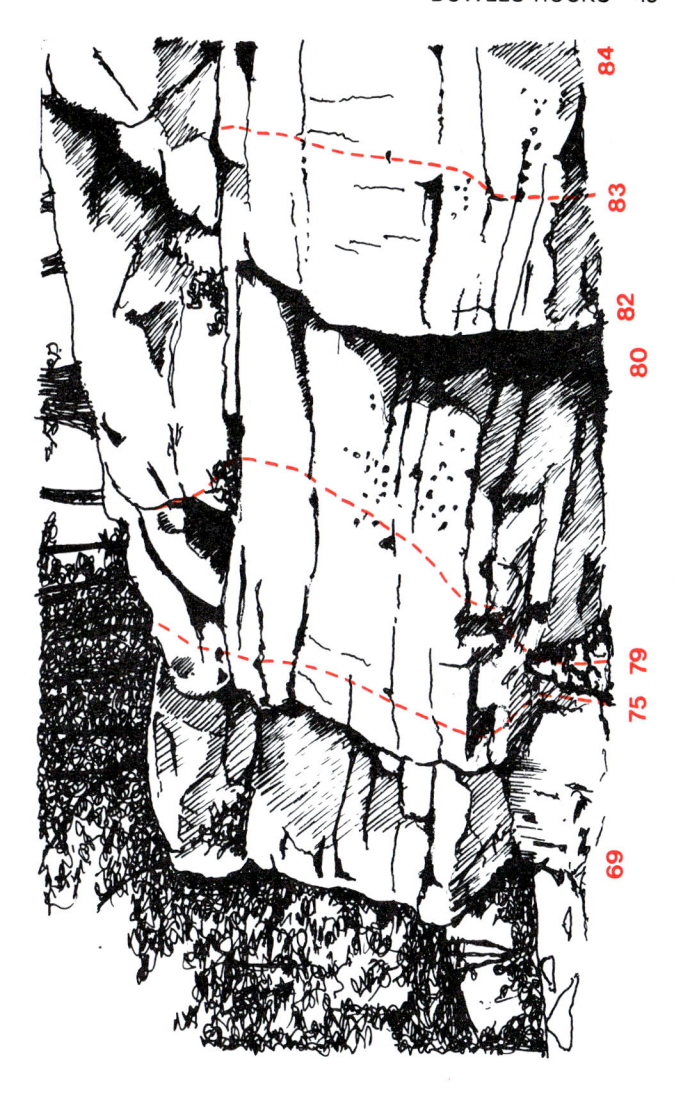

BOWLES ROCKS 43

desperate for the short. From the wide ledge traverse off left or go over the overhangs above near their left end, more 6b.

It is entertaining to jump from the wide ledge on Sandman to the juggy break on Love/Hate and finish up the latter.

*85 Charlie's Chimney 3a
Climb the crack to the roof then traverse some way left and finish in a corner with bolt runners in it.

86 Love 6a(NS)
A hateful route. Eliminate but delightful moves up the right arête of the chimney lead to a heinous overhanging crack to finish (you) - way jingus smee.

***87 Hate 6a
A classic. An awkward move onto the first break is followed by thin moves up the centre of the wall. Pull over the overhang and finish up the crack above. The wall just to the right has similar but slightly harder moves.

**88 Pig's Ear 5c
Climb the crack on small sharp holds to the overhang, which is surmounted slightly to the right. Finish more easily in the same line, or move right and finish up Pig's Nose with further interest.

89 T.T. 5b
The wall immediately right of the previous route is climbed to the ledge below the overhang. Either step right and finish up Pig's Nose or go straight up as for the Ear.

***90 Pig's Nose 5a
Another popular classic. The fine arête is followed easily to the ledges below the top overhangs. Summon up courage, breathe deeply and launch over the bulges above.

91 Koffler 6a
The wall just right of the arête gives one very hard move, after which the difficulties soon ease. Much easier for the tall. The grade is 5b if the breaks running right from Pig's Nose are used.

92 Gully Main Wall 5a
A layback flake on the left wall of Birch Crack is climbed to half-height, whence it is abandoned for earthy ledges above.

The next easy climb provides the usual descent route for this area of the rocks.

93 Birch Crack 1a
A straightforward chimney climb with a triangular slab at its base.

94 Chris 5a
The wall midway between the chimney and the next crack, trending slightly left then back right to a mantelshelf and easy ground.

*95 Kennard's Climb 4a
Not Kenneasy. The first crack right of the chimney moving right at its top to a strenuous mantelshelf finish.

96 Rib 5c
The sandy bulges just left of Dib.

BOWLES ROCKS 45

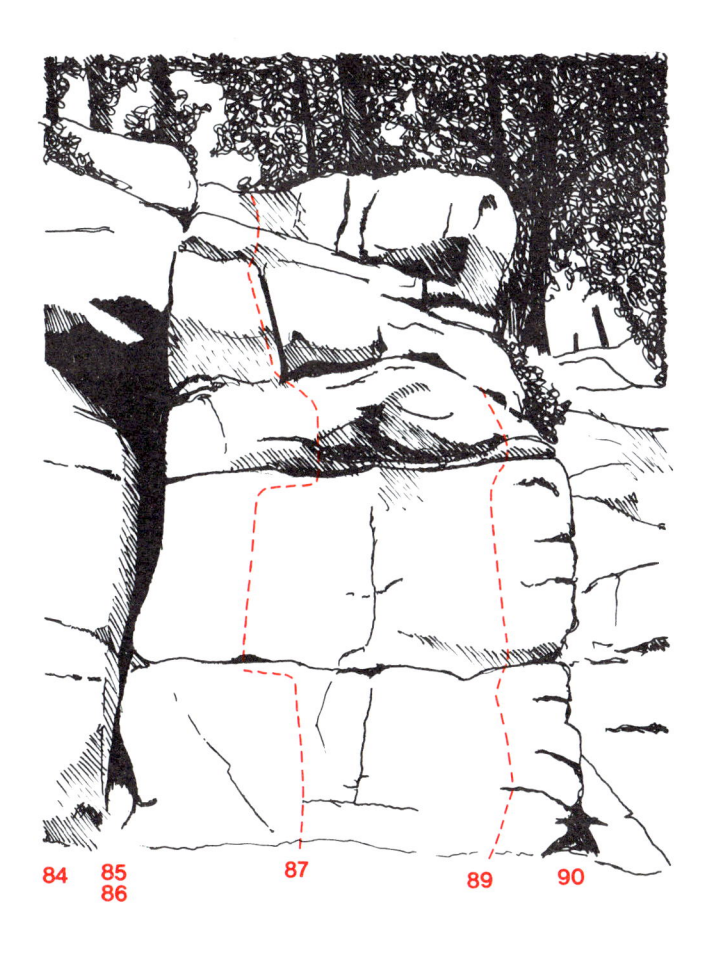

84 85   87   89 90
    86

46 BOWLES ROCKS

*97 Dib 3b
Climb the overhanging crack then move left just below the ledge to an ironstone hold. Mantelshelf onto the ledge and up easy rocks to the top.

98 Corbett Slab 4a
The centre of the pock-marked wall right of Dib is climbed to the ledge. Continue up the right-hand side of the slab and then go up easy rocks above.

99 The Scouter 2b
Climb a blind crack to the right of the pockmarked wall to gain a broad ledge; move left on this to an obvious groove with bolts in it, which is followed to easy ground. The overhang above The Scouter is 5b.

100 Nelson's Column 5a
Start just right of The Scouter and climb the wall without using holds on the next route.

*101 Dival's Diversion 4b
Go delicately straight up about two metres left of the Funnel.

**102 Funnel 4a
A fine route, with thought provoking moves. An obvious scoop in the upper part of the face marks the line; start a little left of this at a short (pink?) crack, or more directly.

103 U.N. 5c
Start a metre right of Funnel and climb carefully up the wall to a mantelshelf onto the wide ledge. Finish with hard moves straight up the front of the block.

104 Chelsea Traverse 2b
A technically interesting low level traverse. Start as for U.N., then traverse left along the lower ledges to the slab at the foot of Birch Crack.

**105 Well's Reach 3a
Bridge three metres up Harden Gully then move out left to follow a crack to the wide ledge below the roof; from here move back right into the gully and so to the top.

*106 The Wrecker 6c(NS)
Well named - a subtle blend of technicality and mindless brutality. The roof is climbed at its widest point using the obvious fist-sized crack. A fist jam here can numb your right thumb for two months. Fun, fun, fun.

107 Harden Gully 2a
The chimney is climbed to the broad earthy gully.

*108 Sylvie's Slab 4a
A pleasant slab to the right of Harden Gully. Finish up the wide crack at the back of the big ledge, if you so desire.

109 Six Foot 4c
Start three metres right of Harden Gully. Climb the wall on slot holds, trending slightly right to finish at the top of Sylvie's Slab.

*110 Larchant 5a
Just to the left of centre of the wall, with cut holds to finish on a broad ledge.

BOWLES ROCKS 47

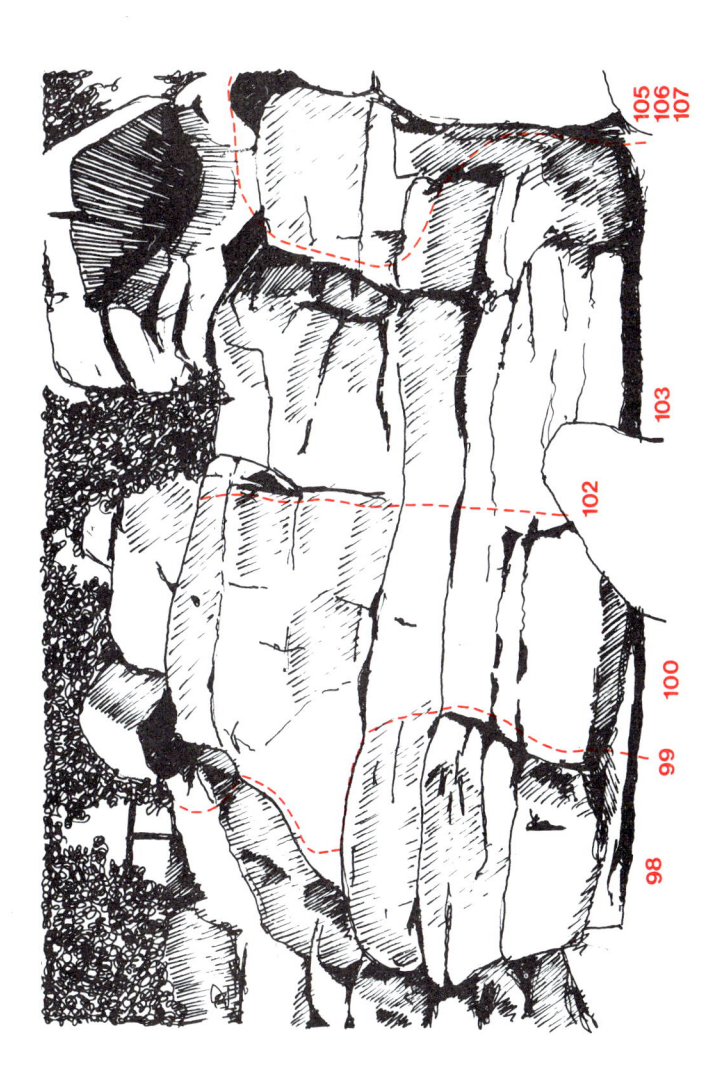

48 BOWLES ROCKS

**111 Hennesey Heights 5b
Go straight up the wall a metre right of Larchant - a good steep climb despite the cut holds.

*An **August Variation** 5b takes the wall just left of October, though it is hardly majestic.*

112 October 4c
Climb a thin crack on good sharp holds, and go straight up to the finish of Fragile Wall.

**113 Fragile Wall 3b
A popular route. Start direct or by traversing in from the right or left. Go up the obvious break at the right end of the wall on immense holds.

*114 Fragile Arête 5a
Do the direct start to Fragile Wall then go delicately up the arête.

An extremely strenuous ultra-low level traverse, keeping the hands below the level of the first main break, is usually begun at Fragile Arête and finished at Harden Gully - 6a.

115 Escalator 5a
Two metres left of Renison Gully. Go straight up on small holds with a mantelshelf to finish. A route has been squeezed in just before the chimney - **Elevator** 5a.

116 Pop's Chimney 4b
The short chimney above the ledge provides a finish to any of the last four routes.

117 Renison Gully 3a
The corner crack is followed to the wide ledge. Traverse easily left to finish.

*118 Lawson Traverse 4a
A worthwhile outing. Start up Harden Gully and traverse strenuously right to Renison Gully with the feet at about two metres.

The Lawson Extension 5b *continues to Nealon's, with interesting sections crossing Seltzer, Encore (rounded hand-traverse), and Rad's Cliff.*

*119 Finale 5c(NS)
Start easily up the wall right of Renison Gully. Pull leftwards with great difficulty onto the wall above the roof and so to the top.

*120 Alka 4c
Go up the nose on good rounded holds and continue up the obvious wide crack above.

*121 Seltzer 5b
The wide kinked crack to the right of the last route. Finish up the thin crack right of the block.

122 Encore 5c
Climb the wall two metres right of Seltzer to the ledge and continue straight up the impending wall to a mantelshelf finish. There used to be

---

5. Devaluation, 5b, Bowles Rocks. *Climber: Dave Jones.* Photo Gordon Stainforth.

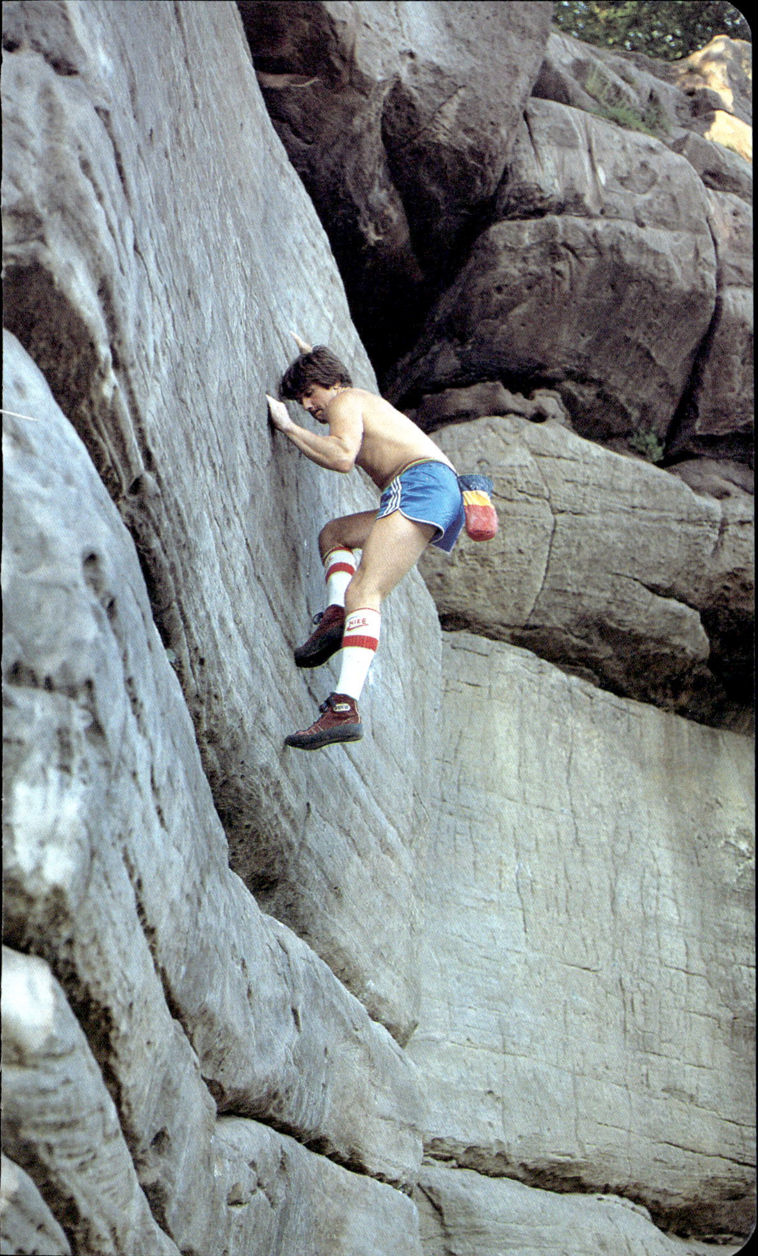
NIKE

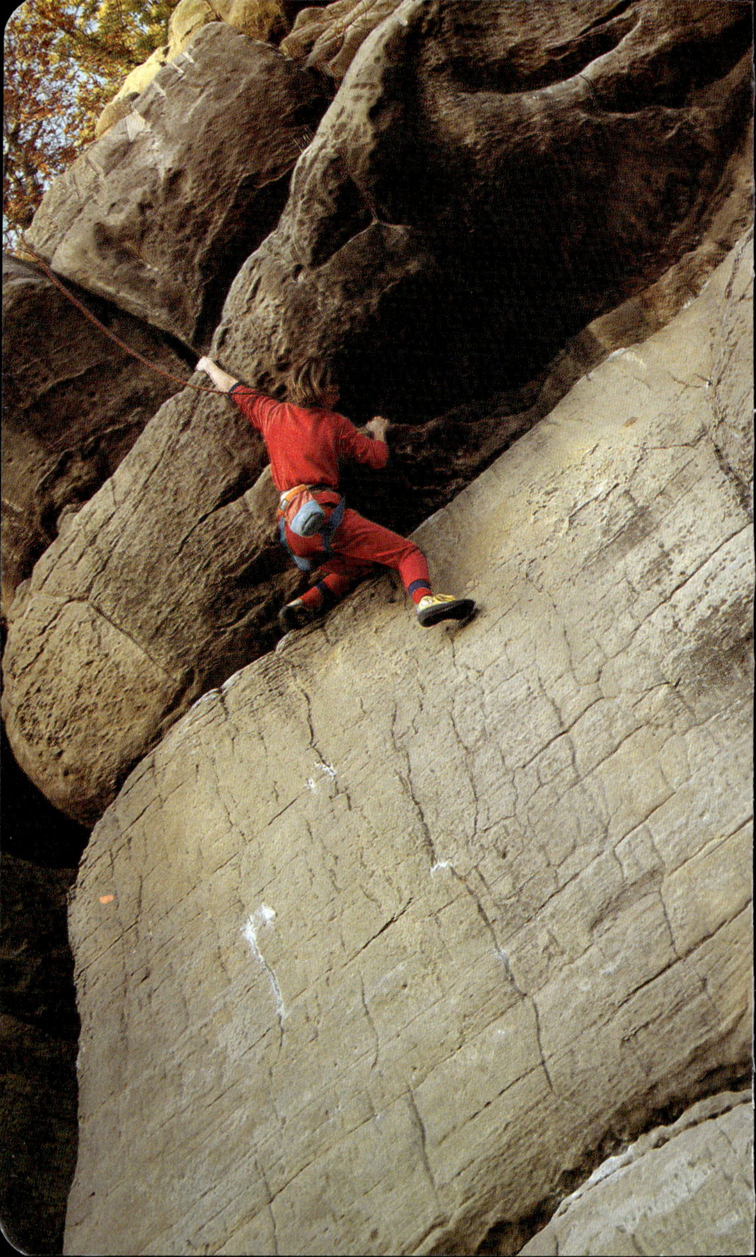

a beech tree to grab here but this collapsed in the storms of October 1987.

123 November 1a
An easy gully to the left of the block.

124 Baby Boulder 4a
The front of the block between the two gullies. It is possible to step left from the top of the block and with 5c moves climb the steep wall.

The next gully provides a very easy descent route.

125 Ballerina 4a
Prance delicately up the steep slab between the gully and Red Peg.

126 Red Peg 2a
Follow a worn crack and mantelshelf onto a broad ledge; continue straight up to finish over or around a little nose.

127 Claire 3a
Ascend the bulging front of the buttress on rounded holds and finish up the left edge of a little slab above.

128 Barham Boulder 3b
Start just to the right of the last route and go up diagonally right to the ledge. Finish as for either of the last two routes.

129 Rad's Cliff 4a
Start two metres left of the gully. Move right on the first break and go up to the terrace. Finish up a short wall below the holly tree.

Just to the right of an earthy gully there is a tall block. The next route goes up the front nose.

* **130 Bovril** 4b
Climb straight up the nose largely on its right side to the ledge. Move left into the gully and pull back right onto the upper block to finish. Ma mightn't approve of this.

131 Wally 4b
A direct line up the wall right of Bovril. It is also possible to start just to the right and climb the wall trending slightly rightwards - 5a.

** **132 Nealon's** 4c
Good climbing. Bridge up beneath the big diagonal overlap to the ledge, and exit up the little square-cut chimney.

133 A Lady In Mink 6a(NS)
Climb the easy right wall of Nealon's to the ledge; pull onto the wall above with some difficulty and make a hard lock to reach the top. The blunt undercut arête to the left of the finish is 6b.

The rocks now become considerably less continuous and more overgrown.

134 Mercator's Projection 3a
Climb easily up the centre of the next buttress and then cross a broad ledge to finish awkwardly from left to right on the overhanging boulder.

---

6. Hate, 6a, Bowles Rocks. *Climber: Felicity Butler.* Photo Dave Jones.

50 BOWLES ROCKS

The next feature is a small isolated rock mass. This is the somewhat overgrown Bowles Buttress, on which there are four short routes.

135 Pat's Progress 3a
A few mantelshelves, starting from the front of the buttress.

136 Dubonnet 4a
Start on the right of the previous route, s'il vous plaît, with a mantelshelf move and continue straight up.

137 William's Layback 2a
An obvious layback in the centre.

138 Index 4b
On the block. Use the index finger in the stalactite/stalagmite to mantelshelf and then go on straight up.

***139 Girdle Traverse** 5c
There are very good opportunities for traversing at Bowles. A complete girdle has been made, of which the more interesting sections have already been described. For instance, a fine outing is to start at Skiffle (37) and follow Orr Traverse (38) to Meager's Slab, stepping down to cross the base of this. Join and follow Pegasus (66), then its extension across Hate (87). Cross Birch Crack (93) low down, and follow Chelsea Traverse (104) to join Lawson Traverse (118) and its extension. Finish at Lady in Mink (133).

BOWLES ROCKS 51

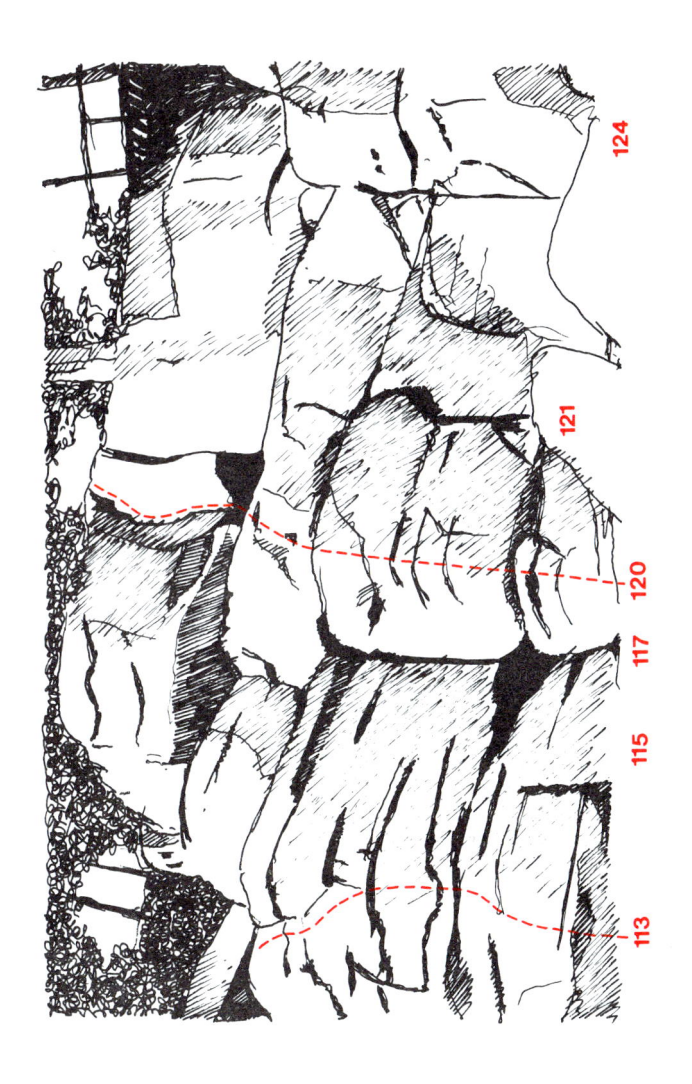

Bulls Hollow OS Ref 569 394

The rocks are situated adjacent to Denny Bottom on Rusthall Common one and a half km west of Tunbridge Wells.

From Tunbridge Wells take the East Grinstead road (A264) along the north side of Tunbridge Wells Common. Turn right some three hundred metres after the Spa Hotel into the Denny Bottom road - signposted to Toad Rock. The outcrop lies through the wood right of this road, one hundred and fifty metres from the junction. Parking is available on the road adjacent to Toad Rock; for this turn right again at the signpost to Toad Rock.

The outcrop is L-shaped, averages about eight metres in height and lies in a secluded position. The ground at the foot of the rocks is in places rather quaggy. The quality of the rock is variable because most of the faces have been quarried in the not too distant past. In some areas holds crumble very easily. The trees above the rocks tend to be well back from the edge. Consequently, a second rope used as a long sling is useful.

AS WITH ALL SANDSTONE CRAGS PLEASE USE A LONG BELAY SLING AND POSITION THE KARABINER OVER THE EDGE OF THE CRAG SO AS TO MINIMISE DAMAGE TO THE ROCK BY MOVING ROPES.

Unfortunately, the outcrop is rarely in condition largely due its secluded aspect and the plentiful shading trees. Despite this, the central area in the region of The Wall provides a concentration of excellent routes.

Contrary to previous practice, the climbs are now numbered from left to right. At the far end of the main crag is a bulging overhanging nose. The first route starts up the slope to the left of this:

*1 Waistline 5a
A high-level traverse along the break above the large overhang. Step off the tree roots, hand-traverse right to the nose and finish over it.

2 Broken Crack 3a
The cracks to the right of the large overhang leading to a tree. Awkward.

3 The Chasm 3b
Go up to a cave in the centre of the face, either direct or by traversing in from the right. The finish is straightforward.

4 Uncertainty 5b
A disgusting route, not to be recommended. Start two metres left of Tree Climb and climb the shattered wall into the groove with the rotten tree stump.

5 Tree Climb 2a
Two wide cracks lead to a tree with exposed roots.

6 Sandcastle 5c
Climb directly up the obvious overhanging sandy nose just right of the tree of Tree Climb.

BULLS HOLLOW ROCKS

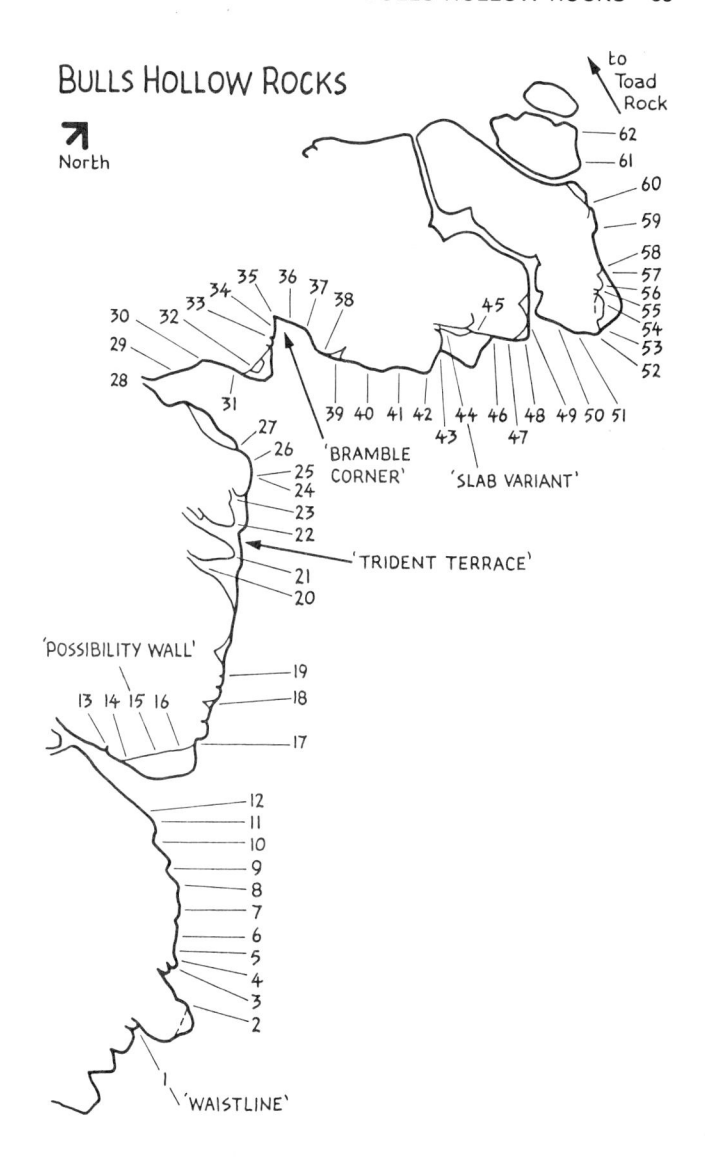

54 BULLS HOLLOW ROCKS

To the right is a yew tree in a break at four metres and another left of this at the top of the crag:

7 Yew Wall 5a
Go up to the left edge of the lower yew tree. Pull onto the wall above on sandy holds moving slightly right, then continue up trending leftwards to the upper yew tree.

8 Poltergeist 5c
Climb onto the ledge right of the yew tree, then up the flake crack and the wall above. The grade assumes the tree is not used.

9 Yellowstone Wall 3b
Climb straight up a sandy crack behind a pair of trees on the ground.

10 Yellowstone Crack 4b
Another sandy crack three metres right of Yellowstone Wall.

11 Taurus 5b
The arête just right of Yellowstone Crack.

12 Minotaur 6b(NS)
An obvious diagonal overlap left of the passageway is climbed on poor holds, with a long reach to finish. Previously a peg route.

Next is a wide passage which eventually leads to the top of the crag. In the right wall near the entrance is:

13 Bridge Crack 4b
Climb into the awkward niche on the right and continue up the crack above. An alternative from the niche is to bridge up at 4a.

*14 The Scoop 6a(NS)
The concave wall just right of the passage entrance is very technical.

**15 Possibility Wall 4b
A steep slab on well worn holds, thin at the top. Very good when dry.

16 Impossibility 5b
Step carefully up the steep slab right of Possibility Wall. Lives up to its name when greasy.

17 Sentry Box Arête 5b
Start round the arête on a ledge two metres up, swing left and climb the arête on its right side without touching the large tree.

18 Sentry Box 4b
Climb straight up the wall to a triangular niche and exit past the tree.

19 Yew Break 1a
An obvious staircase with a tree in it. Follow this rightwards.

To the right is a very rotten green wall. This has been climbed on but is extremely unpleasant and not worth describing. At its right end is Trident Terrace from which a few short unsatisfactory routes start. The terrace can easily be gained on the right.

20 Trident Left 1a
Not if Labour get in. An easy break at the left-hand end of the terrace.

21 Neptune Arête 3b
A short arête to the right with an awkward finish.

BULLS HOLLOW ROCKS 55

22 Trident Arête 3a
A somewhat artificial line to the left of Trident Chimney.

23 Trident Chimney 2b
At the right-hand end of the terrace.

Back on the main wall right of the terrace:

24 Apis 4b
An unsound wall is climbed to a crack which leads up past a small tree to the top.

25 Apis Variation 5c
Climb the wall as for Apis but go straight up the bulging nose to the left, without touching the crack or the tree.

On the left wall of the next bay are:

26 Moss 5b
The wall between Apis and the beech tree. Climb the centre of the wall on rounded mossy holds.

27 Cellar Wall 2a
Wide ledges lead right to a slabby upper section.

28 Coal Cellar 2a
A freak climb (aren't they all?) through a hole between the two converging walls at the back of the bay. It is apparently considered unsporting to use the tree roots to assist the undignified entry - OK chaps. Finish up the wall ahead.

The right wall of the bay starts with:

29 Blasphemy 4a
A short rather dirty crack in a V-groove.

30 Solo 4b
The sandy centre crack with a triangular overhang at the top. Climb the crack to the overhang. Move left onto the wall and finish by the tree. An alternative start, 4c, can be made from the crack on the right; this is followed to mid-height where a move left joins the other line.

At the right end of the wall is a pedestal; the next route starts just left of this:

*31 Conway's Variation 3b
Climb onto the pedestal on the left side and follow the diagonal ramp left to the top.

32 Conway's Buttress 3b
Surmount the pedestal from the right and continue up the short corner to the top, or go up the crack on the right with a small tree.

*33 Conway's Crack 4b
Straight up the twin cracks in the centre of the left wall of the bay.

34 Hanging Crack 5c
Start just left of Bramble Corner. Climb the short wall to gain the steep finger crack. Formerly a peg route.

56 BULLS HOLLOW ROCKS

The next series of routes provides a concentration of some of the best climbs on the outcrop:

*** 35 Bramble Corner 4a
An excellent crack climb. Go straight up the cracks at the back of the bay.

** 36 The Knott 5c
An enjoyable crack climb. The obvious thin crack to the right of Bramble Corner; it gets wider in the upper part. Another old peg route.

*** 37 The Shield 6a(NS)
Very sustained and technical. Climb directly up the centre of the wall between Knott and The Wall trending slightly right at the top.

*** 38 The Wall 5c(NS)
One of the best climbs at the rocks, up the scoopy wall three metres left of Caesar's arête. Start to the left and gain a wide ledge, move up and right then back left to a ledge in the middle of the wall. Continue to the top trending right.

* 39 Caesar 5c
From the recess on Centurion's Groove move left and climb the arête.

** 40 Centurion's Groove 4c
A pleasant route. Head straight up the wall to a recess then follow the shallow groove to the top.

* 41 Pseudonym 5c
A tricky climb that is high in its grade - a pseudo-6a? Climb the thin crack left of the nose to a small sloping ledge. Either go straight up the wall or, easier, trend right to finish.

* 42 Broken Nose 5b
The prominent nose is climbed direct, moving slightly right to finish. The grade assumes that the tree is not used.

43 Slab Chimney 3a
Climb the overhanging square-cut corner to the large platform; continue up the chimney and crack left of the narrow slab.

** 44 Slab Variant 4c
Ascend the broken lower wall to a large platform with a tree. Climb the narrow slab ahead. At the top it is possible to step across to easy ground on the left - taken this way the climb is 3b. The route proper continues straight up the whitish upper wall on the right to the top.

* 45 Time Waits For No One 6b(NS)
The centre of the upper wall right of Slab Variant gives an unusually thin and highly technical sequence of moves. Start on the platform, either direct or better, step across from the slab.

46 Fullmoon 5a
Gain the large platform as for Slab Variant. Move right into the Yew Tree and climb the sandy crack behind it. Simian creatures prefer to climb into the tree from below whilst eating a banana.

47 Eyewash 5b
The steep wall a metre left of Triangle Arête is usually very greasy.

48 Triangle Arête 5b
Climb the arête left of the passage direct. Normally greasy.

The passage provides any easy way up or down and a route:
49 Triangle Climb 2a
Climb the chimney formed by the passage, either inside or near the entrance.
50 Handle With Care 5c
This climbs the wall right of the passage. Start as for Crossply but move left along the ledge to a niche. Then go straight up the crack to an awkward finish. A direct start to the niche gives a more sustained climb.
51 Crossply 5b
Start in the centre of the wall. Climb up to the ledge and then move right to a bulge and a short slanting crack. Climb this and finish on the wall above the gangway.

Round the corner to the right is a wide shelf at head-height.
**52 Gangway Wall 3a
Climb up a short wall at the extreme left end of the shelf; then move up and left to the prominent gangway, which is followed to the top.
53 Square Cut 5c
Climb onto the shelf as for Gangway Wall but instead climb the obvious right-angled arête above.
54 Overhanging Crack 4c
The obvious overhanging crack with a little cave at the bottom. Rotten rock but good jams.
55 Sandy Wall 5a
Start as for Overhanging Crack but move right and pull strenuously onto the wall; continue straight up on good holds.
56 Avalanche Arête 5c
The undercut arête a few metres right of Overhanging Crack. Pull strenuously onto the arête and go straight up to a difficult mantelshelf finish.
57 Fortuitous 5c
The short steep wall immediately left of the groove of Avalanche Route.
58 Avalanche Route 3a
Climb a short rotten wall to a groove and follow this to the top.
59 Birch Tree Wall 3b
Start down and a metre left of the big tree, and go straight up the grooves.
60 Birch Tree Buttress 2a
The groove behind the big tree.

The next buttress has a tree growing out of it at about two-thirds height.
61 Toad Wall 2b
Straightforward but sandy. Go up the centre left of the tree. An alternative start is in the depression to the left trending right to finish.
62 Toad Arête 4b
The arête to the right of the tree growing out from the face.

Eridge Green Rocks OS Ref 555 356

The rocks are situated close to the Tunbridge Wells-Crowborough road (A26), four km south-west of Tunbridge Wells, three hundred metres west of Eridge Church.

Despite recent attempts by the BMC to negotiate an access agreement climbing remains strictly forbidden on these rocks. However, as in the past occasional discreet visits are made by various people, resulting in the few new routes described. The description of routes at this outcrop is purely as a record in case the access situation should ever change. The crag is a designated SSSI.

The main area map gives the best approach to the rocks - that is park where indicated, cross the main road diagonally left to the wooden gate, then follow the path rightwards to eventually reach some old sheds next to a metalled road. Opposite the sheds the rocks can readily be seen through the trees. It is also possible, though not discreet, to drive up the road which starts by Eridge Church. A footpath runs below the entire length of the outcrop, though this (and some of the rock itself) is now obstructed by fallen trees as a result of the October 1987 storm.

The nature of the outcrop as a whole is very varied. It's height ranges from five to ten metres and the condition of the rock varies from clean and solid to very lichenous and friable. This would obviously improve if the routes were regularly climbed. The top of the rocks is heavily vegetated for the most part and, due to the lack of climbers, a few routes have completely disappeared beneath the plant life. However, the quality of the routes is largely good and the outcrop has a unique atmosphere, which seems to gain much from its being little frequented.

In addition to the main outcrop there are two small outcrops in the woods towards Eridge Station - leftwards as one faces the crag. These are called Columnar Buttress and Elephant's Boulder and are described last.

AS WITH ALL SANDSTONE CRAGS PLEASE USE A LONG BELAY SLING AND POSITION THE KARABINER OVER THE EDGE OF THE CRAG SO AS TO MINIMISE DAMAGE TO THE ROCK BY MOVING ROPES.

Starting at the left end of the main outcrop are:

*1 Siesta Wall 5a
Go up an overhanging crack on the undercut left wall and trend right to finish. An eliminate boulder problem takes the nose just to the right, 6b.

2 Innominate Crack 5a
The initial bulge is surmounted outside the crack. Finish right or left or straight up - what else?.

3 Equilibrium Wall 5b
Start just left of Boulder Chimney. Climb the lower steep part moving gradually leftwards to finish by a crack on the left.

ERIDGE GREEN ROCKS

*3A Hottie 6a(NS)
The impending pockmarked wall right of Equilibrium Wall. Climb up to an undercut flake and finish with some difficulty.

4 Boulder Chimney 2b
The width of this passage is somewhat awkward chaps.

5 Libra 5b
Climb the blunt arête just two metres right of the last route.

Several metres to the right there is a large jutting prow. The next route takes the crack on its left.

*6 Hanging Crack 5a
The initial overhang is surmounted by some strenuous moves on good holds. Once in the crack it is comparatively straightforward.

7 Flake Crack 3a
The chimney at the right side of the wall - featuring a flake?

8 Bivouac Chimney 2a
Before the obvious cave.

9 Truncate 3a
The short wall left of the cave, with a twisted tree to finish.

10 Parisian Affair 6a
The short wall above the cave entrance, to the right of and without touching Truncate.

The roof right of Parisian Affair, which is **Too Short To Mention** *6a, has been climbed by leaning across from the left, and thus needs a direct start.*

11 Cave Chimney 2b
The dingy chimney that miraculously appears on entering the back of the cave.

12 6.0 a.m. Route 4b
Start from the right-hand side of the cave and take the crack. The top is rather overgrown.

13 Condom Corner 5c
The grotty rounded arête right of 6.0 a.m. Route is harder than it looks. A climb to be done once only.

Twelve metres further on there are some boulders close to the track offering a few short problems. The next route is on the main wall behind and right of these boulders.

14 Tree Climb 4c
Immediately right of the boulders is a short nose with a small tree in it, so there.

*15 Thin Layback 5b
To the right are a series of small layback holds. This gives a nice little climb with reasonable finishing holds.

16 Scratch 6a(NS)
The wall four metres right of Thin Layback.

17 Amnesian 5b
The cracked groove three metres right of the previous route and behind a large oak tree. A very slimy instantly forgettable route.

ERIDGE GREEN ROCKS
~ SOUTHERN HALF

→ North

Next is a slightly cleaner wall with a large roving tree branch masking it's face.

18　Mosquito 4c
Climb the arête on the left of the wall on good holds.

19　Tiger Moth 5a
The centre of the wall on good holds which should encourage one not to lean back onto the branch but then, why not?

Beyond a short wide chimney is:

*20　Rota 4a
A good jamming crack leads to a twiggy finish.

*21　Demon Wall 5c
Climb straight up the clean pock-marked wall to an obvious curved layback, and a difficult finish. A good route.

22　Tallywackle's Climb 5c(NS)
The wall left of the chimney with a dyno for the small tree to finish -OAP's should note that a dyno is a wild lunge in disguise.

23　Descent Chimney 3b
Straightforward and thrutchy.

24　Bulging Corner 5c
The arête right of the chimney is awkward to start; move round left to finish in the chimney without using the opposite side.

*25　Long Man's Neighbour 4b
The groove to the right is gained from the left or directly with more difficulty. A good and varied climb.

ERIDGE GREEN ROCKS

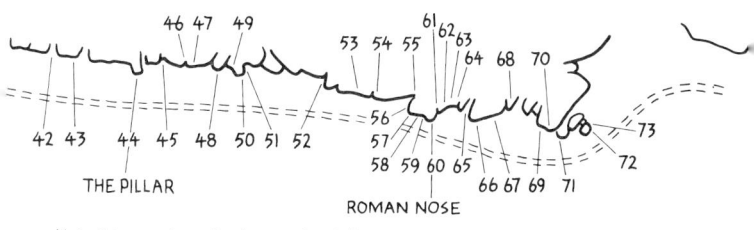

path in this area largely obscured by fallen trees and undergrowth

26 Long Man's Slab 5b
Start two metres right of the last route and pull onto the vegetated ledge. Continue up the mossy slab and finish directly up the headwall.

At this point the rocks extend out to the track. The next route takes the centre of the impressive wall adjacent to the track.

***27 Sandstorm 6a(NS)
A fine route. Pull over the overhang and move left with difficulty to a large pocket. Go up and right into the shallow scoop and follow this onto the wide ledge. Finish direct on very poor holds with a belly flop - not recommended - or traverse left and use the tree branch.

***28 The Crunch 6b(NS)
The impressive blunt arête right of Sandstorm. Start direct or more easily by a long traverse in from the right. Go straight up the arête on well-spaced jugs and small layaway holds to some undercut pockets just below the top, then traverse left and finish up Sandstorm. A direct finish seems possible but would be unpleasantly rounded and sandy.

Next is the Amphitheatre which principally has a crack on its left side, a hard face climb on its back wall, and a chimney on its right side.

29 Amphitheatre Crack 5b
The obvious wide crack some twenty metres right of The Crunch is reminiscent of Curbar's Right Eliminate. The lower portion is awkward and can be very green, whilst the upper section is strenuous.

30 Slug 6a(NS)
On the back wall. Start on a large boulder in the ground by stepping off its right side to reach a pocket. Very strenuous and greasy.

62 ERIDGE GREEN ROCKS

31 Amphitheatre Chimney 3a
A typical High Rocks chimney - a megathrutch in other words - which is climbed foot and knee anywhere, facing any way.

*32 Branchdown 5c(NS)
The mossy right arête of Amphitheatre Chimney.

33 Leech 5c(NS)
The mossy scoop left of Forgotten Crack started on the left.

*34 Forgotten Crack 6a(NS)
The curving crack behind the pine tree stump. It is very difficult getting over the bulge and into the main crack.

*35 Smile of the Beyond 6b
The undercut arête four metres right of the last route is gained from the right, with hard moves to get onto the wall. The wall and short crack above the start provides a slinky alternative finish - **Bernadette** 6b.

36 Torpedo Route 3b
The next chimney is hard to start due to the absence of the right wall for a metre or so. The finish up the front is straightforward. It is also possible to go straight up inside the chimney without the torpedo move.

37 Getafix 5c
Climb the blunt arête to the right of Torpedo Route with a jump to start.

Round to the right is a steep slab:

38 Locust 5c
The crack bounding the left side of the slab.

38A Finance 5c(NS)
A pleasant eliminate on the slab immediately right of Locust - the big layaway hold close to the crack at half-height is kosher. Move slightly right to a pleasant finish over the bulges.

*38B Higher Purchase 6b(NS)†
The centre of the slab. Start as for Finance, shuffle right on the break until a good pocket on the right can be reached then go straight up (crux). Move left slightly to join and finish as for Finance.

*39 Dusk Crack 4c
An obvious line on the right of the steep slab, using the small tree to finish.

**40 The Beguiled 6b(NS)
A brilliant little route. The left-hand end of the impressive pocketed wall round the corner from Dusk Crack is terribly technical, tendonous and tiring.

41 Hour Glass 5b
Six metres right of The Beguiled is a niche at ground level. Climb out of the niche and jam up to the jungle.

**41A Snail Trail 6b(NS)†
Another fine route. Using undercuts make a dynamic move out of the right side of the niche of Hour Glass. Continue directly up the wall above, making use of the obvious large undercut/sidepull near the top.

The next routes are one hundred and fifty metres to the right, past the S-bend in the track. Eventually one comes to a sandy light-coloured

ERIDGE GREEN ROCKS 63

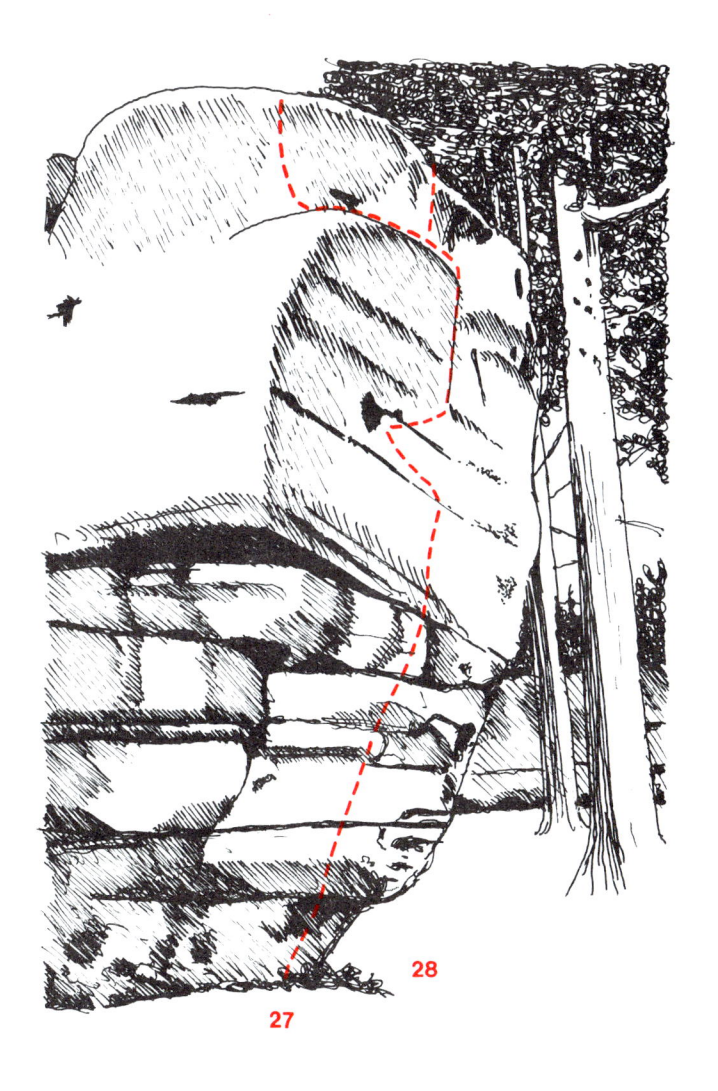

arête - not to be confused with the more impressive The Pillar ten metres further on.

42 Yew Crack 3b
This is to be found about five metres left of the sandy arête and is almost completely blocked by a tree whose root forms an unavoidable 'chockstone' at the finish.

*43 Thrutch 5c
The sandy light-coloured arête. Start on the left and pull over the overhang with difficulty to good holds; easier climbing leads diagonally left to tree roots.

To the right is a steep wall. At the right end of this, on good pocketed rock, is:

44A Triceratops 6a(NS)
Start just right of the arête (but left of the wide ledge); pull up and make very strenuous moves round onto the front face. Finish straight up.

On the next nose is:

44B Kinetix 6b(NS)†
The centre of the wall right of the wide corner crack. A powerful and dynamic series of moves.

**44 The Pillar 5c(NS)
Start on the right-hand side and move up onto the ledge; continue up the front face then move delicately left to the edge and finish straight up. A good route on excellent clean rock.

On the steep wall to the right is:

*45A Waffer Thin 6b(NS)
A highly entertaining (and explosive?) route. Gain the break and make a very hard rockover move to stand up on it. From the good hold on the left jump for the next one and finish strenuously.

**45 Obelisk 5c(NS)
Another fine climb on good clean rock - high in the grade. Climb directly up the sharp arête.

A variant is - **Mein Herr** 6a(NS). *Do the first move of Obelisk, then move slighly right and make a powerful long reach to a good hold and easy ground.*

46 Slanting Crack 3b
The wide (distinctly not slanting) crack right of Obelisk. This is easy until it narrows near the top. An earthy finish.

On the slabby wall to the right is:

**46A Stirling Moss 6a(NS)
A thoroughly enjoyable climb up the wall left of the central groove - thin and technical but with holds in all the right places.

*47 Scooped Slab 5b
Start at the right end of the wall and climb diagonally left to the groove in the centre. The finish is rounded and very awkward. A direct start is also 5b.

ERIDGE GREEN ROCKS

47A Snap, Crackle...POP!...Splat 6b(NS) †
Start as for Scooped Slab but go straight up to the leaning, pocketed wall. Undercuts and a dynamic move enable the top to be reached.

48 Black Crack 3b
The very short corner is hard to start and a tight thrutch all the way.

On the attractive sandy coloured buttress to the right is:

*49 Yellow Soot 6a(NS)
Climb the main wall left of Dilemma. Strenuous climbing on slightly sandy rock leads to a tricky finish.

*50 Dilemma 5c
Start just left of the forward point of the broad arête. Trend slightly right to finish over the bulge, which is a little obstructed by vegetation.

*51 Iron Man Tyson 6a(NS)
Climb the wall and arête right of Dilemma, starting on the right. Interesting moves.

Twenty metres or so right of the last route and three metres right of another short crack is:

52 Toadstool Crack 4a
The straightforward but narrow crack bounding the left-hand end of a fine steep fluted wall.

**53 Steelmill 6a(NS)
Take the centre of the fine flakey wall to an awkward finish. A very worthwhile route when dry.

**54 Touch Down 5c(NS)
The wall right of Steelmill would also be good if it ever lost all its grease.

55 Green Bollard Chimney 2a
Fifteen metres further right again is another High Rocks type chimney. It is half filled with debris, shaded by a holly tree and well worth avoiding.

The next feature of the rocks is a prominent overhanging nose with a crack on either side. The arête on the left is Asterix.

*56 Hadrian's Wall 5b
The easy-angled wall on the left of Asterix is climbed by a rising traverse from the left corner. Alternatively the traverse line can be reached from directly below, halfway along.

**57 Asterix 5b
Start round to the left and then climb directly up the arête. A pleasant climb.

*58 Fly By Knight 6a(NS)
The slabby wall just right of Asterix. Delicate balance moves lead to large layaway holds to finish.

*59 Remus 4c
The narrow crack on the left of the nose. Another pleasant climb.

60 Roman Nose 5b(NS)
The nose between the cracks. Start up Remus, then step right onto the nose; thin layaways lead to the top. A direct start over the little roof is 6b(NS).

ERIDGE GREEN ROCKS

61 Romulus 5b
The deeper crack on the right. Start awkwardly on poor rock and move up until the crack is reached. This goes more easily but with few holds.

The next three routes are on the wall right of Romulus, the condition of which is quite variable.

*62 Good Route...Poor Line 5c(NS)
The vague line of grooves a metre or so right of Romulus.

63 Good Route...Good Line 5b(NS)
The groove line just right of last route, initially taking the obvious layback.

64 Layaway 5b
The shallow scoop five metres right of Romulus is currently in very poor condition.

On the next smaller buttress there are three routes:

65 Capstan Wall 4a
Follow the line of the crack on the left of the buttress, with good holds.

*66 Concorde 5b
Climb straight up the arête.

67 Shanty Wall 5a
Go straight up on small lichen-covered holds, then step across to a rake on the right and so to the top. There is a lot of vegetation here at present.

The next four routes are behind dense undergrowth, and are not worth any effort to get to.

68 Bugbear Buttress 5a
Straight up the centre. Short but strenuous.

69 London Corner 2b
Obviously the position is of interest, if nothing else.

70 Jughandle 2a
On the wall to the right.

71 London Wall 2b
Just right again, and in some contrast to its eponymous northern counterpart.

On the next block, which is close beside the track, are two routes.

72 Eric 5a
Start by a ledge just left of the front nose. Go up and trend left to the top.

*73 Fandango 5c
Start right of the nose, and go straight up. The only obvious feature is a welcome horizontal break at mid-height, before a strenuous finish. An interesting route.

Fifty metres further right, there is a little buttress with three routes.

74 Keystone Face 4c
The face left of the chimney. The final move is on small holds.

75 Keystone Crack 2a
Go easily up the obvious chimney.

ERIDGE GREEN ROCKS 67

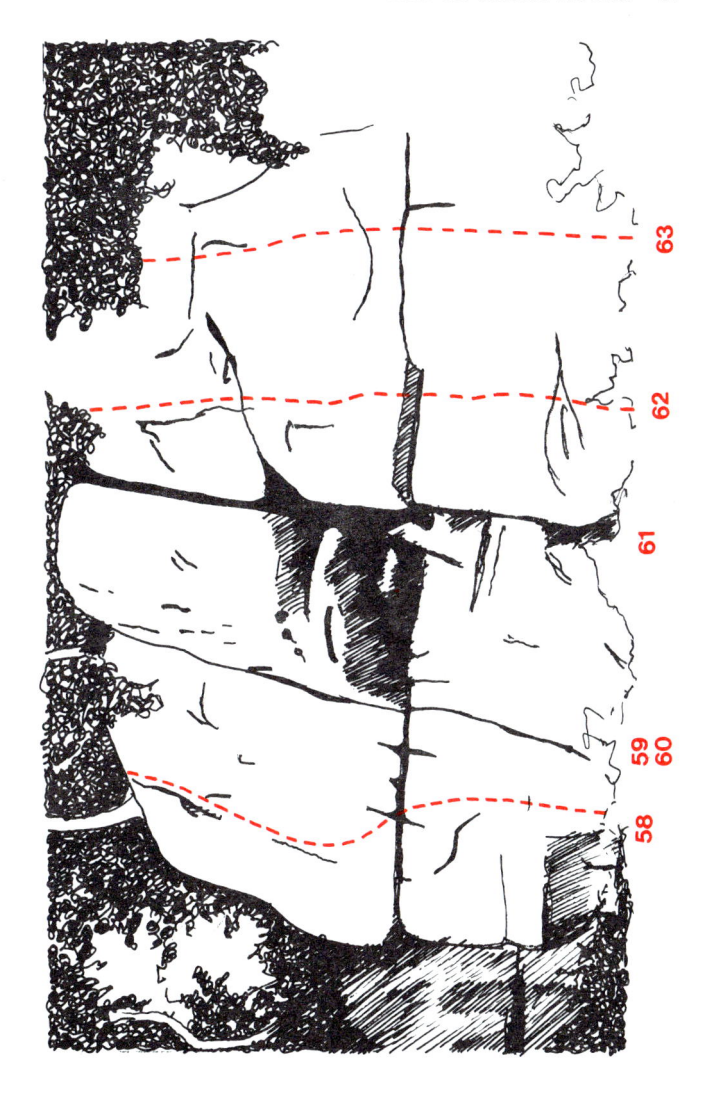

68 ERIDGE GREEN ROCKS

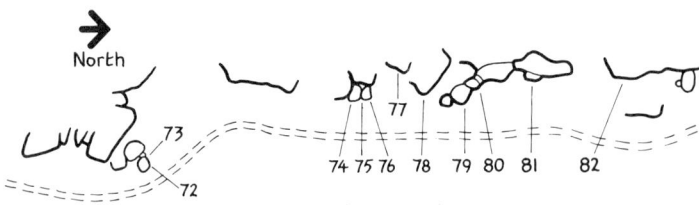

path obscured by broken trees, etc.

76 Keystone Wall 3b
Right of the chimney. Very green chaps - like martians?

Next is a series of small buttresses. On the first is:

77 Hartleys 4b
The most obvious crack in the centre of the wall.

78 Flutings 4b
A steep climb on good holds starts on the arête, and finishes either on the front, or on the side wall.

On the second buttress is:

79 Fontainebleau 5b
Is somewhere else and bears little resemblance to this. A strenuous layback flake, very undercut at the base, and awkward to start. Quite a grinder.

80 Fernkop Crack 4b
Difficult to start, due to the absence of the right wall at the bottom. Rather vegetated.

On the fourth buttress is:

81 Pedestal Wall 4b
A small platform jutting out from the wall is easy to attain. The wall above is also easy apart from the final move.

82 Crackpot 4b
The crack in the centre of the fifth block.

Continuing along the track one comes to the prominent Eridge Tower. This is a semi-isolated rock mass with good routes taking good lines, so there.

**83 Barbican Buttress 4b
Climb a crack to a ledge at the foot of a narrow slab on the left. Finish up the slab.

*84 Steamroller 5c(NS)
Straight up the centre of the impending, pock-marked wall.

***85 Battlement Crack 5a
A good climb. Climb the crack to the overhang, move left and continue up another crack to finish with increasing difficulty.

ERIDGE GREEN ROCKS ~ NORTHERN HALF

**86 Portcullis 5c
Another good climb. Go up the crack to the niche below the square block-shaped overhang. Pull over this on sandy holds to the top. A variation finish takes the left wall of the tower after the niche - 6a(NS).

87 Eridge Tower Route 5a
A scramble up the lower part leads to the upper overhanging crack, which is climbed on sandy holds.

88 Tower Girdle 5b
The Tower can be girdled just below the overhanging top portion.

89 Shirt Rip 5c(NS)
On the green wall immediately right of, and set back from, the Eridge Tower. Take the thin slanting crack at the left end.

90 Three Hands Route 5b
The greasy crack two metres right of Shirt Rip. Good when dry.

The next route is twenty metres further along the track, where the height of the rhododendrons decreases.

*91 Twin Slabs 5a
The lower slab leads to a ledge halfway up. The upper slab is a square-cut shallow chimney, climbed by bridging, with a thin finish. Both this and the next route are well worth the jungle bashing to experience their delights.

*92 Tiger Slab 4b
Climb up the lower wall to a broad ledge. The upper wall is ascended facing right, by an awkward movement up a short crack, from the top of which step left and climb a thin slab. An alternative (5b) finish is possible on the right.

93 Green Crack 2b
Well obscured by rhododendrons and appropriately named.

Close to the track again is:

94 Gully Rib 3b
The obvious easy-angled rib where a small rock mass projects near to the track. Currently rather overgrown.

95 Cave Corner 5a
The lower wall is climbed at its most forward point a metre left of the low wide cave. Continue up the upper part by a steep slab on the left.

96 Cave Climb 5b
Take the lower wall immediately above the cave. Move left and climb the upper wall at its most forward point.

This last route marks the end of the main outcrop.

The two outlying outcrops mentioned in the introduction are on the south side of the metalled track. The dirt track at the entrance to the woods that leads south is followed. A right fork is taken and after about 300 metres a white round buttress can be seen 50 metres to the right. This is:

97 Columnar Buttress 4a
This is the main route and is centred around the obvious huge handle hold.

98 Primrose 4c
Follow the rounded flake just right of the last route.

If the dirt track is followed for another 150 metres, a larger green buttress on the right becomes apparent. This is called Elephant's Boulder or Elephant Wall. The first three routes are on the low left end of the outcrop.

99 Heffalump 4a
A very short route up the easy-angled rock on the right side of the equally short passage.

100 Elephant's Tail 3b
Start in the gully on the left, step round to the front and up.

101 Y Crack 4a
Why not? The obvious Y in the front of the boulder.

102 Elephant's Head 5c(NS)
The very left end of the sheer wall, just round the corner from Y Crack.

**103 Diagonal 6b(NS)
A fine looking line with equally good climbing. The right-to-left overlap left of Mammoth Wall, with a tricky exit at the top.

*104 Mammoth Wall 5b
On the recessed wall. Start six metres right of the gully and climb the layback crack. Move left to finish via small ledges.

ERIDGE GREEN ROCKS 71

Harrison's Rocks   OS Ref 532 355

The rocks are situated about one and a half km south of Groombridge, along the west edge of Birchden Wood close to the now-closed railway line between Groombridge and Eridge Stations.

They are approached by heading south from Groombridge, passing the old station on the left. At the first fork go right and after two hundred metres turn right again down a narrow lane, signposted as Birchden Wood and Harrison's Rocks. A car-park with toilet facilities is soon reached beyond which motor vehicles are not permitted. There is a donations box at the car-park exit. This money is put towards the maintenance of the toilets (often with soft toilet paper), the car-park and the rocks themselves. The continuation of the lane as a dirt track leads from here through Birchden Wood past another signpost to the rocks. One usually arrives at the top of the gully between routes 79 and 80.

Any difficulties incurred when using the car-park area or the rocks should be communicated to Terry Tullis, South East Area Committee Representative of the BMC, telephone Groombridge (089 276) 238. Large parties wishing to use the Rocks should first apply to The Sports Council (London and South East Region), 160 Great Portland Street, London, WW1N 5TB, telephone 01 580 9092.

Harrison's Rocks remains the best known of the outcrops described in this guide. This seems to be due to the large number of good climbs at most grades of difficulty. There are, perhaps thankfully for most, far fewer chimneys than at High Rocks. The rocks face west and can be a suntrap in the summer - trees permitting - making them a very pleasant evening venue. The rock is not always as sound as it may appear even on the more popular routes. Care should therefore be taken when soloing and in the positioning of top-ropes - large apparently solid blocks at the top of the crag are often not as stable as they seem.

Harrison's Rocks is actually owned by climbers. It was purchased by the British Mountaineering Council (BMC) and is held in trust by the Sports Council. The intention is solely to preserve the climbing facilities. To this end, the following conditions have been drawn up by the BMC/Sports Council Management Committee for Harrison's Rocks:

1. AS WITH ALL SANDSTONE CRAGS PLEASE USE A LONG BELAY SLING AND POSITION THE KARABINER OVER THE EDGE OF THE CRAG SO AS TO MINIMISE DAMAGE TO THE ROCK BY MOVING ROPES. This is of prime importance for the preservation of the rocks and cannot be emphasized enough. Belay bolts have been placed in some areas to encourage this practice. Ropes should not be put directly through these because they will be worn out fairly quickly if you do so and then require replacement.

2. Abseiling is prohibited.

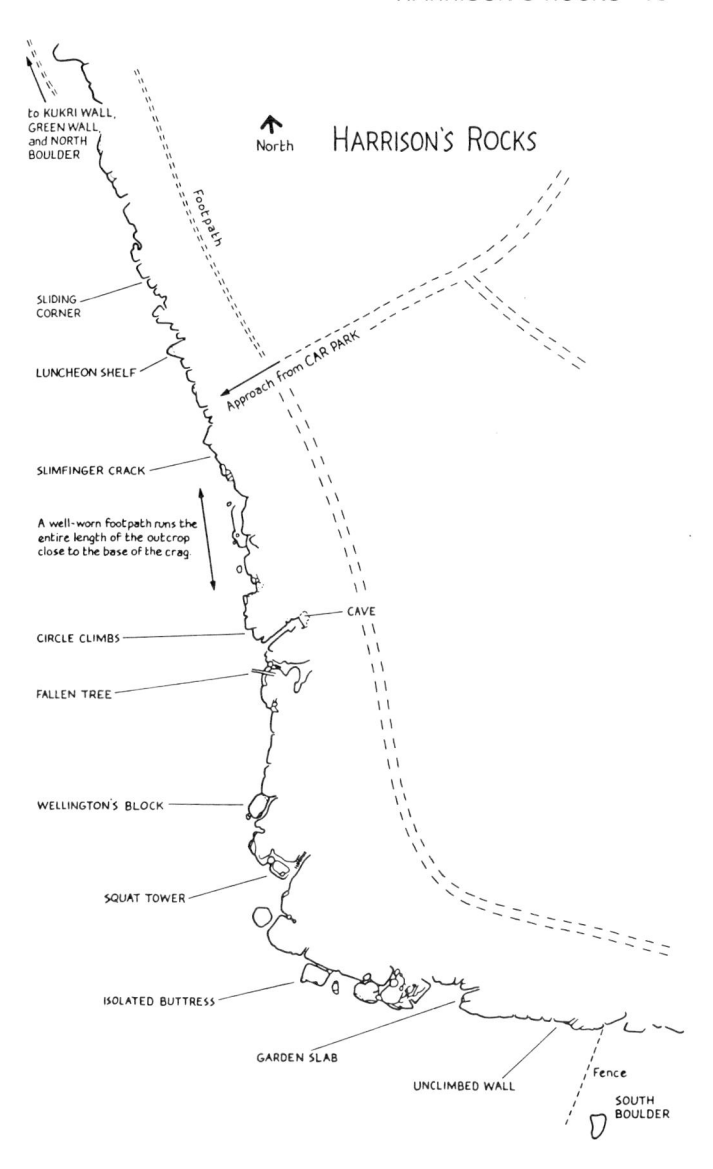

3. No aid climbing or leading with pegs, wedges, bolts or conventional protection devices. The choice lies between top-roping or soloing.

Furthermore, access to the crag is through Forestry Commission land. Therefore, to maintain good relations with the Commision:

4. Camping, the lighting of fires and stoves, and the playing of transistor radios etc is prohibited. Please avoid any unnecessary noise.

5. Please pick up your litter, and other peoples if necessary. There are bins in the car-park.

The imposition of rules is clearly an anathema to most climbers but is entirely necessary because of the fragility of the environment. The Rocks are suffering badly from erosion due to moving ropes at the tops of climbs and heavy foot traffic leading to a drop in ground level below some routes. The typical result of this is progressively easier finishes to some routes and harder starts to others. The rope grooves are cemented in by the Management Committee from time to time but with care this should not be necessary. Unfortunately, it is more difficult to check the ground erosion though steps have been taken. These consist of laying down extensive amounts of gravel to improve drainage and shoring up the paths with planks and stakes. So far this seems to have been a successful policy.

In a change from previous practice, the climbs are now described from left to right; starting with the North Boulder which is some way left of the main crag and which sports a number of boulder problems:

On the side facing the main crag there is a 3a, with 5b problems to either side. The centre of the passage wall gives a 6b lunge for a jug. The arête to the right is 6a. The north face has a 5a problem using a large undercut, a 5b problem up the centre and another 5b with undercuts just to the right. The right arête is the same grade. The west face has a 6a over the nose on the left, a 5c up the flutings in the centre and three more 6a problems gradually working right.

Thirty metres right of the North Boulder is Sandown Crag, which is now much more open than before due to the clearance of trees and vegetation. It is characterised by a tree stump on the right at the top. Three routes have been described:

1 The Ramp 2b
At the left end of the buttress is a ramp which is followed leftwards to a dirty finish.

2 D.J. Face the Music 5c
A thin and technical problem up the steep wall between the ramp and the crack.

3 Central Route 3a
This pleasant and worthwhile route takes the obvious central crack line of the buttress.

A few other little problems are possible to the right of Central Route but are not worth describing.

There now follows a large number of low buttresses and intermittent

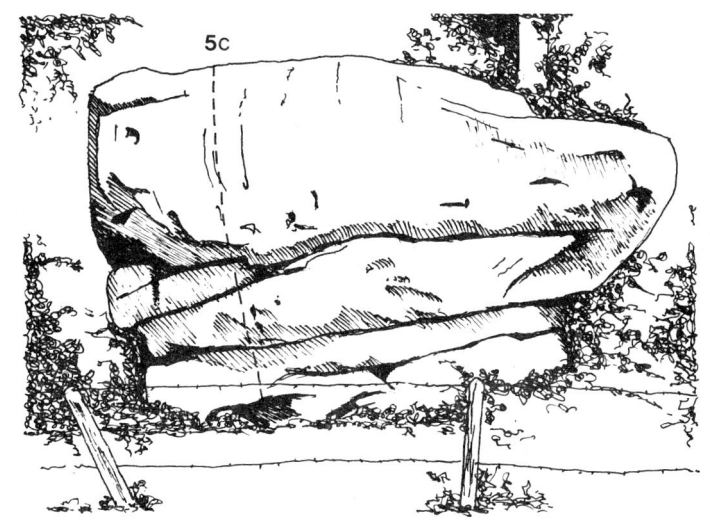

North Boulder – West Face

faces. Although a number of little problems are possible here, there is only one recorded route in this area. This is to be found on a low buttress with a slab about forty metres right of Sandown Crag.

4 Usurer 3a
Despite the name this is a climb of little interest. Start at the lowest point, climb the right-hand end of the slab and finish amongst the holly above.

About twenty five metres further on is Green Wall, which is now quite open and thus very often dry. There is a large beech tree stump at the top and just left of centre. A number of little problems can be done at the left end but the first route is:

5 Teddy Bear's Picnic 5c
The short wall 1½ metres left of the beech tree has thin holds and is deceptively difficult.

6 Central Groove 4a
The groove right of the tree stump, with an awkward start behind a holly bush and a move right to finish.

*7 Dynamo 5b
Go straight up the wall left of Usurper and finish between the two grooves.

*8 Usurper 5b
There is another groove about three metres right of Central Groove; start just right of this and move left into it.

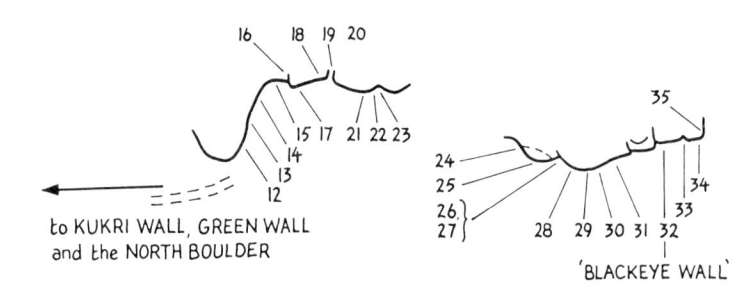

Another fifteen metres right is Kukri Wall with three routes.

9 Breadknife Buttress 4b
The left wall is tricky at the top.

10 Kukri Wall 3b
Climb the faults in the middle of the wall.

11 Kukri Wall Direct 4b
The middle of the right wall on small holds and somewhat obstructed by holly.

More broken rocks follow, after forty metres of which Eyelet Wall is to be found.

12 Ringlet 5b
Start as for Eyelet but as soon as possible move across left onto the arête and up this.

*13 Eyelet 4a
A strenuous problem on good holds up the overhanging bulge. The Eyelet itself disappeared years ago.

14 Singlet 4b
Go straight up to the right-hand tree stump.

15 Dave 2a
Mantelshelf and then go up to the tree roots.

16 Don 2a
A short wide crack in the corner.

17 Toad 4c
The nose to the right of Don.

18 Elastic 5b
The wall left of Tight Chimney is awkward.

19 Tight Chimney 3a
Face right and climb with the left leg in, if you want to that is.

20 Tight Chimney Slab 4b
Traverse right out of Tight Chimney on the first ledge and go up the slab

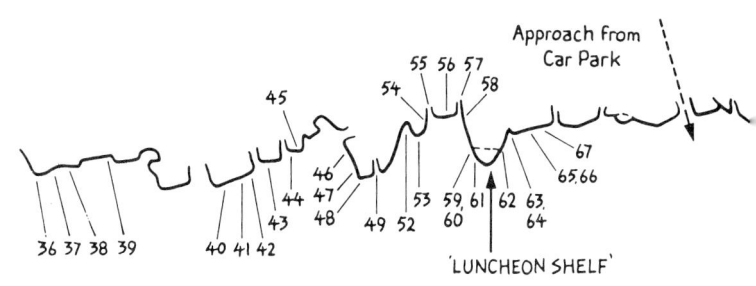

HARRISON'S ROCKS — NORTH

Approach from Car Park

'LUNCHEON SHELF'

just beyond the nose. A direct start from below is possible at about 6a.

21 Sullivan's Stake 5b
A tricky climb in the centre of the triangular wall.

22 Gilbert's Gamble 4b
Gain a ledge just left of the Ejector crack and go delicately to the top.

23 Ejector 4a
The crack in the centre of the face is aptly named.

23A Sand Piper 6a
The thin cracks in the steep slab just right of Ejector.

Further along the path the next low face left of a chimney gives two routes.

24 Trip of the Psychedelic Tortoise 5c
The short wall and overlap left of Carrera gives a deep and meaningful experience, man.

25 Carrera 5b
Start up the flake left of Open Chimney; move right and then back left to finish.

26 Open Chimney 2b
This can be done facing either way or not at all.

The next buttress gives five routes largely with rounded sandy holds.

*27 Cottonsocks Traverse 4b
Sandy to start with but worth the effort. From the foot of Open Chimney make a gradually ascending traverse right until the break below the top is reached. Continue across the remaining Root Routes to the foot of the rocks in the next bay. Finish up Route 2 or a little further right.

28 Root Route 3 5b
The rounded nose right of Open Chimney has very poor sandy holds - it is thus very strenuous and easy to fall off of.

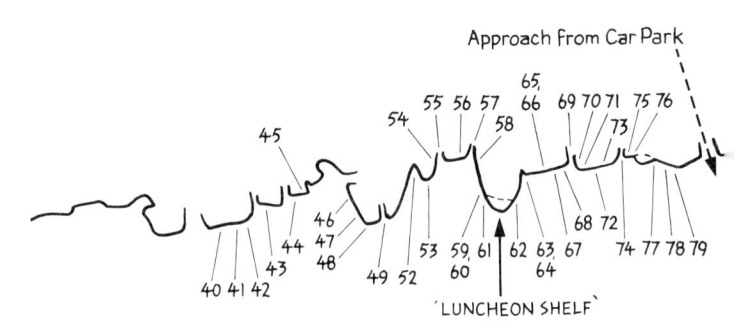

29 Root Route 2 5b
Start at deep positive pocket hold in the middle of the wall; stand up on this with difficulty and go on up tending a little left to finish.

30 Root Route 1½ 5a
Start two metres right of Route 2 and go straight up.

*31 Root Route 1 3b
Start at the right end of the wall and gain the first break. Traverse left to join and finish as for Route 2. A direct line from the start to the tree roots is 3b.

The next buttress has some short problems of some technical interest for those who have done all the longer problems.

32 Blackeye Wall 5c
Climb the thin crack until it is possible to hand-traverse left on a rounded ledge and make a very awkward mantelshelf into the niche.

*33 Slanting Crack 5c
The diagonal line in the centre of the wall is frequently green and much harder than it looks.

*34 Counterfeit 5c
Forge up the wall immediately left of Right-Hand Crack on small finger holds.

*35 Right-Hand Crack 4a
The wide crack with a stump at the top. A 3a climb can be done up the small buttress right of the crack.

The next buttress is small and vegetated with two cracks in the upper part. Recent ground excavation has made the three climbs a metre or so longer.

36 Wisdom 5b
The thin lower wall and the left-hand crack.

37 Fang 5b
Climb the centre of the bulging wall between the two cracks. The fragile stump at the top should be treated with care.

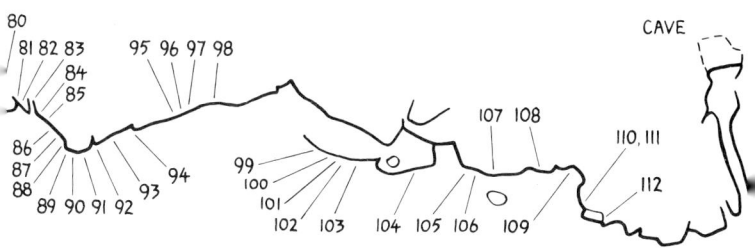

HARRISON'S ROCKS — NORTH CENTRAL SECTION

38 Incisor 4b
The lower wall and the right-hand crack.

The next climb is a few metres right on a short green slab, somewhat hidden at the top of a slope:

39 Weeping Slab 5a
A steep slab that is usually wet and impossible. Also known as 'The Monk's Slippery Slide'.

A little further on the line of the rocks is more continuous than previously. The next feature is Slanting Holly Buttress with three routes:

40 Sticky Wicket 5c
Follow the obvious crack on the left of the buttress to an unpleasant finish through grease and holly bushes. Hard Very Slimy would be a better grade.

41 Rotten Stump Wall 5c
Climb the next short crack on its right side. A long reach follows to the next break, which needs to be dry to hang onto. The rotten tree has long since disappeared.

*42 Sliding Corner 5b
Start in the chimney right of the buttress, move left and then go straight up on very awkwardly placed holds.

43 Fingernail Crack 2a
The short crack on the left side of the steep slab.

44 Dinosaurus 5c
On the buttress right of the steep slab. Go up the gully two metres then move right onto a wide sloping ledge. Step up and right onto a break and finish on the front face.

45 Smiliodon 5c
A direct start to Dinosaurus. Climb the crack in the centre of the wall to the break. Move right to layaway holds and then back left to finish. It is 6a when climbed direct all the way.

Next is a broad gully with a wall on its right side:

46 Tomcat/Simon's Wall 5c
The left end of the wall. Start behind the holly bush and go up on small holds.

47 Panther's Wall 6a
Very technical. Climb the wall left of the arête of Snout using some obvious deteriorating undercut holds.

48 Snout 5b
The rounded arête at the end of the wall with awkward balance moves on sandy holds leading to an easy finish.

*49 Snout Crack 3b
This is best done facing left, giving a straightforward and surprisingly good route.

50 Guy's Problem 5c
The arête right of Snout Crack.

51 Mantelpiece 5c
A short problem gaining the niche left of the tree.

52 Beech Corner 3a
The tree gets in the way but the climb up its left side is strenuous. The line on the right side of the tree is 5a.

**53 Blue Peter 5c
Climb the steep arête starting on the left. Step (shep?) back left to finish.

An eliminate has been climbed up the steep wall immediately right of the arête, which is **Madness** *(5c) because:*

**54 Blue Murder 6a
Climbs the impending crack in the left wall of the bay with increasing difficulty to the break. Finish either directly above the crack or move strenuously a little right and then go up.

55 Slab 3b
Not a slab at all, more of a contorted chimney really. The wide crack on the left of the slab. The kink is the tricky bit.

**56 Slab Direct 4c
A nice and (therefore?) unusual climb for sandstone. Make a delicate step onto a large foothold in the centre of the slab and climb directly to the top.

*57 Slab Crack 5b
The corner crack gives awkward jamming and bridging moves - recommended, if this sort of thing appeals.

*58 Lager Frenzy 6c(NS)†
Can be had but most will resign themselves to a Hangover of some sort. The cracks in the centre of the overhanging wall are followed to the break where a move left allows the top to be reached. Move back right to mantelshelf on a jug.

---

7. Long Layback 5a, Harrison's Rocks. *Climber: Dave Turner.* Photo Ben Pritchard.

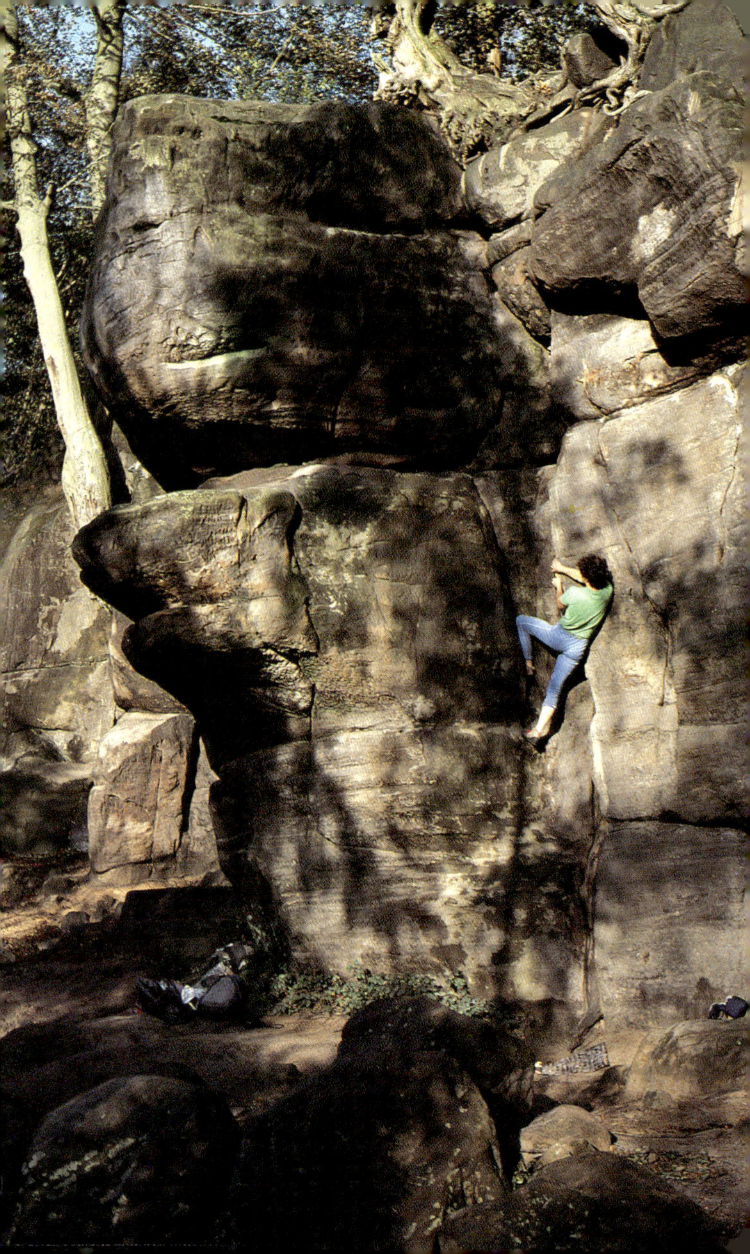

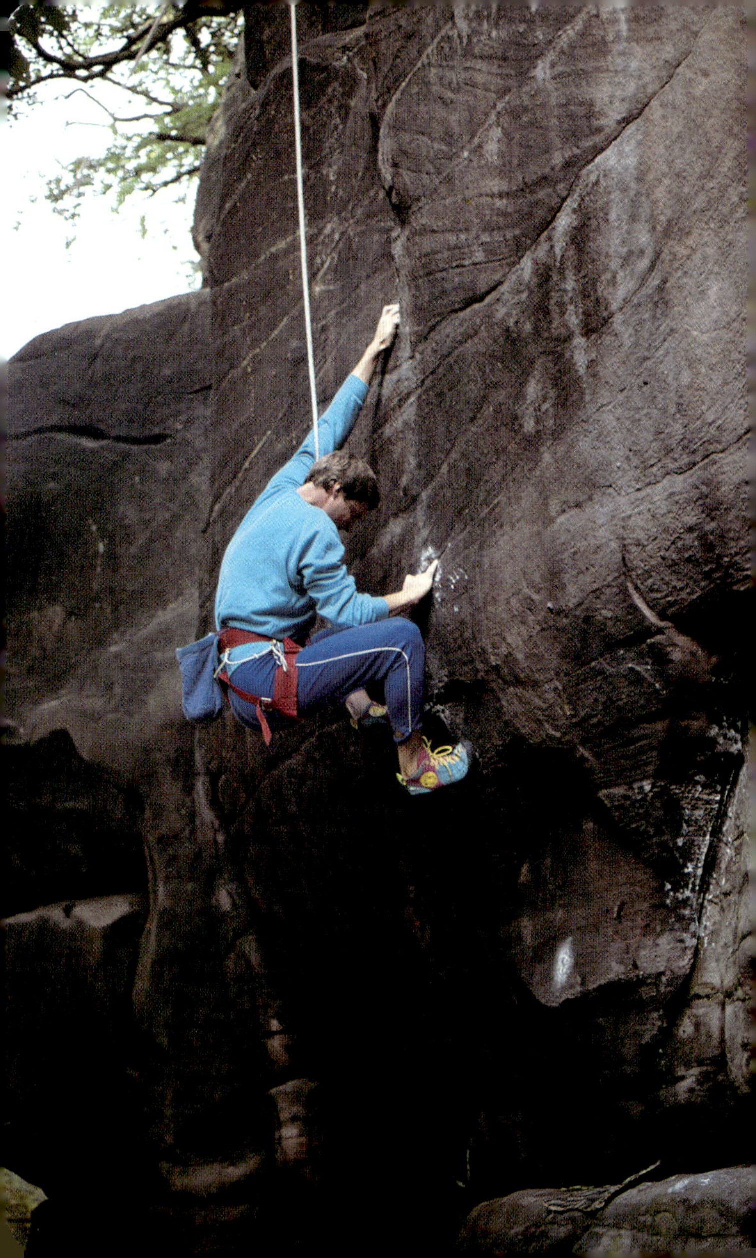

HARRISON'S ROCKS

59 Celestial's Reach 6a
Start on the right edge of the wall. Go up to the main break with difficulty then step left and finish more easily up the wide crack. Alternatively, swing left from the bottom of the crack and finish up the steep nose on good but spaced holds, 5c.

60 Stardust 6a(NS)
Follow Celestial's Reach to the break then move right and pull over the bulge to finish up the shallow groove.

To the right is the Luncheon Shelf which can be gained in a number of ways. The various finishes can be combined with any of the starts.

61 Hangover II 6a
Start immediately below the left edge of the overhang and make a hard move up to gain a sandy ledge. Hand-traverse right to the centre and mantelshelf onto the Shelf. The **Centre Finish** 6a is undercut and makes use of a large pothole and small fingerholds above.

A strenuous variation to Hangover II is **Hangover I** *6a. Start as for Celestial's Reach then hand-traverse right to join and finish as for Hangover II.*

***62 Hangover III** 6a
Do people ignore you? Want to get noticed? Start at the right-hand corner of the overhang. Make a long reach to a slanting jug, swing out left on the break and traverse to the centre. Mantelshelf with difficulty onto the Luncheon Shelf. Take the Luncheon Shelf Finish or the **Nose Finish** 6a(NS) † a metre to the left.

A good direct line on Hangover III goes straight up from the slanting jug with a heel-hook in the break on the left.

***63 Luncheon Shelf** 5c
Start as for Long Layback but at the top of the parallel cracks traverse left onto the wide shelf - 5a. Finish up the wall above the Luncheon Shelf about two metres left of Long Layback.

****64 Long Layback** 5a
A classic climb up the big corner with the parallel cracks. The start is now very polished.

****65 The Flakes** 6a
Another classic route. Pull into the niche right of the corner then go up gradually right to the roof using the thin flakes. Hand-traverse right to the leaning crack and finish awkwardly up this. Please try to minimize rope abrasion on the rock to the left of the final crack.

***66 Flakes Direct** 6a
Start as for The Flakes but instead of moving right go straight up the crack above the niche. Finish directly over the top overlap. Holds on Long Layback are avoided entirely.

****67 Coronation Crack** 6a
Follow the thin crack in the middle of the wall to join and finish as for Flakes. The middle section gives precarious jamming for the technician

or a powerful undercut move for those of the ramboid tendency. Finish straight up as for The Flakes.

68 The Limpet 6b(NS)
A good but eliminate route that has now had many ascents. The arête left of Dark Chimney is climbed almost totally on its left side. At the top overlap finish direct or swing a metre left and then go up.

A strenuous traverse has been made along the high-level break of The Flakes wall by starting up Dark Chimney and finishing up Long Layback - **Vampire's Ledge** 5b.

***69 Dark Chimney 2a
The classic easy route of the rocks is also a very popular climb - the adjectives popular and classic don't always go together, particularly with Sandstone chimneys.

70 Dark Chimney Buttress 5a
Climb the left-hand end of the wall right of Dark Chimney. Move right onto the ledge and finish straight up.

71 Nut Tree 6b
The very rounded arête at the right end of the wall is touch and go.

72 Spout Buttress 5c
The crack just round the arête is very hard to start.

73 Spout Crossing 5a
Climb the recess to the left of the Spout to the first ledge. Either finish direct with further difficulty, or move right into the Spout and go up this a metre, followed by a traverse right to finish up Pelmet.

*74 Windowside Spout 2a
The obvious chimney.

There is a multiplicity of routes on the next wall, of which Bow Window is the original. This is distinguished by a 'milestone' block at the foot and a 'triangular pocket hold' on the smooth wall "above.

75 Casement Wall 5b
An eliminate climb on the wall immediately right of Windowside Spout chimney. Go straight up to the Pelmet ledge and continue up the jam crack to the top.

*76 Pelmet 5b
Take a direct line up the wall 1½ metres left of Bow Window to the jam crack of Casement Wall. The triangular pocket may be used for the right hand but it can be avoided. Alternatively, climb the first five metres of Bow Window then hand-traverse across to the crack.

**77 Bow Window 3b
A justifiably popular climb. Start on the milestone and follow the obvious break via the triangular pocket to beneath the overhang; pass this on the right to finish up an easy wide crack. A **Direct Finish** 5c pulls leftwards onto the wall above the overhang.

78 Finger Stain 5b
The middle of the convex wall right of Bow Window has good positive holds.

HARRISON'S ROCKS 83

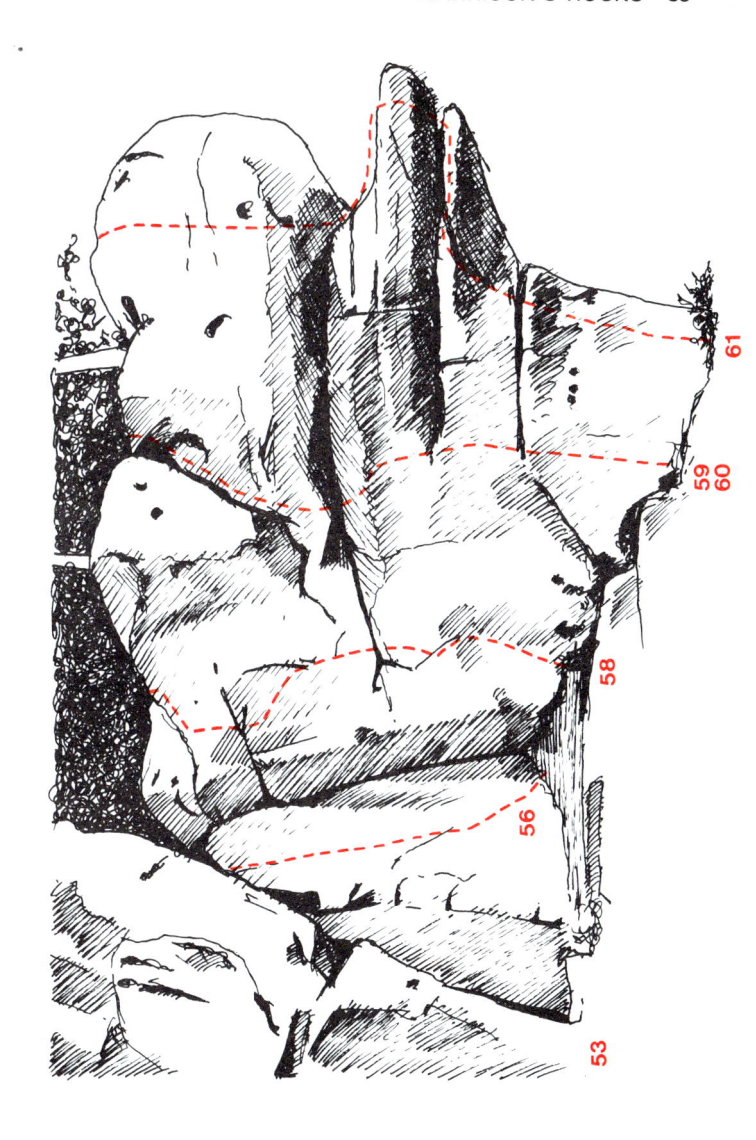

*79 Sashcord Crack 4a
Short but good which is what counts. Never mind the quality... Climb the centre of the bulging wall left of the descent gully. Finish up the wide crack on the left or traverse off right. The small block directly above the crack is 4b.

At this point a steep, well worn path leads to the top of the rocks. This is the usual descent used when approaching from the car-park. To the right of this is:

80 Giant's Staircase 2a
This consists of three tiers, the second of which is a tricky balance problem.

81 Arrow Crack 2a
Straightforward. Finish up the short wall above.

82 Gardeners Question Time 5b
The short wall just right of Arrow Crack.

83 Longbow Chimney 2a
Another straightforward but often greasy route.

The wall to the right has seven routes.

84 Grist 5c
Climb the arête just right of Longbow Chimney using an obvious pocket at mid-height. Mantelshelf and then climb the short wall above.

*85 Quiver 5c
Follow the line of flakes two metres right of Longbow Chimney; an awkward start.

*86 Toxophilite 5c
The next line of flakes below and left of a small holly tree in the wall.

There has been some confusion over the years between the names of the next two climbs (caused by very ambiguous descriptions in the first place); the following seems to reflect current general consensus:

*87 Little Sagittarius 5c
Start below and right of the holly tree and make an awkward mantelshelf onto the wide ledge. Climb the wall above with a delicate move to reach a thin layback hold, followed by a difficult stride right into a scoop. Finish straight up to the beech tree.

**88 Sagittarius 5a
Start directly beneath the overhanging arête. Hand-traverse the first break leftwards until a restful standing position can be gained. Step up the slab delicately to a scoop and exit on the right to an easier finish. A start a metre to the left is 5b, while a metre left again it is 5c.

89 Archer's Wall 5c
Start just left of the overhanging arête and go straight up in the same line to the top, where else?

90 Archer's Wall Direct 5c
Start directly below the overhanging arête and go straight up it, including the final move.

**91 Stupid Effort 5a
Start as for the previous route but go straight up trending slightly right

HARRISON'S ROCKS 85

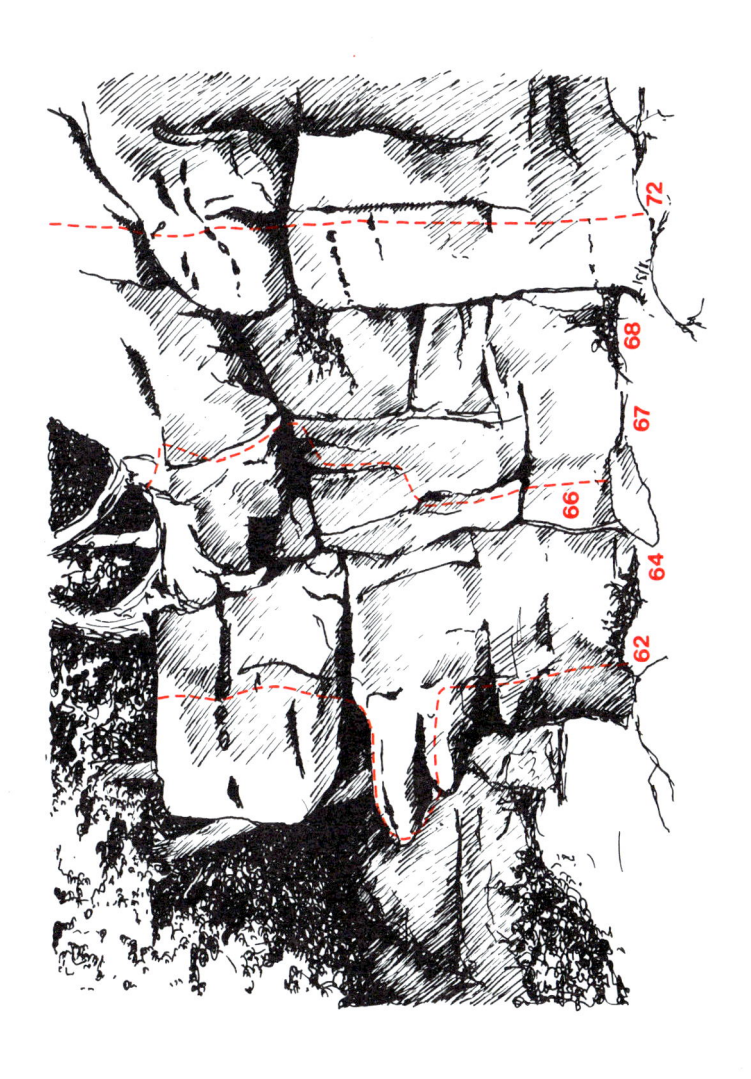

to a ledge; from here make an awkward mantelshelf onto the next sloping ledge. Step left to the edge and finish up this.

**92 Long Crack 4b
Start in the corner and follow the crack. It is most difficult in the constricted centre section. Either continue easily up the crack or move left and join Stupid Effort.

**93 What Crisis? 6c(NS)
A technical and powerful route. Gain the chipped peg-hole in the wall right of Long Crack and somehow use this to reach the crack above where another very hard move follows. (The climb was formerly **Crisis** 6a(1pt). Please do not aid sandstone routes with pegs etc. because of the inevitable damage the rock suffers as a result).

***94 Slimfinger Crack 5c
A classic climb which can be done with great elegance. Step onto the ledge below the crack and follow this to a pleasant finishing groove. Alternatively, finish over the bulge on the right.

*95 Vulture Crack 5c
Climb the steep crack to the break. Move out left and go up the wall on small holds. An interesting diversion is to continue moving left past Slimfinger and What Crisis? to finish up Long Crack - **Missing Link** 6a(NS).

96 The Sting 6a
Start on the undercut wall just right of Vulture Crack and go directly to the top. Be (bee?) careful with the holds.

*97 Horizontal Birch 3a
The birch disappeared years ago. Climb the crack to the overhang and traverse out left to finish.

98 Downfall 4b
Ascend the next crack to a platform; then go up the impending wall on the left which is somewhat easier than it looks.

Next is a bay with a low wall at the back which gives some worthless problems. The Pig Tail Slabs follow with three routes, very popular with instructional groups.

99 Left Edge 2b
Guess where this goes? Climb the left end of the slab.

100 Original Route 2a
Either go directly up the centre of the slab two metres right of the edge or, start a little further right and step left into the line.

101 Big Toe Wall 3b
Do the right-hand start to the last route but continue to a standing position on the second break. Traverse right a metre to a hidden layaway and then go straight up.

102 Greasy Crack 4a
The wide greasy crack four metres left of Giant's Ear is best avoided at all costs.

*103 Giant's Ear 5a
The obvious ear-shaped flake at the right end of the face is climbed with increasing difficulty to the platform. There are two possible finishes,

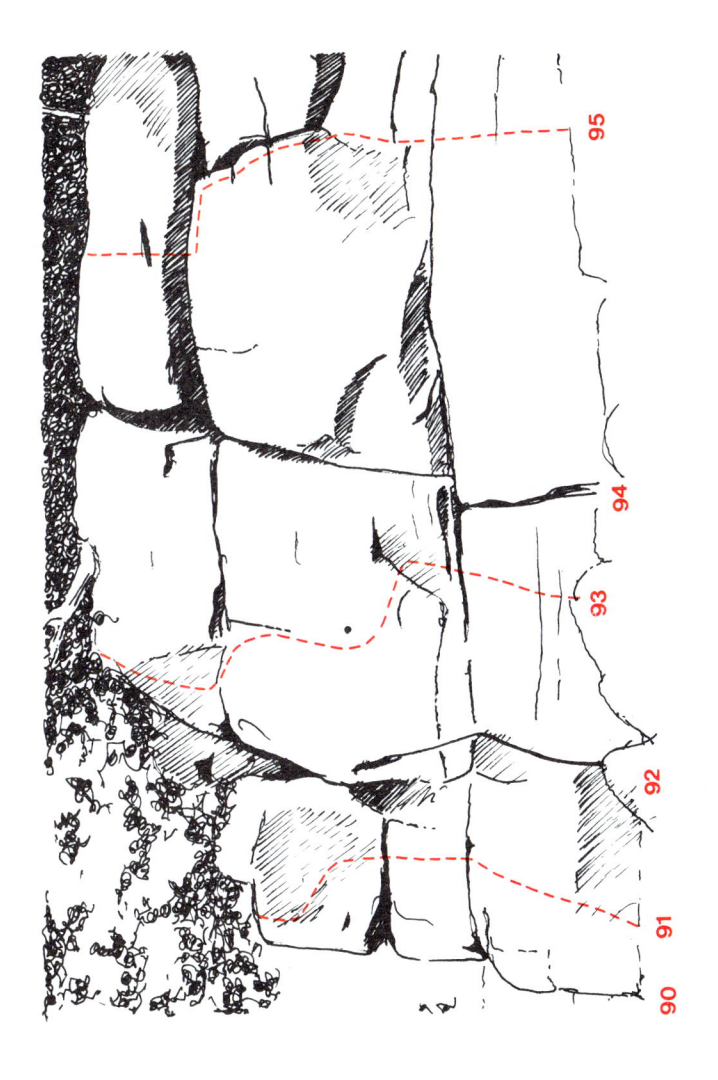

HARRISON'S ROCKS 87

HARRISON'S ROCKS ~ SOUTH CENTRAL SECTION

often climbed as routes in themselves. The first is 3b taking the centre of the wall, moving right to finish. The second is a direct finish to the first - 4a.

104 Junend Arête 2a
An artificial line up the right edge that is ideal for novices. The first part is now overgrown with holly so it is best to start on the platform.

A low greasy wall now follows with three poor routes.

105 Fallen Block Mantelshelf 4a
Mantelshelf into the triangular niche from the left, whence a tallish person can just reach the edge with the finger tips - otherwise tough luck.

106 Fallen Block Eliminate 5b
Climb the short wall just right of the previous route using small pocket holds; then continue over the bulge above to reach a tree root.

107 Fallen Block Wall 5a
Start up a crack behind the fallen block; hand-traverse three metres left then move into the triangular niche and continue more easily to the top.

A little further on is:

108 Snake's Crawl 1a
A weird little route which enters the rock via a hole to the left of the Little Cave, or by another further left, to emerge halfway up the face. Finish up the short wall above.

109 Little Cave 2a
The wide chimney left of Signalbox Arête.

The wall now becomes higher and is in the form of huge blocks.

**110 Signalbox Arête 4a
A good route. Traverse in along a broad ledge from the bay on the left to the steep blocky nose, which is climbed on good holds.

111 Sinner's Progress 5a
Worthwhile if in condition. Start as for Signalbox Arête but continue along the ledge of Sinner's Wall, behind the sapling and into the cleft. Go up a metre to a ledge and traverse right on this, moving down to the

HARRISON'S ROCKS

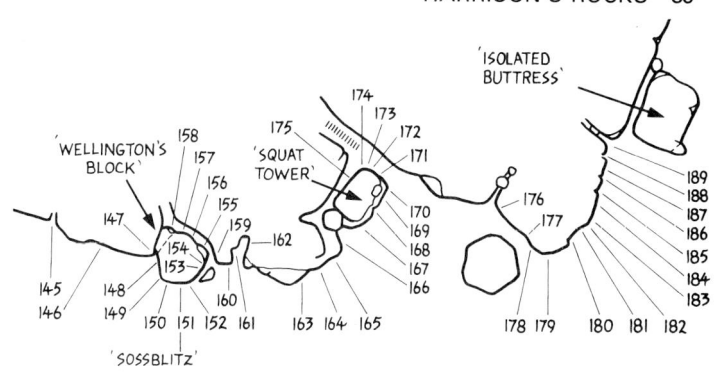

niche of Saint's Wall. Continue across the Circle climbs and down to the ground at the foot of Short Chimney. Known as the **Saint's Decline** if taken in reverse.

112 Sinner's Wall 3a
Climb the next crack to the platform - usually much harder due to the grease. Traverse right along this to behind a sapling in the next crack on the right and follow this easily to the top. There is an ungradeably greasy direct start up the thin crack below the sapling. It is also possible to go straight up the chimney above the start.

113 Saint's Wall 5c
Three metres right of the previous route is a very low break in a smooth wall. Start at the left end of this and with difficulty gain the next ledge. Move right into the niche and exit from this up the cracks above. A start can be made at the right end of the initial break using a shallow rounded pocket, 6a.

114 Glendale Crack 6b
To the right is a thin peg-scarred crack. This is climbed to gain the usually greasy and thus deceptively difficult ledges above.

115 A Killing Joke 6c †
The blunt arête right of the previous route has a vicious boulder problem start. The rest is considerably easier.

116 Left Circle 6a
A groove in the wall left of the corner marks the line, which only just merits the grade. The initial moves are very thin, after which the difficulties rapidly ease.

A micro-eliminate has been climbed up the wall between the Circle routes - **Take That Effing Chalk Bag Off, or I'll Nick Your Rope and Give It to Terry "The Chainsaw" Tullis and He'll Keep it For Ever and Ever** 6a.

**117 Right Circle 4a
A straightforward climb up the corner apart from the tricky strenuous start. The original Circle Climb moved into Left Circle at the first break.

118 Bloody Sunday 5b
The narrow wall immediately right of the corner.
119 Good Friday 5b
The front nose gives steep climbing on poor holds.
120 Small Chimney 2b
Very few positive holds; face either way.
121 Small Wall 5b
Two tricky layaway moves, the first using a good layaway hold very close to the chimney. It is possible to start on the right and step left into the line.

To the right is an easy way down.

122 Long Stretch 5b
The front of the block between the two passages is much harder for the short.

On the low block right of the passage is:

123 Coffin Corner 4c
A grave problem to be taken seriously. Start at the base of the passage, gain the first break and move right to finish.
124 The Bolts 6a(NS)
The sandy bulges on the front of the boulder with a hard mantelshelf or belly-flop to finish.

On the right side of the block is the St. Gotthard Tunnel which gives:

**125 St. Gotthard 4a
A varied route of some interest. Climb the chimney to the top of the low block. Step across right onto the main wall and traverse right for two metres. Move up, then go diagonally left on good holds to an awkward move into a recess and easier ground.

Through the St. Gotthard Tunnel and up on the right is a steep wall below the finish of St. Gotthard:

126 Long Reach 5a
Another inspired piece of route-naming. Ascend the left end of the wall on good holds with (surprise, surprise) a long reach for the top.
127 Simplon Route 4a
Climb the wall to the recess of St. Gotthard by bridging or 4c face climbing.

Back on the main wall is:

128 The Nuts 6a
A thin crack to the right of St. Gotthard chimney is climbed with difficulty to the wide ledge. Move a little left and monkey up the steep wall above.
129 Rowan Tree Wall 5a
The cracks left of the next recess and below the leaning tree are followed to the upper ledge. Finish up the slab on the right using small holds - you could try using big ones but they aren't there.

HARRISON'S ROCKS 91

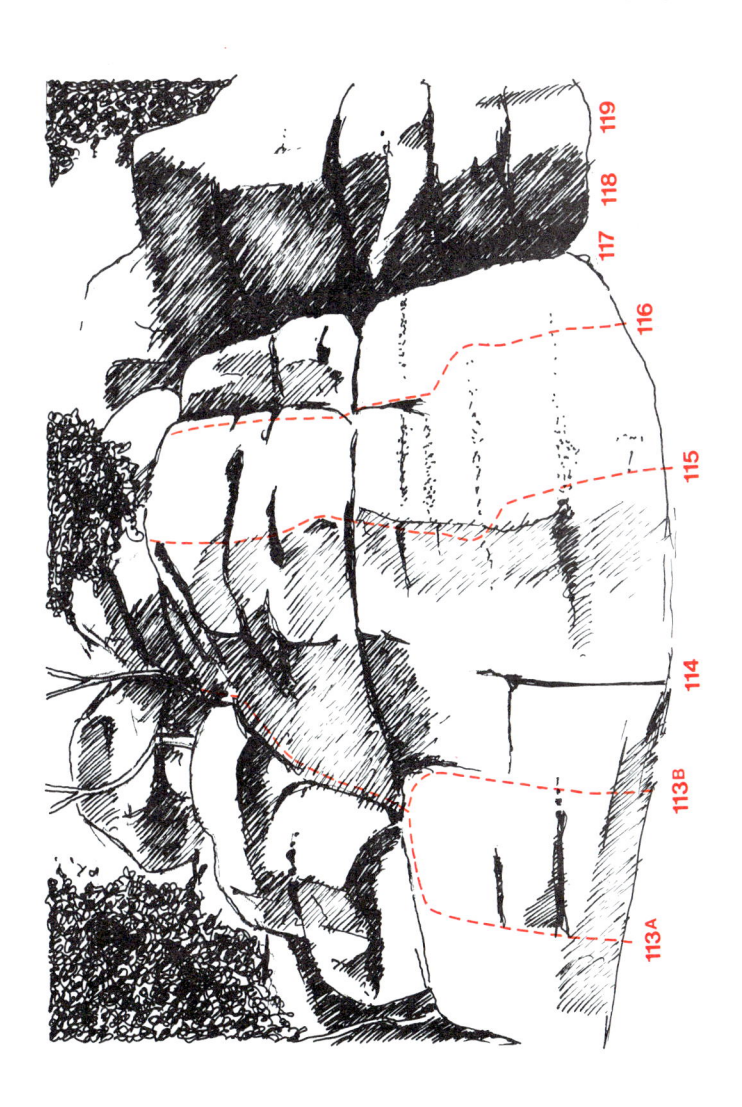

The next feature is a wide recess with two cracks on either side. The right-hand crack is The Sewer, which provides the start for the next two routes.

*130 The Sandpipe 3b
Start as for The Sewer but at the top of the initial wet crack step across the base of the wedge-shaped block into the crack on the left; follow this to the platform and finish up the corner.

131 Sewer-Rowan Connection 5a
Follow The Sandpipe to its crack but traverse further left into the next crack (Rowan Tree Wall) and finish up this.

*132 The Sewer 4c
A fairly popular route, guaranteed to drain your strength. Climb the wet crack and continue up the pod right of the wedged-shaped block to a platform. Finish straight up the crack above.

The next two climbs also have a common start at The Sewer:

133 Sewer Wall 5c(NS)
Start as for The Sewer but from the top of the wet crack traverse right onto the wall and climb the next crack to the upper ledge. Traverse right to a difficult finish at a break with very poor holds. Sandy in places and harder than it looks, especially in the upper crack.

***134 Monkey's Necklace 5b
A long route well worth the rope manuvres. Start as for Sewer Wall but continue the traverse round the nose for a further six metres to a second more obvious crack - Monkey's Necklace Crack; climb this for four metres then trend diagonally right to the top. There is a powerful direct start to the Necklace Crack - **Primate Shot** 6b(NS) †

**135 Orangutang 5c
Start at some undercut ledges below and left of the Necklace Crack. Go up to the traverse line of that route and either continue as for that route or carry on straight up the bulging wall with further interest.

*136 Monkey's Bow 6a(NS)
Start just left of the right edge of the front wall and gain a standing position on the first break. Hand-traverse left towards the Monkey's Necklace Crack and finish up a short crack just right of it.

137 Baboon 6a(NS)
Similar to the previous route but make the traverse at the next break up.

138 Moonlight Variation (Brookslight) 6a(NS)
Start as for the previous two routes, but carry straight on up the impending wall keeping a metre or so left of Moonlight Arête. A direct start is possible.

***139 Moonlight Arête 4b
A fine route straight up the scooped wall two metres left of the gully, starting with an easy traverse in from the gully.

**140 Starlight 4c
Start as for Moonlight Arête, but move back right to the broad arête and follow it to the top.

The next passage provides an easy way down. A short problem has

HARRISON'S ROCKS 93

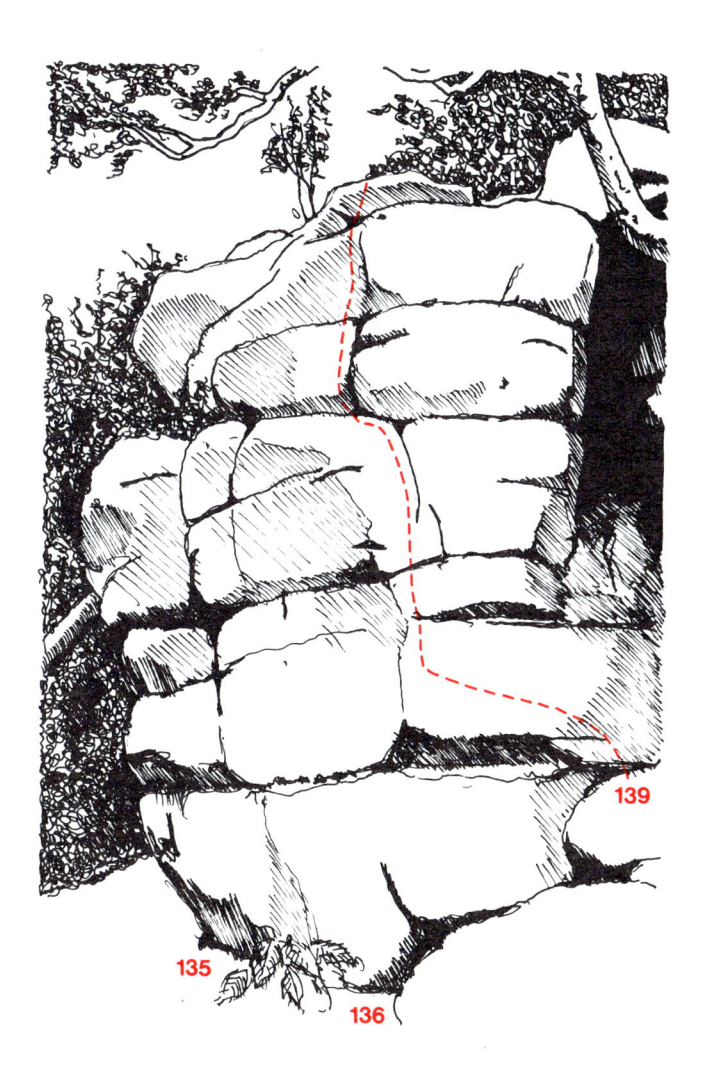

135 136 139

been climbed on the left side of the gully - **Matt's Fingertip** 5a. *To the right of the gully the rock is very greasy and has no routes except for:*

141 Bostic 6a(NS)
A problem of adhesion. The bulging greasy arête at the right end of the wall and immediately left of Noisesome Cleft No.1. This route very rarely sees an ascent for obvious reasons.

142 Noisesome Cleft No.1 2b
Climb the crack to the top, moving onto the left side when necessary. In good conditions the slab above Bostic may be climbed.

143 Noisesome Wall 5b
Start as for Noisesome Cleft No.1, or with more difficulty just to the right, and climb diagonally rightwards. Greasy.

144 One-Two Traverse 5a
Barely worthwhile - should be One-Two Avoid Traverse. Start at the top of Cleft No.1. Descend a metre to a ledge, which can be traversed, with a downwards step, all the way right to Cleft No.2.

145 Noisesome Cleft No.2 3a
The next wide crack some distance to the right.

146 The Sod 5c
Absolutely. The dirty greasy crack eight metres left of Passage Chimney. Follow the slimy crack to near the top, then either bushwhack off left or continue straight up. Horribly unpleasant. (Until recently 5c(2pts), utilising two slings for aid).

147 Passage Chimney 2a
The chimney left of the Block. The climb goes up the outside on well worn holds. The inside is often taken as an easy though usually muddy way down. The passage can be chimneyed or grovelled at any point along its length.

Next is the Wellington Block, which sports some excellent hard routes and a couple of good lower grade routes to boot. The first route takes the steep wall right of Passage Chimney:

*148 Forester's Wall Direct 6a
Climb the wall to the left of centre to the break and continue to the top in the same line, keeping left of the crack of Forester's Wall. The first break can also be gained on the right.

A line has been climbed directly up the arête to the right, joining Forester's Wall at the break but continuing straight up as for Bonanza Direct Finish - Indian Summer 5c(NS).

**149 Forester's Wall 5b
A good climb. Start on the right side of the arête; move up a little, then swing left and make strenuous moves to gain a wide ledge. Traverse left to the middle of the face and climb a crack and bulges to the top.

*150 Bonanza 5c
Follow the previous route to the ledge on the arête. Go up a little then traverse right about two metres and surmount the bulges with difficulty. A direct finish before the traverse is also 5c.

***151 Sossblitz 6a
A pumpy little number. Start in a niche to the left of the arête. Pull

HARRISON'S ROCKS 95

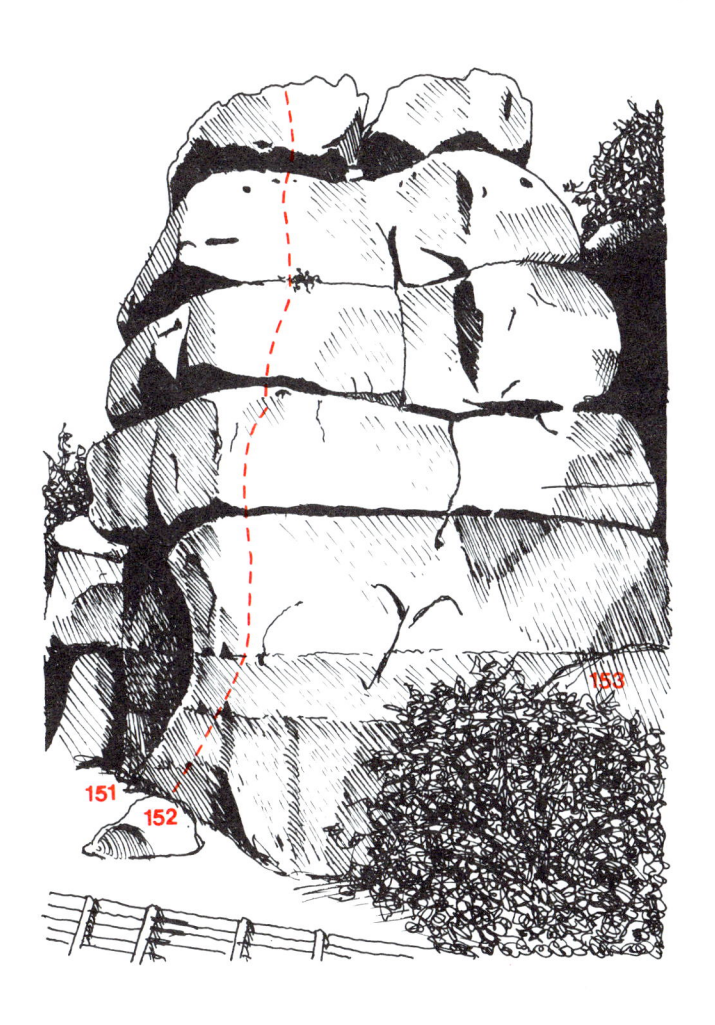

round the overhang on its right side to a standing position. Continue up past a letter box slot, then reach up right for another such slot and finish direct.

** 152 The Republic 6b(NS)
The front nose of the Block gives a fine route with hard moves between rests. Climb directly on the arête on its right side. Once standing on the third break move a little right and mantelshelf on ironstone holds. Finish straight up. (The route was originally done with a jammed sling-knot for aid and a brief excursion into The Niblick - **The King** 6a(1pt)).

*** 153 The Niblick 5b
A classic and varied route up the front face of the Block. Step off the wide flat boulder and go up a thin crack to the break; move left and layback into the square-cut niche above. A steep slab follows with an awkward wide crack to finish.

154 Pincenib 6b(NS)
An eliminate with some good moves up the face right of The Niblick. Gain the first ledge easily, then pull onto the wall using the crescent-shaped flake without using the right edge. A tricky move then leads to a scoop and easier ground.

An easier alternative to Pincenib, 5b, is to climb the right edge itself which, despite the presence of the back wall of the passage, is a good route of some technical interest.

** 155 Wellington's Nose 3b
A popular route. Start at the front end of the passage and chimney up it until it is possible to step across onto the Block. Go straight up to the overhang and either go over it, or traverse right for two metres to finish more easily up Sabre Crack. Another alternative, **Pince Nez** 4c, is a leftwards hand-traverse below the finishing crack of The Niblick to finish over the front nose of the block.

The next three routes are hidden on the passage wall of the Block:

156 Lady Jane 5c(NS)
Gain the ledge a metre left of Sabre Crack then climb the wall above with a peculiar mantelshelf move in the middle.

157 Sabre Crack 3a
The wide crack in the centre of the wall is harder than it looks.

158 Caroline 5b
The wall just right of Sabre Crack.

There are no routes on the greasy right wall of the passage. On the small buttress right of the Block is:

159 Wellington Boot 6b(NS)
The middle of the wall facing the Block making use of the thin crack and ironstone holds above.

160 Belts and Braces 5b
The extremely sandy nose of the block left of the chimneys, finishing up the rounded grooves on its right side.

---

9. The Republic, 6b, Harrison's Rocks. *Climber:* Dave Turner. Photo Ben Pritchard.

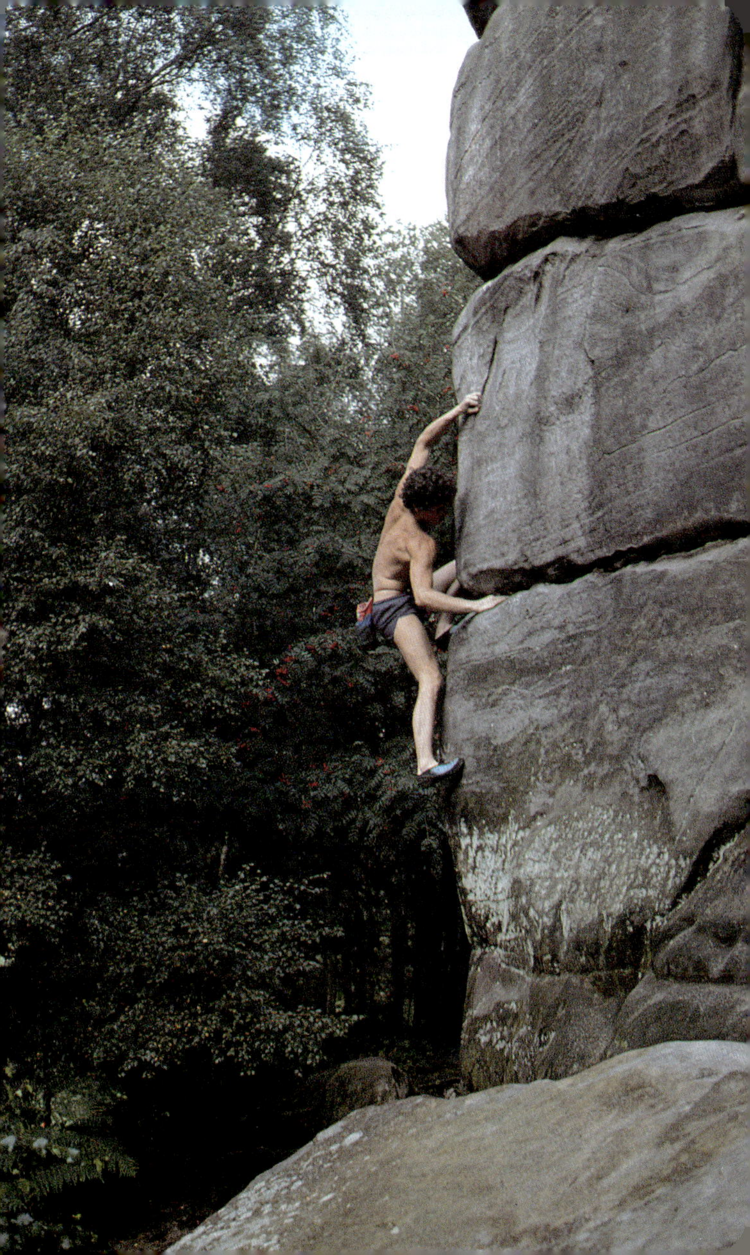

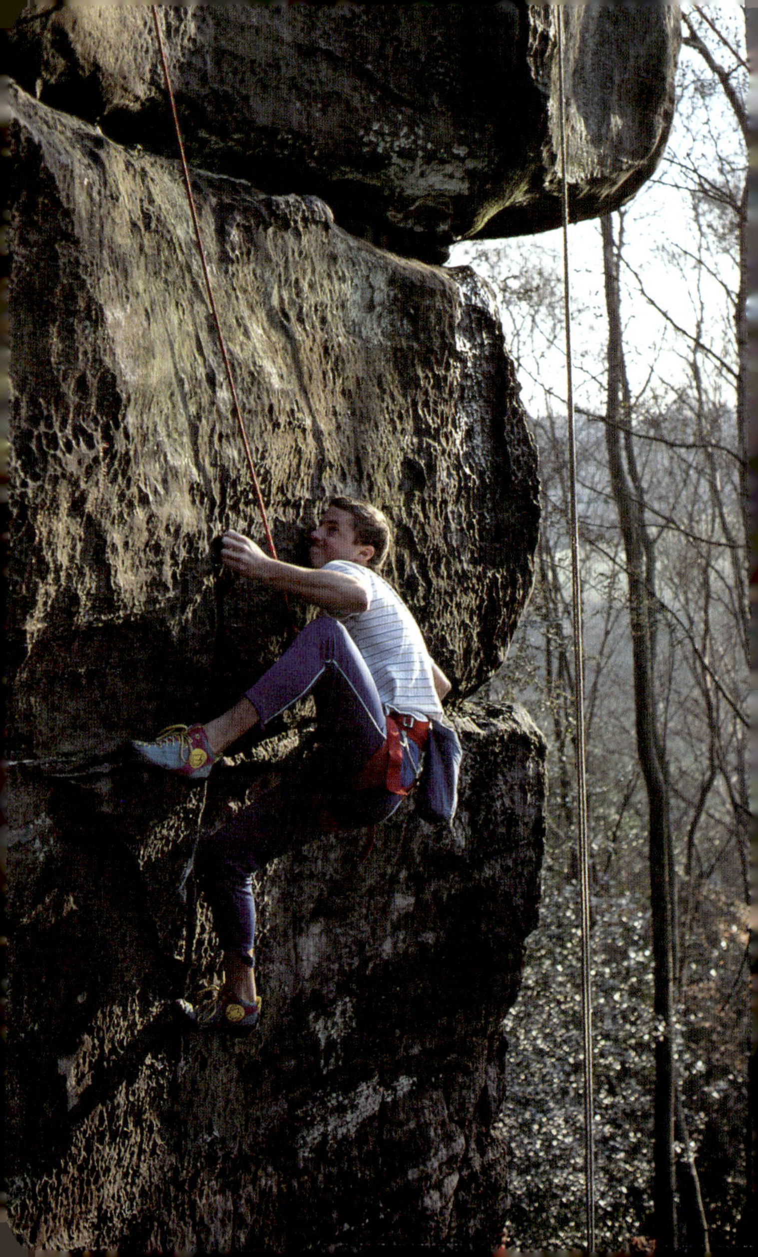

161 Jetsam 2b
The left-hand sandy chimney.

*162 Flotsam 3a
The right-hand chimney is the better of the two.

Round the corner to the right is a short steep wall.

163 Wildcat Wall 5c
Start at the left end of the wall by an oval pocket and go straight up to a strenuous mantelshelf onto the ledge, and easy ground.

164 Woodside Blossom 6a
The short slanting crack to the right is used to reach the break, which provides a difficult mantelshelf. Finish up the short wall above. This route is usually greasy and unclimbable.

165 Deadwood Crack 4c
The shallow sandy crack leads awkwardly to the rounded ledge. Finish up the narrow groove. The overhang above and set back from this route provides a mildly strenuous boulder problem.

*166 Tame Variant 2b
A somewhat sandy but popular climb which meanders up the the wide ledges at the right end of the wall. The crack formed by the jammed boulder on the right can also be climbed.

To the right is the Squat Tower. Belays for the routes on its front face are best arranged using a very long sling fixed high on the tree beyond the back of the Tower.

167 Stag 5c
An awkward unsatisfying route. Using good holds gain the blunt arête two metres left of The Vice. Climb the arête and then pull onto its shoulder to a mantelshelf finish.

**168 The Vice 4c
A popular route. Start in the centre of the face then climb the crack on well worn holds. Traverse out right to finish.

*169 Toevice 6a
Climb the shallow, narrow crack two metres right of The Vice. Very tricky.

170 Handvice 5c
Follow the thin crack three metres right of The Vice to an awkward exit where it ends.

171 Birch Nose 5b
The front right corner of the Squat Tower has very poor sandy holds.

The next climbs are on the side walls of the Squat Tower, next to a passage, with some now broken stone steps, leading to the top of the crag:

172 The Clamp 5a
The centre of the short wall left of Corridor Route. The first holds are reached from the boulder on the right. A direct start is now much harder - 5c - due to ground erosion.

---

10. Wooly Bear, 6c, Harrison's Rocks. *Climber: Mike Ratcliffe*. Photo Dave Turner.

173 Corridor Route 4a
Start from the upper end of the stone steps and climb the passage face at the extreme right-hand end.
174 Rhapsody Inside A Satsuma 5a
The arête right of Corridor Route.
175 Quasimodo 4b
From the centre of the back wall of the Tower traverse left all the way round to the front of the boulder and finish up The Vice.

On the right of the passage is an expanse of broken vegetated rock of little interest to climbers except perhaps for providing a good landing point after having leapt off the Squat Tower. Further right on a wall by a large slabby boulder are three routes which rarely come into condition:

176 Knight's Gambit 5b
A balance move is made onto the first ledge two metres from the left end of the wall; from here move up and then make an awkward step to a ledge and small tree below a crack. Climb the crack.
177 Knight's Move 5c
Start as for the Gambit but traverse right along the first break for four metres, where a long stretch is made to reach a left-hand pocket. A right-hand mantelshelf follows, after which move delicately up right to another pocket. A further mantelshelf on the right leads to an easy finish.
178 Reach for the Sky 6a(NS)
The blank wall left of Set Square Arête, starting three metres left of that route and finishing at the small tree on the top. Necessarily dynamic for most but easier for the very tall.
*179 Set Square Arête 5b
A thought-provoking route directly up the arête opposite the large boulder.

Just right of the arête is:

179A Sandbag 5c(NS)
Balance onto the ledge, then stretch for the next break if you can. An extremely difficult mantelshelf move is made to finish.
**180 Sunshine Crack 4c
A good climb of its type up the obvious wide crack. Begin on the ground and finish at the top.
*181 The Knam 6a
Not an obvious enil and rarely dry. Start in a recess 2 metres right of Sunshine Crack. Pull onto the shelf using holds on the right-hand side of the recess. Continue up the wall and pull onto the next shelf with great stress.
*182 The Mank 6a
An overhung scoop a few metres right of Knam marks the line. A move (or jump) is made to an obvious jug and the scoop gained. Small holds beneath the overhang lead up to the ledge. Finish up the groove.
**183 Piecemeal Wall 5c
The next feature in the wall is a shallow crack in a bulge. Start slightly right of the crack and climb it. Move right and up to the rounded ledge.

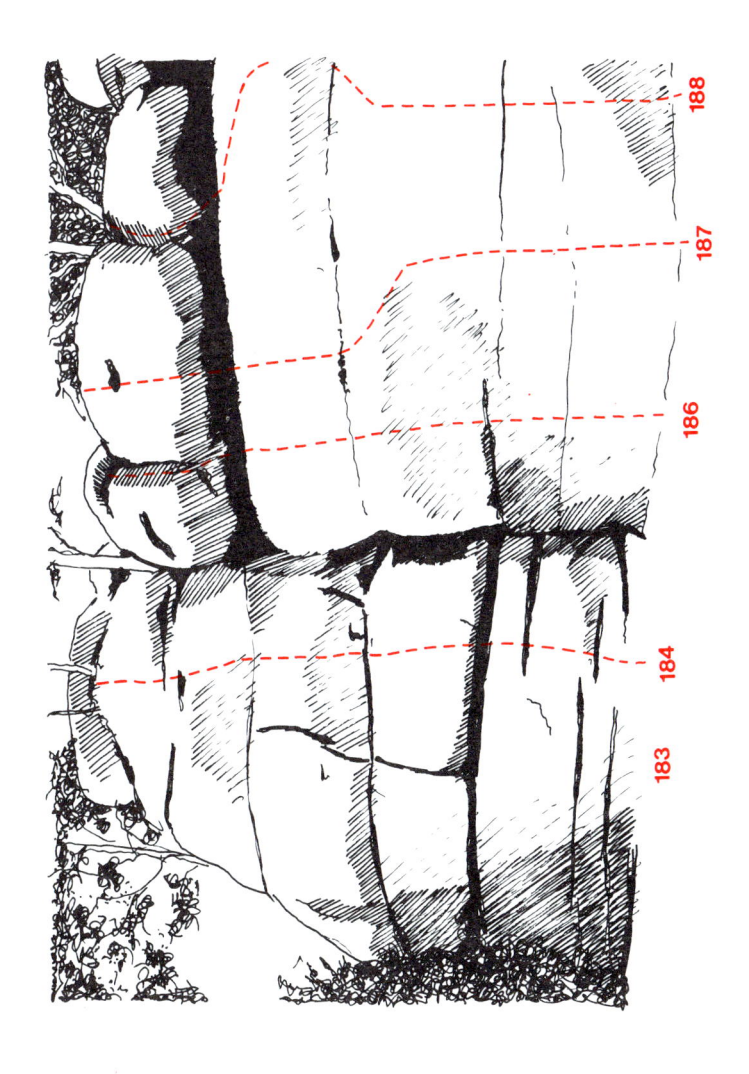

HARRISON'S ROCKS 99

Make a short traverse left and go up a scoop leading left to finish over the block above.

184 Karen's Kondom 6b(NS)
A sticky problem. The middle of the bulges right of Piecemeal Wall. Either finish direct or more pleasantly up the chimney on the right. One can also finish up Piecemeal Wall.

** 185 The Chimney 2b
A good and popular climb. Follow the chimney easily (or perhaps with difficulty) to beneath the overhang; move left below this and continue up to the tree. Alternatively, traverse right on the (platform past the finishing crack of Reverse Traverse to the next crack (Two-Toed Sloth) and finish here - **Chimney and Traverse** 3a.

186 Reverse Traverse 5c
Start just to the right of the chimney and go over the bulges following the vague grooves to the broad ledge. Finish up the wide crack above.

187 Eric 6a(NS)
Find a way up the wall two/three metres left of Two-Toed Sloth, keeping right of the previous route. Move delicately onto the ledge and surmount the top overhang with some difficulty.

* 188 Two-Toed Sloth 5a
Start just left of the passage by a large stalactite. An unusual but nice move is made to reach a jug on the first ledge; mantelshelf onto this then meander up the slab to finish easily up the wide crack above. There is a 5b problem up the edge to the right of the start.

Just to the right is a gully, which leads very dirtily to the top of the rocks. On the right of this is:

189 Arustu 5b(NS)
The obvious greasy buttress would be good if it ever dried out but is usually unclimbable.

The next feature is the Isolated Buttress which gives some of the best climbs at Harrison's. Access to the top is provided by the large jammed boulder bridging the right end of the passage. Alternatively, there is an obvious exposed long step across the midpoint of the passage. The belay bolt on the top should be backed up if possible.

** 190 North-West Corner 5c
Start just left of the arête and climb onto and up it on small but good holds to an awkward balance move. Finish in the depression right of the block or straight over it.

A hybrid route - **Diagonal** *6a(NS) - starts up North-West Corner, then makes a strenuous finger-traverse across the second break of Woolly Bear to join and finish as for South-West Corner.*

** 191 Woolly Bear 6c(NS)
Very technical and fingery climbing directly up the centre of the wall to join West Wall. The crux can be avoided by swinging right on the second break to go up just left of the arête, 6b. Either finish up West Wall or step right and join South-West Corner.

*** 192 West Wall 5c
A classic trip. Climb the left edge of the wall to the big overhang.

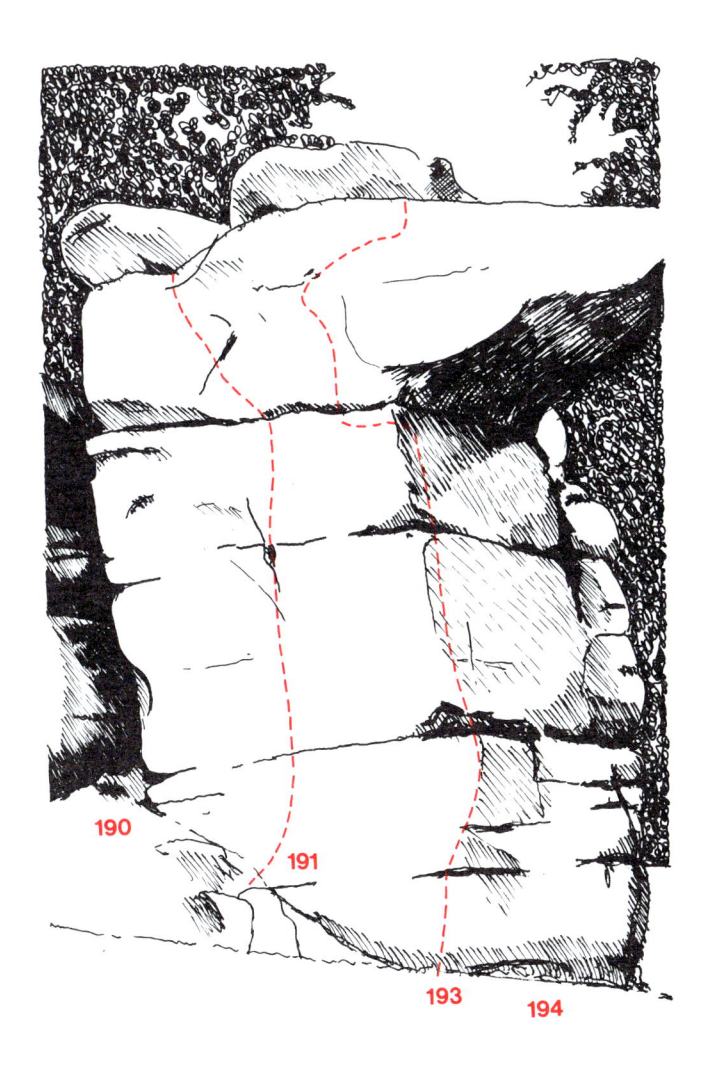

HARRISON'S ROCKS 101

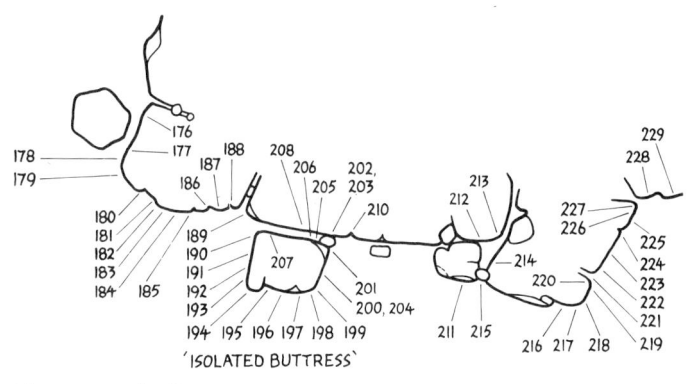

Harrison's Rocks – South

Traverse left until half way across the wall then make a hard move up using an undercut and finish direct.

**193 South-West Corner 6a
Start as for West Wall to below the overhang, then move round the arête and gain the obvious undercuts up and to the left. Move back right to finish. A finish can be made straight up from the undercuts, at the same grade when dry.

***194 Isolated Buttress Climb 4c
Start in the middle of the wall below the big overhang. Small holds lead up and right to the rounded rib. Now either climb the rib, or the wall just left of the rib, to a broad ledge. Finish up the crack above. Alternatively, traverse right to finish more easily up the crack of Birchden Wall - this gives a long interesting climb requiring two ropes.

A barely independent eliminate takes the narrow wall immediately left of Edwards's Effort - **Edwards's Wall** 5c.

*195 Edwards's Effort 6a
Start up the niche in the front face and go up to and climb the flared often greasy crack above to the wide ledge. Finish as for Diversion.

**196 Diversion 5c
Start on the right side of the niche. Go up moving left a little to the second break then hand-traverse two metres right. Make hard moves up to a hidden jug and move right onto the ledge. Either finish up a crack just left of the Birchden Wall crack, or go up the steep slab just to the left of this - 6a.

***197 Birchden Wall 5b
A classic route, high in the grade. Start up the shallow groove two metres left of the rounded arête of the buttress. A technical move up leads to fine climbing on the wall above - finish up the wide crack.

The narrow space between Birchden Wall and Birchden Corner gives:-
Pan 5c.

HARRISON'S ROCKS

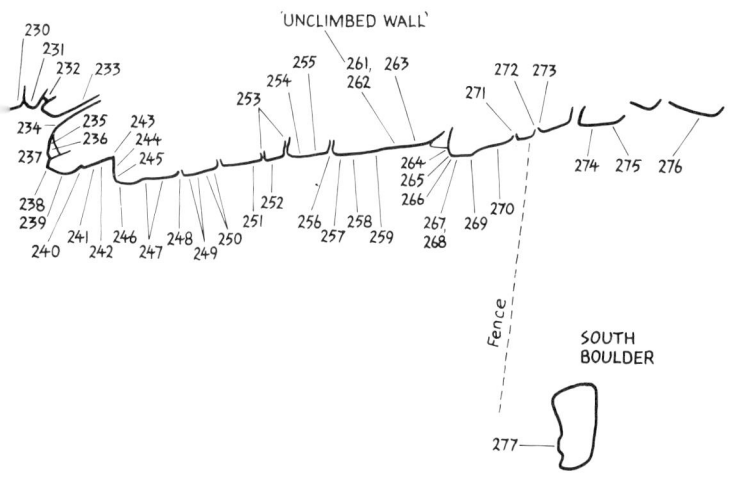

198 Birchden Corner 5c
Start on good holds beneath the arête. Go up for three metres, then pull left onto the wall and continue up via a thin diagonal crack. Move a little right to finish.

*199 Crowborough Corner** 5c
The crack just right of the rounded arête. At half-height pull blindly left onto the arête and finish delicately straight up. The arête itself has been climbed direct from bottom to top at 6a.

It is possible to continue straight up where Crowborough Corner pulls left - **Mr Spaceman** 6a(NS).

200 Wailing Wall 5c
The layback crack in the centre of the wall is followed to its end, where a hard move is made to reach the main break; standing up on this can be very easy or very difficult!

There is an eliminate route up the centre of the leaning wall right of Wailing Wall, the grade of which is increasing as the small holds gradually break off - **Wailing Eliminate** 6b(NS).

*201 Boysen's Arête** 6a
The short impending arête below the boulder bridge; go round this on the outside and up the bulging wall above. Short but fingery and technical.

***202 Boulder Bridge Route** 2b
Chimney up (back-and-foot) halfway along the passage. Sidle left to the Boulder and continue traversing, with some exposure, across the

top of Wailing Wall to finish at Crowborough Corner. Alternatively, climb the main wall behind the Buttress to the boulder bridge on good but often greasy holds - 3a.

*203 High Traverse 5c
Traverse round the Isolated Buttress in either direction at about the level of the boulder bridge. Various starts and finishes are possible, whilst belaying is difficult.

**204 Girdle Traverse 5a
A low-level traverse of the Isolated Buttress starting at the foot of Wailing Wall. Hand-traverse left to Birchden Corner where a move up is made onto front face; continue along and pass the rib of Isolated Buttress Climb with difficulty to join West Wall. Either follow that route, making an interesting and very long 5c route, or jump off.

The next three routes are on the back wall of the Isolated Buttress and are graded assuming bridging methods are not used. They are described left-to-right as you look at them.

205 Powder Finger 6b(NS)
Climb the wall a metre or so right of Boysen's Arête. Go straight up all the way to the top. The last hard moves over the triangular block are often very greasy and can be avoided.

206 Bloody Fingers 6a(NS)
A direct line two or so metres left of Green Fingers, giving similar but slightly harder climbing.

*207 Green Fingers 5c
Start a metre left of North-West Corner and climb the steep wall on small holds, finishing left of the block at the top.

Still in the back passage but back on the main wall are:

208 Badfinger 6a(NS)
Climb the lower and upper walls opposite Bloody Fingers. Usually, an unpleasant route.

209 Bolder Route 5b
The wall directly opposite Powder Finger is normally very greasy.

To the right of The Isolated Buttress the main wall is heavily shaded by trees and is usually green and greasy. A few metres right of the passage is:

210 Jagger 5b
A poor and usually slimy route. Shake (like Elvis, not Mick) up the shallow crack to the ledge; continue up the wall above using the tree.

Just up the slope to the right there is a descent route behind a large tree; to the right of this is a feature formed by a large boulder known as the Big Cave.

211 Cave Wall Traverse 5b
Go up the green recess on the front of the boulder to its top; from here move right and follow Smith's Traverse but continue on past its finish to the arête and into Crack and Cave; carry on at the same level beyond to finish by Grant's Groove.

HARRISON'S ROCKS

*212 Big Cave Route 2 2b
Entertaining. The left-hand crack on the back wall of the Cave. Finish through the hole at the back.

**213 Big Cave Route 1 2a
A popular climb. The right-hand crack on the back wall is best climbed by facing outwards for the most part.

214 The Wallow 6a(NS)
If you stand in the cave and face right there is a concave wall. Climb this near its right edge on small holds and continue more or less directly up to the top. Easier for the tall.

*215 Smith's Traverse 2a
This is better than it looks and interesting for novices. From the top of the large boulder in front of the Big Cave, traverse right across the face on the wide ledges until past the overhang then go easily up to the top.

On the main wall by the path again is:

215A Baldrick's Boulderdash 5b(NS)
A very direct line up the wall just left of Forget-Me-Not. Bridge up using the block to gain the first ledge, then go straight up and surmount the final overhang on good holds.

216 Forget-Me-Not 6a
The tenuous crack-line three metres right of the passage. Pull into the crack from below and follow the vague cracks to Smith's Traverse. Finish over the bulge above by the very thin crack.

217 Second Chance 6a
Start up the flared crack with great difficulty - it is easier (5c) to swing in from the left. Continue straight up the wall to join Smith's Traverse.

*218 Last Chance 5c
A short crack just right of the previous route is reached and climbed on excellent sharp holds. An awkward mantelshelf leads to the horizontal break and the top.

**219 Spider Wall 5b
Start by a large pothole in the lower wall two metres left of the arête of Cave Wall. Climb straight up into a shallow niche, make a delicate move left onto the ledge and finish easily.

*220 Cave Wall 5b
Climb the arête immediately left of Crack and Cave. Small holds lead to the horizontal break; surmount the bulge with difficulty to finish. It is nicer to move left and finish up Spider Wall.

**221 Crack and Cave 4a
A misnomer since vandals dislodged the boulder that formed the Cave, though it nonetheless remains a good and popular route. Climb the corner crack direct to easier ground and the top.

222 Grant's Wall 6a
Climb the wall two metres right of Crack and Cave to the ledge, then move a little left into the corner and overcome the overhang on good holds.

*223 Grant's Groove 6a
The shallow groove two metres right of the previous route is frequently greasy but gives a good climb when dry.

**224 Grant's Crack 5a
The obvious groove in the centre of the wall is hard to start. At the top of the crack move awkwardly left beneath the overhang to reach easier ground.

225 Thingamywobs 5b
The next thin greasy groove and the wall above. The face just left of the crack gives some eliminate 5c climbing - start up the crack.

226 Whatsaname 5b
The blind crack between Thingy and Thingamywobs.

227 Thingy 4b
Climb the short rounded nose at the right-hand end of the wall.

The next buttresses are very rounded and bulging but are broken by a number of wide cracks:

228 Rum and Ribena 4b
A wide crack leads to the earthy ledge. Another wide crack leads to the finish.

229 Rum and Coke 5b
A line two metres right of Rum and Ribena; move right on the break and finish up the wide crack.

230 Cunning Stunts 5b
The product of a shining wit? The wall three metres left of Scout Chimneys. Start at an inset vertical flake and go straight up to the yew tree.

231 Cabbage Patch Blues 5b
The bulging slimy wall between Cunning Stunts and Scout Chimney. "Suck your way up to a flat hold, then up and slightly right to the top." Hard for the short.

232 Scout Chimney 1a
The straightforward chimney immediately left of the passage - the other chimney left this is 2a.

233 Back Passage 3a
A short wide crack in the right wall of the passage. It is much harder if the wall behind is not used.

234 Araldite Wall 5c
Just left of the right edge of the passage. Gain a ledge and then follow the shallow groove to finish. This is often very wet and a grade harder.

*235 Garden Slab Left 5a
Climb the left side of the slab at its weakest point.

236 Tiptoe Thru The Tulips 5b
An eliminate between the two original slab routes, with a finish over the block at the top.

*237 Garden Slab Right 5a
Delicate. Start from a block a metre left of Biceps Buttress and go straight up trending right near the top. An interesting variation is to start up this route, then traverse across the slab at half-height and finish up the Left Route.

*238 Biceps Buttress 5b
The bulging arête where the wall changes direction is easy until the

HARRISON'S ROCKS 107

finish, which is pretty awkward. A variation start can be made by following Muscle Crack to the first break and then hand-traversing left to the arête.

239 Finger Popper 6b(NS)
The wall and bulges a metre left of Muscle Crack, with a nasty hold somewhere.

240 Muscle Crack 6a
Also known as The Graunch, which might tell you something? Small holds left of the wide overhanging crack lead to a rest beneath it, where you still have time to reconsider your presence. The crack itself is as strenuous and thrutchy as it looks.

*241 Crucifix 6a(NS)
The centre of the wall between Corner and Muscle Crack, starting a little to the left.

242 Hector's House 6b(NS)
Start a metre or so left of the corner and go straight up to a hard finish. Good value.

243 Corner 5c
Guess where this goes? Either start direct or as for Hector's House, moving into the corner at about three metres. It is frequently wet and unpleasant and 6a.

*244 Philippa 6a
A good climb. Start as for Shodan to the break, move left a metre and go up to and over the bulges above.

*245 Shodan 5c
The overhanging wall to the left of Half-Crown Corner on crinkly sharp holds. Go straight up to the first ledge, step right to the arête and follow this to the top.

An eliminate route - **On The Edge** 6a(NS) - *goes up just right of Shodan, moving into Philippa to finish.*

*246 Half-Crown Corner 5b
Start left of the angle of the buttress. Pull with difficulty into a niche then move up and right onto the wall, which is followed more easily to the top.

247 Wander at Leisure 4c
Several possibilities of about the same standard on the steep wall between Birch Tree Crack and Half-Crown Corner.

*248 Birch Tree Crack 3b
Follow the steep strenuous crack to the tree roots.

249 Birch Tree Variations 5c/6a
On the wall just right of the crack there is a stalactite at three metres; this can be gained from the left or the right with another hard move to reach the top. The grade depends on which holds you allow yourself.

250 Birch Tree Wall 4c
The wall three metres left of the polished stump trending slightly right to the top. Another less satisfactory climb starts a metre to the right -4b.

HARRISON'S ROCKS 109

Next is a wide crack containing an old polished tree stump giving an easy way down. The wall just to the right provides a 5c move using a big stalactite for the left hand.

251 The Scoop 5c
Technical and delicate moves into and out of the scoop in the wall right of the stump. The right arête is awkward but the same grade.

252 Pullover 5c
Start on the left or right and climb the undercut bulges to a strenuous mantelshelf in the centre. Finish up the little wall above with an interesting move. There is a 4c hand-traverse at half-height.

*253 Easy Clefts 2a
The chimneys on either side of the undercut bulges; the right-hand one is better.

*254 Senarra 5a
Start in the middle of the wall, move up then climb the wall on its left side, trending a little right at the top to finish. Can be started further left.

**255 Hell Wall 4c
A good and popular climb up the right-hand side of the wall. The start is the hardest part after which the holds improve.

**256 Charon's Chimney 3a
Straightforward and a good climb when dry. A name that sticks (Styx?) in the mind.

The next wall sports some fine open face climbs:

*257 Baskerville 5c
A technical climb up the wall a metre right of the chimney without touching it or Far Left. A little harder (hounder?) than the next two routes.

**258 Far Left 5c
Start two metres left of Elementary and go up to a break; move right and make thin moves to the top or finish direct. A climb for the well read?

**259 Elementary 5c
A good route. Start up the prominent cracks left of Unclimbed Wall. Layback the final crack to finish. If this is very greasy step into Far Left; use the small holds Watson the wall and perhaps with sheer luck (Sherlock?) gain the top.

260 Desperate Dan 6a(NS)
Start where Unclimbed Wall steps off the ground and go straight up to the second break. Move slightly right and, using a small pocket hold on Unclimbed Wall Direct Finish, make thin technical moves to finish just left of the tree.

A more independent direct finish to Desperate Dan takes the wall right of the final crack of Elementary, using small layaway holds - 6b(NS) †

***261 Unclimbed Wall 5b
An excellent and popular route. Start two metres left of two obvious potholes in the face. Step up and move right, then use the potholes to

reach the break. Move right again and make a hard move to gain the crack and ironstone holds above.

*262 Unclimbed Wall Variations
A **Direct Start** to the two potholes is 5c. A better Direct Start straight up to the finish is also 5c via a curving layaway. There is a fine technical **Direct Finish** - 6a - up to the right side of the tree.

An eliminate, blinkers essential, takes the narrow piece of rock between Right Unclimbed and Unclimbed Wall Direct Start - **Jingo Wobbly** 6b(NS). *It is necessary to do the adjacent routes beforehand to know which holds are in bounds.*

264 Sunray 5a
A poor route. From the first narrow part of the chimney climb the short wall on the right.

265 Solstice 5c
Climb the steep wall immediately left of the arête, avoiding Sun Ray at the finish.

*266 Bulging Wall/Zig Nose 5c
Start as for Zig-Zag or more directly up the arête (harder) and go straight up the bulging nose with tricky moves to get to the ledge. Finish direct.

***267 Zig Zag 5a
Start just right of the arête below the bulge at three metres: go up to this, move right two metres and climb the cracks to the break. Finish straight up or traverse back left to the nose and up this to the top. It is possible to go up before the cracks are reached.

*268 Todd's Traverse (Boundary Wall Traverse) 5a
Start up and move right on Zig-Zag; keep traversing at this level across Rift and Witches Broomstick to finish up Neutral. Tricky when greasy.

The starts of the following three climbs have become easier since the building of 'The Beach' raised the ground.

*269 Rift 5c
A steep wall with a fingery undercut start, three metres right of the start of Zig-Zag. Climb straight up the wall, using good pinchgrip holds near the top. Unfortunately, one of the initial holds has recently been "improved" by vandals unknown.

A direct line just left of the next crack in 5c.

270 Witches Broomstick 5c
A crack with an undercut start.

The bulge and wall just left of the next crack is 6a.

271 Neutral 6a
It's hard to be neutral about this slimy offering. Just left of the fence is another crack with a difficult undercut start.

Outside the boundary fence and on private land are:

*272 Meat Cleaver 5c(NS)
A chop route? The crack directly above the fence is gained from the left.

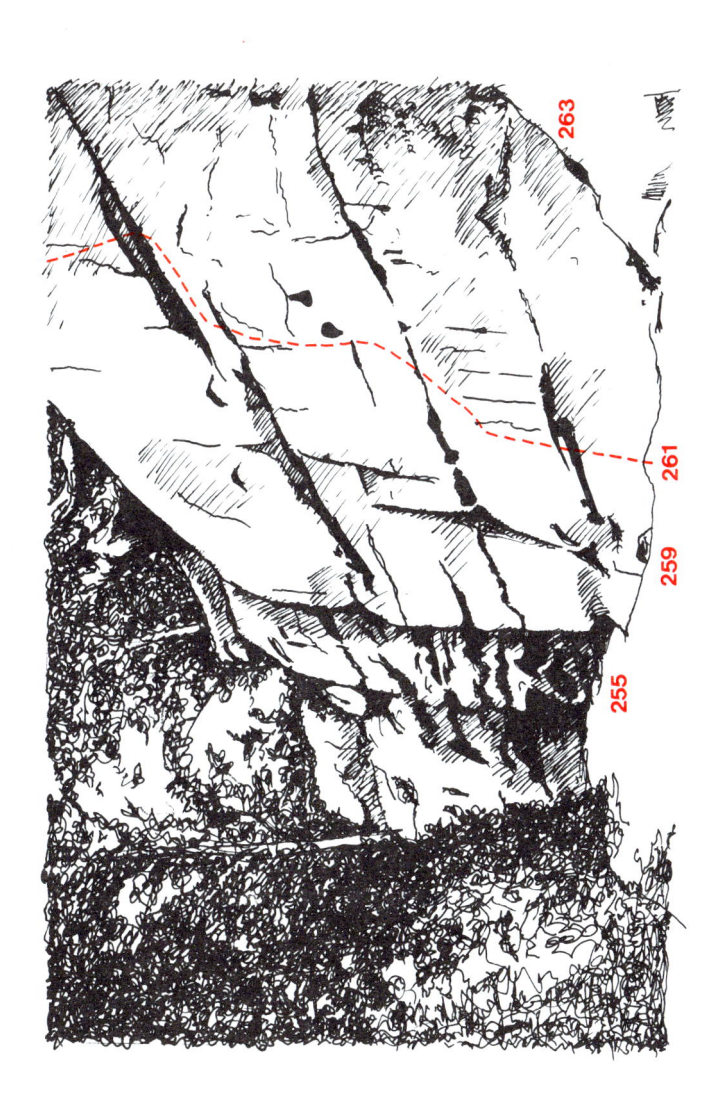

HARRISON'S ROCKS 111

273 Holly Tree Chimney 2a
Obvious
274 Nose and Groove 3b
Traverse in from the left, step up into the groove and climb it.
275 Golden Crack 4b
A variation start to the groove of the next climb. Traverse left at the top of the crack into the groove.
276 Far South Wall 4b
Obvious.
277 South Boulder 4b
A fine slab with small holds. A step to the right enables one to pass the small overhang at half-height.

The Girdle Traverse
A girdle traverse has been made of the substantial part of Harrison's, giving over five hundred metres of climbing. The original route started at Far South Wall (276) and finished at the foot of Slab (55) and is thus nearly four hundred metres long. This was later extended and some of the walking sections eliminated, giving another hundred and fifty metres. In certain areas harder traverse lines were climbed as exploration proceded. The worthwhile sections have already been described, while the whole route appears never to have been done in a single outing.

---

11. Philippa, 6a, Harrison's Rocks. *Climber: Geoff Pearson.* Photo Dave Jones.

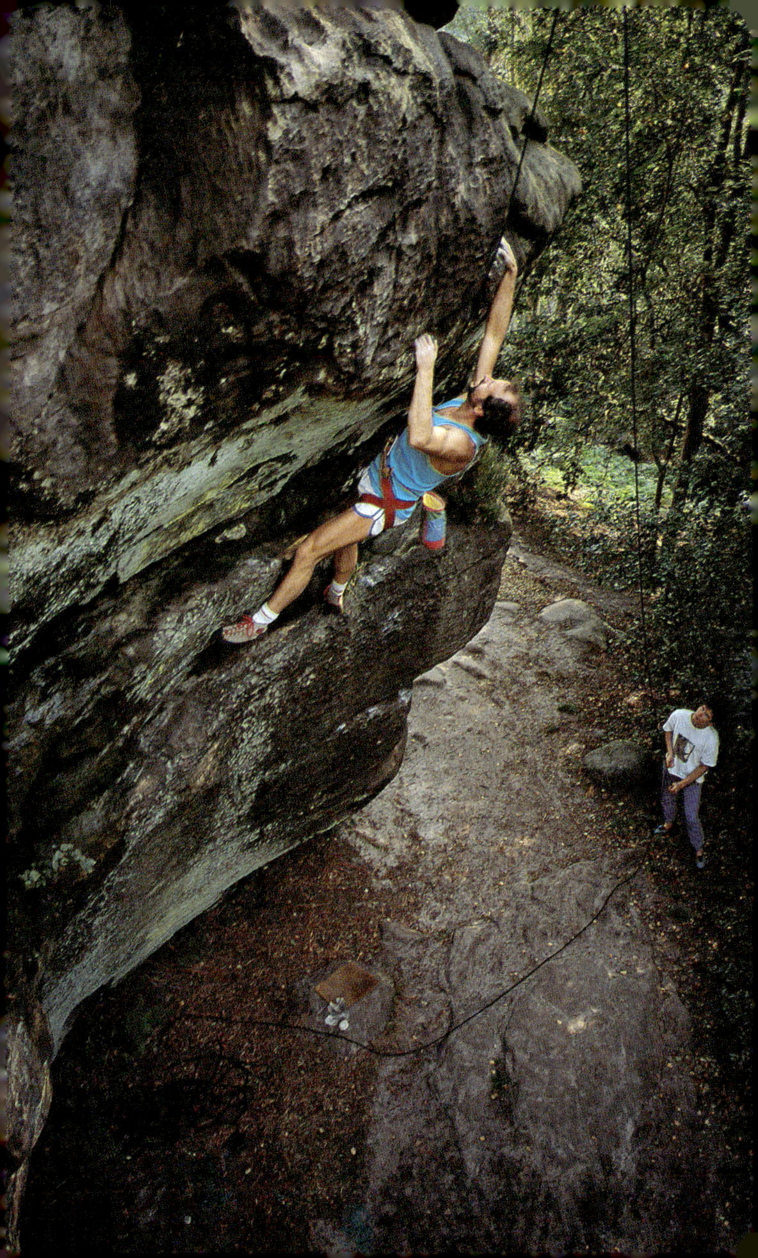

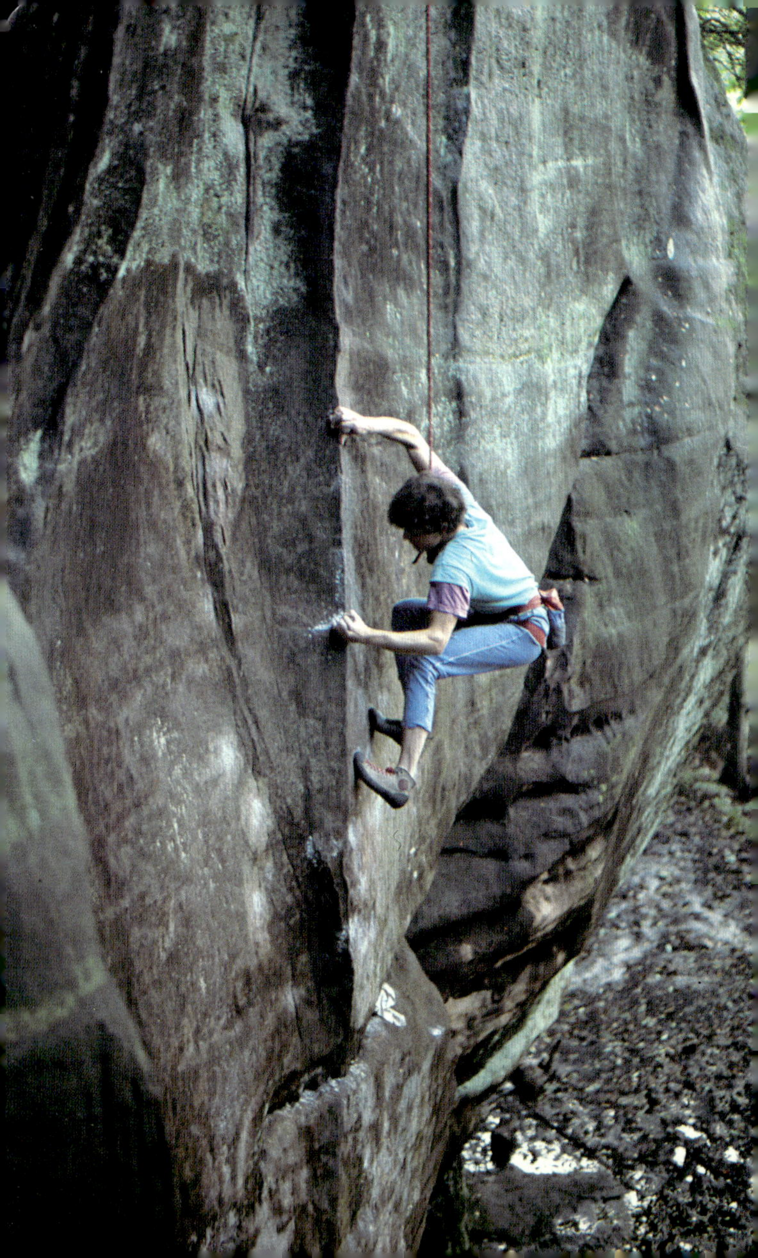

High Rocks   OS Ref 562 382

The Rocks are situated about two and a half km west of Tunbridge Wells and 3 km north-east of Groombridge, opposite the High Rocks Hotel, and are readily approached from either direction. Take the East Grinstead road (A264) from Tunbridge Wells. After two km, on Rusthall Common, a left turn signposted to High Rocks is taken. This leads to a railway bridge, immediately beyond which the High Rocks Hotel and entrance to the rocks are found. From Groombridge follow the road from the railway station to the south, which arcs round to the northeast. After two km take a left fork, which leads to the Hotel and rocks.

The rocks in the gardens opposite the hotel and enclosed by fences belong to the High Rocks Hotel. They are open to the public for an admission fee: currently £1.50 (!) for climbers and, for some unknown reason, £1 for non-climbers. The Continuation Wall, left of the gardens, has different owners but no access problems have been encountered. This section is readily accessible either about 400 metres from its left-hand end at a path under a low railway bridge next to the road, or by a vague footpath by the start of the bridge near the hotel.

As the name implies these are the highest rocks in the area but, although their steepness gives an impression of even greater height, they never exceed twelve metres at any point. The whole outcrop consists of a main wall some four hundred metres long largely facing north. The Continuation Wall is less continuous in terms of height and route quality.

High Rocks is probably the best outcrop for high grade climbing when in condition. In addition, there are numerous chimney climbs for connoisseurs of such esoteria, which can be climbed all year round. The rate of drying could be improved if some trees and vegetation were to be pruned. However, the possibilities are limited because of the gardens, although there was some useful natural pruning in the October 1987 storm. Indeed, the rhododendrons and abundant trees give the crag a relaxed and intimate atmosphere during the summer months, in complete contrast to the Bowles Bustle and the Harrison's Hordes.

High Rocks has been designated a Site of Special Scientific Interest (SSSI). At one time Nature Conservancy Council (NCC) moves suggested a climbing ban, though this was subsequently diffused by negotiation. However, the NCC is still worried about rope burns destroying features such as polygonal markings. These are very common in areas such as Fontainebleau but rare in the south-east. Particular care should be taken in the area of Infidel and, of course, in general. There are a number of rare mosses and other plants to be found here, so please don't destroy any flora unnecessarily.

AS WITH ALL SANDSTONE CRAGS PLEASE USE A LONG BELAY SLING AND POSITION THE KARABINER OVER THE EDGE OF THE

---

12. New Route, High Rocks. *Climber: Dave Turner.* Photo Ben Pritchard.

CRAG SO AS TO MINIMISE DAMAGE TO THE ROCK BY MOVING ROPES.

Climbers are admitted to the grounds by permission of the Proprietor. No camping or bivouacing is allowed at the rocks. The entrance to the climbs opposite the Hotel is in the Advertisement Wall to Mulligan's Wall area - route numbers 142 to 160.

The climbs are described starting with the Continuation Wall area (outside the hotel grounds). The first sizeable rock wall on a large buttress has a large pothole at three metres, which can be entered and leads via a series of clefts to Limpet Crack and Bottle Chimney further right.

1 **Birthday Buttress** 5a
The arête left of Pothole Crack. Start just to the left and go up until it is possible to move onto the arête and finish direct.

2 **Pothole Crack** 4b
The crack which sweeps up right from the hole, with a very awkward move onto the ramp.

3 **Gibbons Progress** 6a
A steep route some four metres right of Pothole Crack. An undercut hold is used to leave the ground, after which go slightly left through a scoop to a difficult finish.

4 **Rake's Progress** 5c
Either climb straight up three metres right of the previous route or trend more easily rightwards to finish near Limpet Crack.

*5 **Limpet Crack** 4a
Strenuous climbing leads to a rest ledge near the top and an easier finish.

6 **Finger Wall** 5b
The wall two metres right of the last route on small holds.

7 **Sombrero Wall**
The bulging arête below the finishing tree of Stalactite Wall has not been climbed recently due to erosion of the sandy holds and of the ground at the start. I take my hat off to anyone who can (or wants to) climb this now.

8 **Stalactite Wall 3b
A good route starting from the foot of Bottle Chimney. Traverse diagonally left on good holds to the arête and finish slightly left of the top nose.

9 **Stalactite Wall Direct** 5a
As for Stalactite Wall but finish straight up by the large flake.

10 **Poacher Corner** 5b
Start as for the previous climb but go straight up the arête.

11 **Bottle Chimney** 3b
A wide start leads to a tight finish that forces the climber outwards. Face left.

12 **Independence** 5b
Start in the shallow scoop a metre right of Bottle Chimney. Climb this

HIGH ROCKS 115

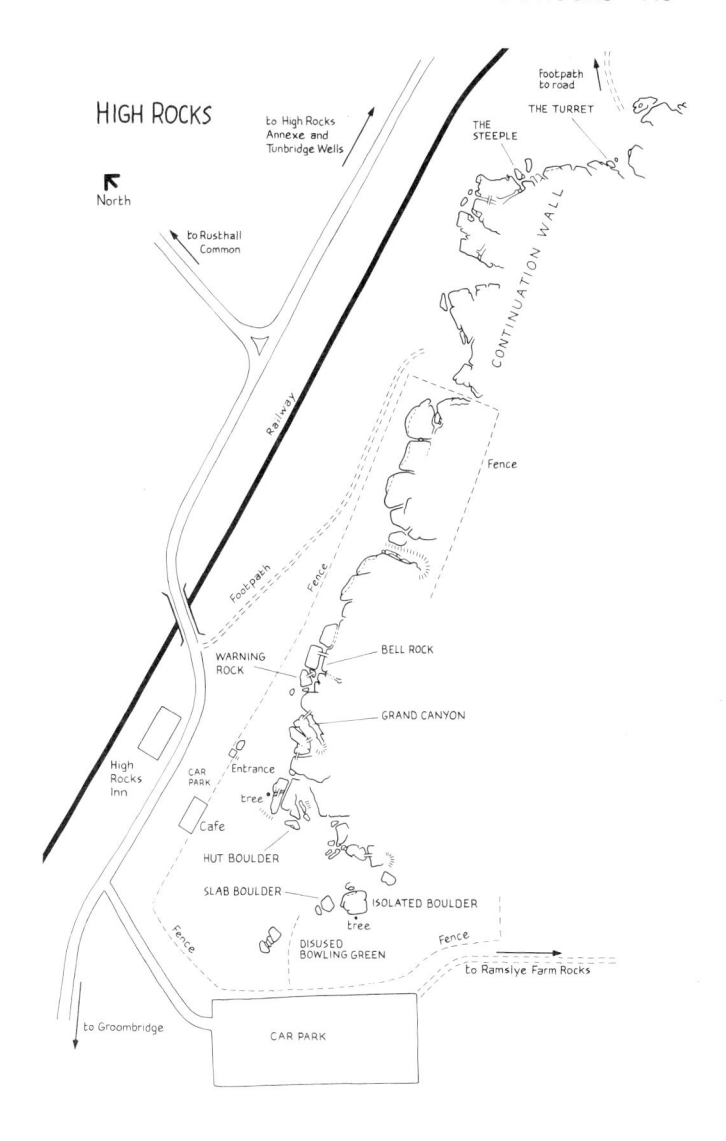

116 HIGH ROCKS

HIGH ROCKS ~ EAST (CONTINUATION WALL)

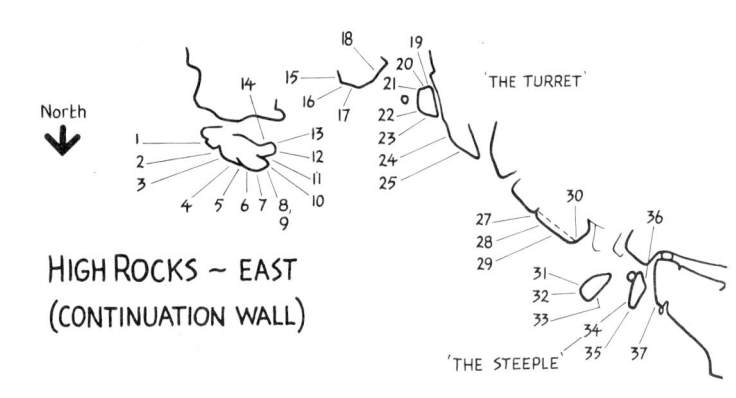

on poor holds, then move slightly right and pull onto the projecting bulge on small holds. Finish straight up.

13 Jug Arête 3b
Immediately right of Independence.

14 Wobbler Wall 4c
The very short wall right of the arête with a shaky final move.

The following problems are on the next boulder before the more substantial Turret Face.

15 Yom Kippa 5b
An awkward little route up the middle of the left wall of the boulder; fast climbing seems to be the best approach.

16 Motza 5b
A line over the bulges on the front of the boulder with hard finishing moves.

17 Green Slab 5b
The obvious slab on the front of the boulder and right of the previous route. Go easily up to the second ledge and an interesting finish.

18 Nosh 5a
Start at an obvious hole just round the corner from Green Slab. Either go straight up or move more easily right then go up - 4c.

The next large buttress is the Turret, with five routes:

19 Left Edge 5b
The left side of the left face is hard at the top. A nice climb.

**20 Turret Face 4b
Start a little right of the last route and go up, gradually moving right, to eventually finish on the front face. A more direct finish is 4c.

HIGH ROCKS

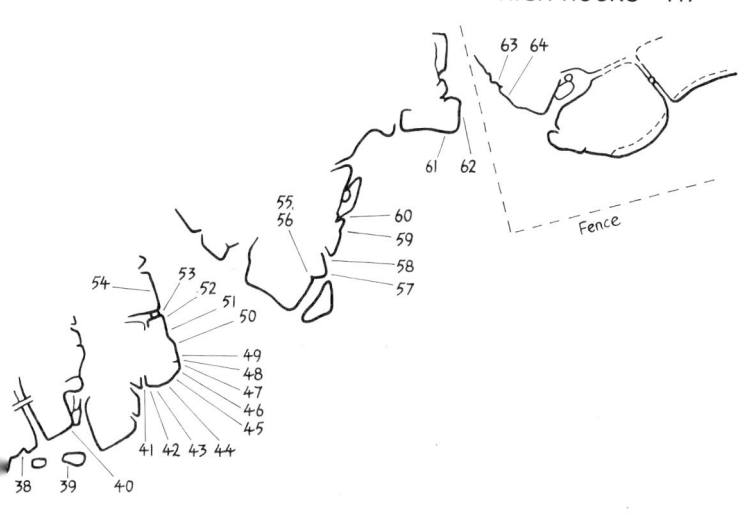

21 Drunkard's Dilemma 5b
Start below the overhanging arête right of Turret Face. Pull very strenuously over the bulge using a good layback hold, moving very slightly left then back right to finish as for Turret Face.

22 Windy Wall 5a
Start by an obvious crack in the front of the block. Traverse diagonally left from the ledges below the top to join and finish as for Turret Face.

A harder variation on Windy Wall is to swing left from the first ledges of that route to a sloping ramp hold, then up on better holds to finish more or less direct - **Nigg Nogg Variation** 5c(NS).

23 Turret Wall 2b
Step up the right-hand edge at the front of the Turret. Much harder when greasy.

There are three routes on the boulder which adjoins the Turret:

24 Twinkle Toe Slab 5b
Up the steep slab just right of the Turret. A delicate climb on small mossy holds.

25 Limpet Wall 5a
The ledge to the right of the previous route is gained by a "thoughtful move". The crack above is not very useful for holds.

26 Awkward 5b
Start up the right face of the boulder, move left to the edge and make a hard move to gain a small ledge on the arête.

Beyond the next bits of broken rock is a tree stump:

27 Rake Buttress 2b
An uninteresting climb but useful for beginners. Step off the tree and meander up to the nose above, with a tricky reach for a tree route to finish.

28 Elephant's Umbrella 5c
Start under the yew tree right of the last route. Pull strenuously over the overhang, using holds to the right of the crack.

29 Parrot's Parasol
A direct line three metres right of the yew tree. The start has not been done since some crucial initial holds went AWOL; perhaps the paracetamol.

30 Parrot's Wing 3a
Not a Budgies' Roundabout. A very short unsatisfactory crack.

On the boulder in the centre of the broad gully is:

31 Two Bit 4a
The front left-hand corner of the block.

32 One Bit 3b
The front arête. The middle of the front face is 5c.

The next feature is a steep-sided pinnacle on the slope in front of the main wall, called the Steeple.

33 Steeple Back 3b
The back left edge of the Steeple.

34 Steeple Direct 5a
Start on the left front arête, go straight up and traverse right to the arête. Awkward.

35 Obverse Route 4c
Start just to the right of the previous route. Climb up and out onto the left side face, and up this to an awkward finish.

36 Ordinary Route 2b
On the right-hand side of the Steeple and near the back. Straightforward and the easiest way down.

The next part of the main wall gives some short bitty climbs.

37 Two Mantleshelves and Cave 3a
An exceptionally contrived non-route. The mantelshelves are two small broken boulders, leading to a finish up a short chimney in the main wall.

38 Barefoot Crack 5a
Face right at the bottom. The start is tricky but soon eases. Usually unpleasant. The wide crack to the left is 5b.

*39 Scotland Slab 1a
The line straight up the middle of the slab is ruined by the cut holds but as such is a useful beginners route. Can be climbed feet first or with no hands.

40 Stepped Buttress 2a
A straightforward series of barely worthwhile mantelshelf moves.

41 Midway Chimney 2b
A short chimney in the corner. The left-hand chimney is 2a

HIGH ROCKS 119

42 Going To The Pub 5c
Is a much better idea, however good the route. Nevertheless, when they're shut, begin two metres right of the chimney and go straight up with some difficulty.

*43 Camelot 6a
Start five metres right of Midway Chimney. Climb the impending crack with difficulty and finish up the wall above.

*44 Lady of the Lake 5b
The steep wall three metres right of Camelot, trending left at first and then back right.

45 Shalot 5b
The right-hand arête of the Midway block, with a series of mantelshelves to finish.

46 Midway Traverse 5a
A twelve-metre-leftwards traverse on an obvious line from the lower part of Tunnel Chimney to Midway Chimney.

47 Whiplash 5b
The left arête of Tunnel Chimney.

48 Tunnel Chimney 2b
The strange leftward curve is difficult to negotiate.

49 Rubber Panty 5c(NS)
Not a little kinky. The green and lichenous arête right of the last route.

50 Taurus 5b
Start just left of Hangman's Wall and go up awkwardly leftwards.

51 Hangman's Wall 5c
This is climbed mainly in the crack.

52 Prickle Corner 5c
The awkward bulging arête to the left of Icicle Passage.

53 Icicle Passage 2a
Straightforward thrutching.

54 Green Gilbert 4c
The very mossy slab just right of the previous route is harder than it looks.

Next are some low buttresses followed by some steep quite impressive but mossy slabs with no routes at all - probably best left that way. The next feature is a large yew tree above a slab, which provides some good boulder problems.

55 Starboard Chimney 3a
The chimney behind the yew tree has a tricky undercut start.

56 Anchor Chain 4c
Cross the nose by broad ledges from Starboard Chimney to reach Port Crack above the constricted part.

*57 Battleship Nose 5b
Go straight up the nose between Starboard Chimney and Port Crack, with a tricky finish.

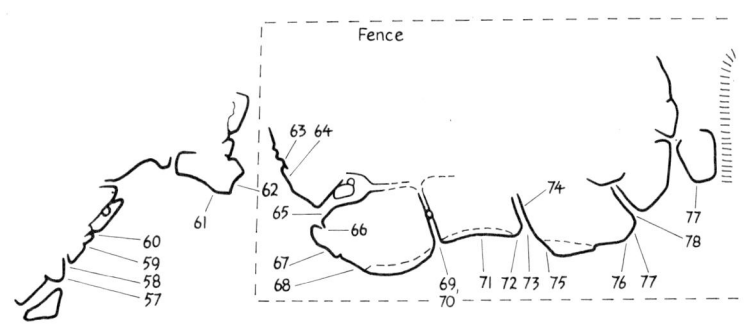

HIGH ROCKS – CENTRAL SECTION

Fence

*58 Port Crack 4b
A steep clean-cut crack with a constricted middle part that forces the climber out of it.

Beyond the next impressively steep and blank wall is:

59 Paul Skinback 5c
The thin discontinuous corner crack two metres left of Overboard has poor holds.

60 Overboard 4b
Climb three metres up a crack to the oak, then move right onto a ledge and up.

The next climbs are about thirty metres right, on a low block just right of which is the tasteless new fence marking the start of the Hotel grounds.

61 Finger Fiend 5c
A short route just to the left of centre of the steep front wall. The name is a hint.

62 Demon Digit 4a
This short route is to be found round the corner from Finger Fiend, just right of the little chimney.

To the right of the fence beyond the gully is a block, the front left arête of which gives:

63 Pure Arête 5b
The finishing holds often need to be dug out.

64 Peace On Earth 5c(NS)
Start as for Pure Arête but hand-traverse right at about two-thirds

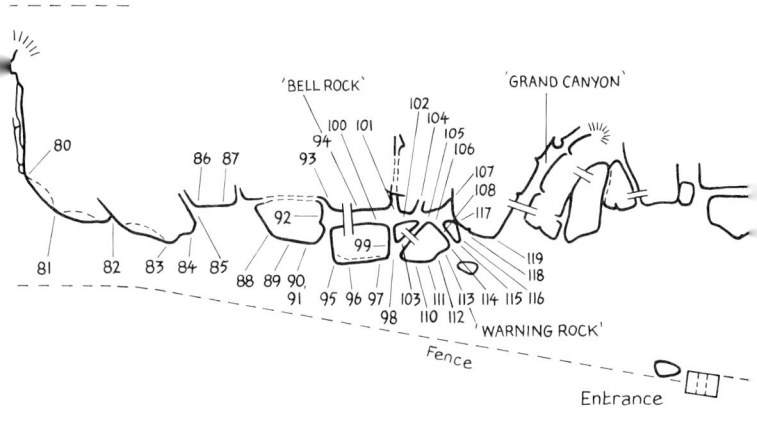

height towards the centre of the block. Go straight up when the time feels right - direct start needed.

65 Orion Arête 5c(NS)
The arête immediately left of Orion Crack and just right of the little passage.

**66 Orion Crack 4a
A good climb up the shallow crack leading to a platform and the wall above.

67 Scimitar 6a
Start at the steep crack three metres right of the previous route and go straight up. The initial moves are usually greasy but this is a good climb when in condition.

***68 The First Crack 6b(NS)
Usually has the last laugh. The fine imposing crack about ten metres right of Scimitar. The first section gives very hard jamming - best left to connoisseurs with large rolls of sticky tape. The middle section has better holds and leads to a finish straight up the wall above.

*69 Missing Link 6b(1pt)(NS) †
Impressive and perhaps not possible for the short. Start up Anaconda Chimney. On the break at four metres traverse left past the first nose to the second one. Use a sling round a stalactite to lean out and reach over the bulge to slot holds. Hard free moves follow to gain the upper wall, which is climbed to the top.

**70 Anaconda Chimney 4a
A relatively pleasant chimney climb. Climb the chimney facing left at first to a ledge at three metres, after which the climbing is much easier.

71 Bolt Route
On the wall between the chimneys. A possible free climb so please don't destroy the rock further by aid climbing.

72 Rattlesnake 6a(NS)
An eliminate line but good climbing nonetheless. Start up the next route and swing onto a ledge on the left arête when it is in reach. Layback the arête to a tricky finish.

73 Boa-Constrictor Chimney 4b
Tight? From the ground just inside go up the narrow front portion facing left. At the top traverse inwards across the wide part and exit on the right.

At the back of the chimney is:

74 Boa by the Back 4a
Up the back facing right, to the top of a projecting bulge on the right wall. Climb the narrow crack at the back to the chockstone; this is hard until the chock is reached. Finish at the back.

75 Venom
A peg route up a good line five metres right of the chimney. Don't peg it please.

*76 Adder 6a(NS)
Start at the Needle's Eye and follow the thin crack. Previously an aid climb and usually very greasy but an impressive line.

77 Aid Route
On the wall between Adder and Cobra Chimney. This route used a combination of pegs, wedges and bolts. Please don't damage the rock by putting any more in.

78 Cobra Chimney 4a
Wherever (if ever?) you climb this it is too wide for comfort.
On the small block left of the steps is:

79 Sorrow 5b
Climb straight up the front of the defaced buttress on good holds, with a mantelshelf to finish.

Just right of the steps is:

***80 Steps Crack 5b
The fine-looking crack right of the passage was the early classic of the rocks. Exit left at the top.

**81 Moving Staircase 6b(NS)
Start in a cave six metres right of Steps Crack and go strenuously up to the first break. Pull out right onto the obvious rampline and follow this with escalating difficulty to finish up the steep slab above its end.

Round the corner is a large concave wall with no routes or discernible holds and is thus suitable for abseiling. The next feature is:

82 Chockstone Chimney 2b
Facing right, climb a crack in the right wall; go outside the chockstone and into the recess in the right wall. Go up this and then step across to the second chockstone to an earthy exit left.

83 Judy 6c(NS)
The centre of the massive overhanging wall gives an impressive climb that packs a mighty Punch. A desperate boulder problem start on the right leads to an obvious traverse line into the cave; exit up then left from this to a semi-rest on a large flake; hand-traverse right to finish up the wide crack in the overhang. The route is easier (6b) and perhaps more enjoyable with a leg-up to start.

84 Ragtrade 6a(NS)
The arête down and left of E Chimney.

85 E Chimney 3a
Similar to Cobra Chimney but somewhat shorter.

An easy descent route is to be found at the back of the chimney.

86 Designer Label 6a
A technically interesting climb but more of a soiled second than catwalk material. The right arête of E Chimney is climbed on its left side to start with and then on the front.

87 Recess Wall 3a
Ascend a short chimney on the right. Traverse the wall leftwards on a broad ledge and out at the far end with an exposed step.

Back on the face by the path is:

*88 Salad Days 6b(NS)
An excellent route starting up the front left arête of the wall. Gain the thin ledge above some large pockets and mantelshelf onto this using the small pockets above. Move right along the first break and make enjoyable moves up the long thin flake. Step left at the next break to a sandy finish.

*89 Leglock 6a(NS)
An obvious crack in the wall right of Salad Days is gained from the right with difficulty. Follow this to near the top then traverse left round the corner and up. One may avoid the start by not doing the route, or by traversing in from Cut Steps Crack along a line of stalactites.

*90 Cut Steps Crack 5c(NS)
Surprisingly this follows the cut steps in the steep slab right of Leglock. At the first break traverse right to the nose. Lean over to the crack in the opposite wall and climb it to its end. Move left and climb the centre of the final block. Two ropes are needed to belay this "adventurous route."

91 Too Tall For Tim 6a(NS)
Go straight up from the start of Cut Steps Crack, with an impossibly long reach for excessively short people.

At the back of the wide passage, which is the easterly end of the Transverse Passage, is:

92 Strangler 5a
In front of and to the left of the slanting chimney is a short crack; climb this and then either move left to continue up the chimney or step right into the slanting chimney.

93 Dead Wood Chimney 2b
Climb a crack in the right wall of the slanting chimney. Traverse outwards at the top and finish either by an earthy exit on the left or by stepping across to the right, followed by a stomach-traverse over the chockstone. The whole chimney can also be climbed at the back with an exit through an earthy hole.

*94 Bell Rock Transverse Passage Route 1 5a
Chimney straight up the cleft, which is slightly wider at the top, to the bridge. There are two rest ledges on this impressive looking route.

Back on the main face is:

**95 Krankenkopf Crack 5b
A few metres right of the wide passage. Strenuous kranken on excellent jams in the steep crack leads quickly to the niche and a much easier wide crack to finish. This was one of Martin Boysen's "Desert Island Climbs" so it must be good.

**96 The Dragon 6a
Climb the overhanging crack five metres right of Krankenkopf to a ledge. Move left and go up to an inverted scoop which provides a good undercut hold; there is a good hold above and to the right of this. A fine enjoyable climb after the start.

*97 Robin's Route 6a
The bulging crack four metres right of the previous route gives thuggish climbing best left to the bumpy boys. Finish easily up the wide crack above. There are some equally Ramboesque starts about three metres right and two metres left of the original - both are 6b.

In the next passage is:

98 Wye Chimney 4a
Indeed? Start with a mantelshelf problem, putting a hand on either wall, then wedge up to a ledge on the left wall. Climb back-and-foot up to a higher ledge on the same wall and traverse outwards to finish just inside the huge block which crowns the chimney.

99 Slab Chimney 2b
Use holds on the left wall to gain a ledge. The slabby part above is surmounted by wedging to a large ledge again on the left. Now step across to the right wall and make a stomach-traverse round a corner to finish up a short crack.

100 Insinuation Crack 2b
Similar to Slab Chimney in character but tighter and with an easier finish straight above.

100A Hidden Arête 5b
The arête to the left (as seen from outside) of Insinuation Crack. Follow the arête to a ledge, move slightly right and finish with a hard mantelshelf.

The next nine routes centre around the continuation of the Transverse Passage:

101 Bell Rock Passage 4a
Straight up at the Transverse Passage end to a ledge on the left wall. Finish by a through route, or an outside route.

HIGH ROCKS 125

102 Bell Rock Transverse Passage Route 2 5a
This is climbed back and foot. Similar to Route 1 but narrower.

103 Smooth Chimney 4a
Back and foot straight up facing left to finish.

104 Spider's Chimney 3b
This also seems to be best done facing left. An earthy finish with holly.

105 Bell Rock Transverse Passage Route 3 4c
Semi-bridging movements up the passage a metre right of Spider's Chimney.

106 Giant's Stride 3a
Climb the chimney at the Transverse Passage end, step across to the right wall and go along a ledge high above the Transverse Passage to the back corner of the Balcony. Finish up the inside.

107 The Chute 4a
The sandy and slimy lower crack is climbed with difficulty facing left. Later, a hand is stretched across the Transverse Passage to enable the overhanging chockstone to be passed. Finish easily above or step across to the Balcony.

108 Warning Rock Chimney 2a
Walk from the back up to the highest point of the floor. Climb a nail scratched sloping ledge, facing right to reach the Balcony and continue to the top on the outside.

109 Labyrinth
An amazing route? Between Deadwood Chimney and the Balcony all the chimneys and passages have a more or less continuous ledge some two to three metres from the top. The route traverses this ledge and can be started or finished anywhere. The grade is dependent on the parts that are climbed.

Three metres right of the wide passage leading to Wye Chimney is the start of:

110 Dysentry 5c(NS)
Climb the thin overhanging crack then move left along the ledge to gain the chimney, which is climbed for three metres. Traverse back right along a rounded ledge until a slanting crack is reached; finish up this and over a doubtful block on the left.

**111 The Prang 6a(NS)
Start round the corner from Dysentery. Jump for a high jug hold and use a long slanting flake to gain a line of stalactites; follow these left to the nose and for two metres more. Climb the wall, using a very small edge to make a long reach to the next break, and finish up the pock-marked block.

*112 The Lobster 6a(NS)
An impressive line up the Warning Rock. Climb the crack until it peters out. Make a hard move to reach the break, which is unfortunately always very greasy and tricky to hold with one hand - easier and better if you clean the ledge beforehand.

At the top of the next two routes are some rare polygonal rock formations of great scientific interest - see crag introduction. Please

HIGH ROCKS 127

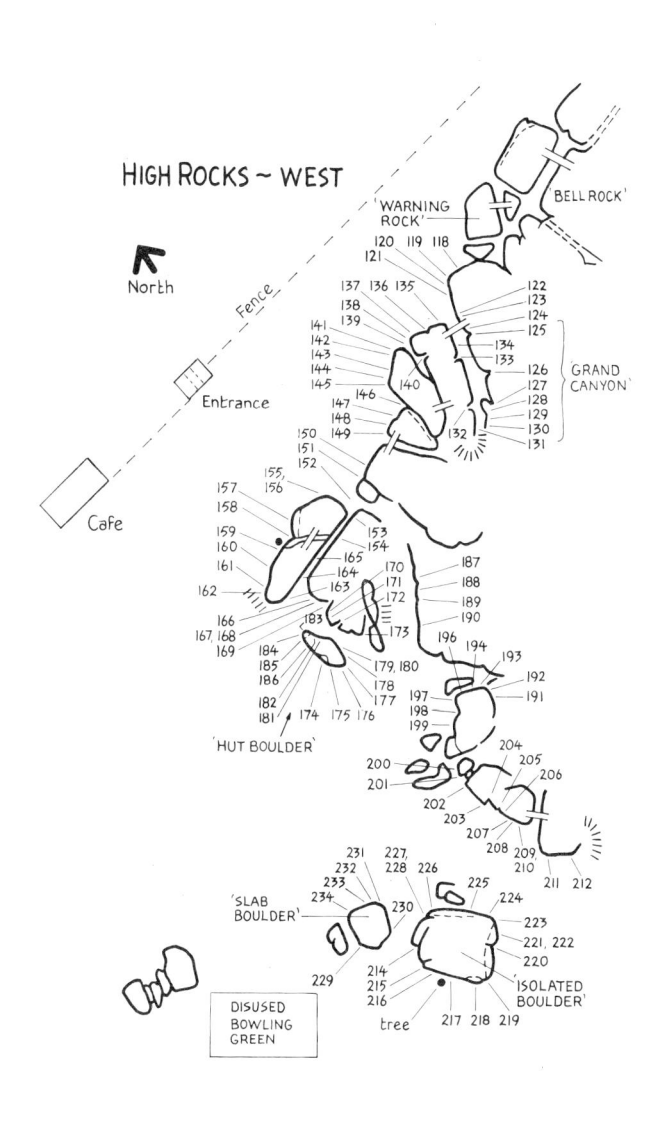

take great care with belays and ropes so as not to damage them - the (long) belay sling for Infidel is best placed such that the krab is on the break beneath the large final overhang.

***113 Infidel** 6a
A climb of great difficulty and atmosphere - only added to by the accompanying inscription. Start up the inverted scoop just right of the corner and go up to the break. Move right and stand up with difficulty; make a frustratingly long reach to the next break, from which go up to the roof and traverse off right. Direct finish...?

*114 Henry the Ninth 5b
The rib immediately left of Warning Rock Chimney, climbed on its left side. The upper part can be climbed either by laybacking or monkeying. Strenuous either way but nice.

*115 Warning Rock Buttress 3b
Step up into the front end of Warning Rock Chimney and climb it to the level of the Balcony. Step up into the recess on the left wall and so to the top.

**116 Jaws 5c
Climb the overhanging right-hand side of the Warning Rock Buttress, starting about two metres in on the left side. Move up, then go left by bridging until able to pull into the crack on the opposite wall; follow this to the tree. A gripping solo.

117 Balcony Direct 4b
Bridging up the entrance to Bell Rock Transverse Passage is followed by back-and-foot work facing the Balcony, which is attained on the front side.

*118 Boysen's Crack 6a
Narrow, earthy and often damp - nothing personal mind. The rounded crack two metres right of Jaws. Awkward jamming leads to a rounded often dirty ledge and easier ground. Good when clean and dry.

119 Conchita 6a(NS)
The nose on the left of the entrance to the Grand Canyon is extremely awkward and technical.

The following sixteen routes lie on the walls of the Grand Canyon, the deepest and widest cleft at the rocks. This gives a large number of classic High Rocks jamming cracks.

120 Marquita 5c
The first crack on the left wall of Grand Canyon gives a good jamming problem.

*121 Lucita 5c
Start four metres right of Marquita and traverse left into an S-shaped crack.

122 Slant Eyes 5c
Start as for Lucita then follow the obvious pockets diagonally right to a long reach for a tree stump to finish.

---

13. Krait Arête, 6b, High Rocks. *Climber:* Gary Wickham. Photo Dave Turner.

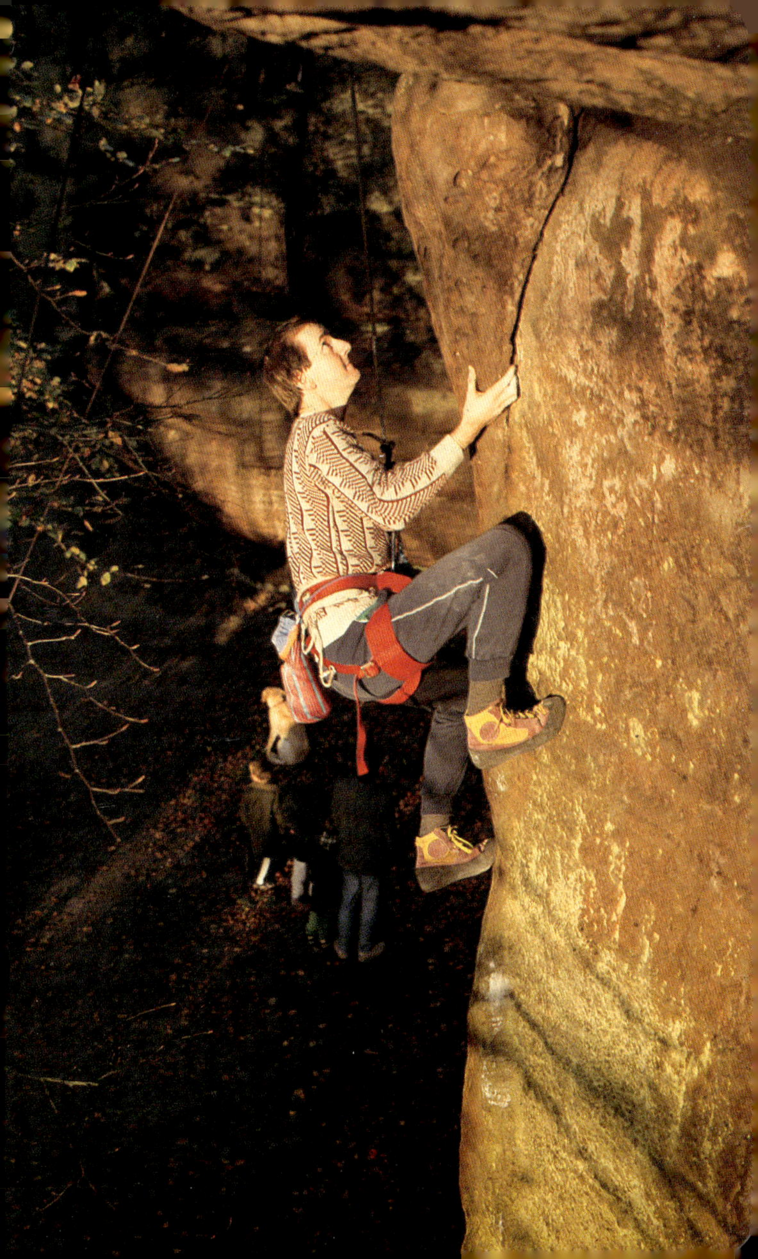

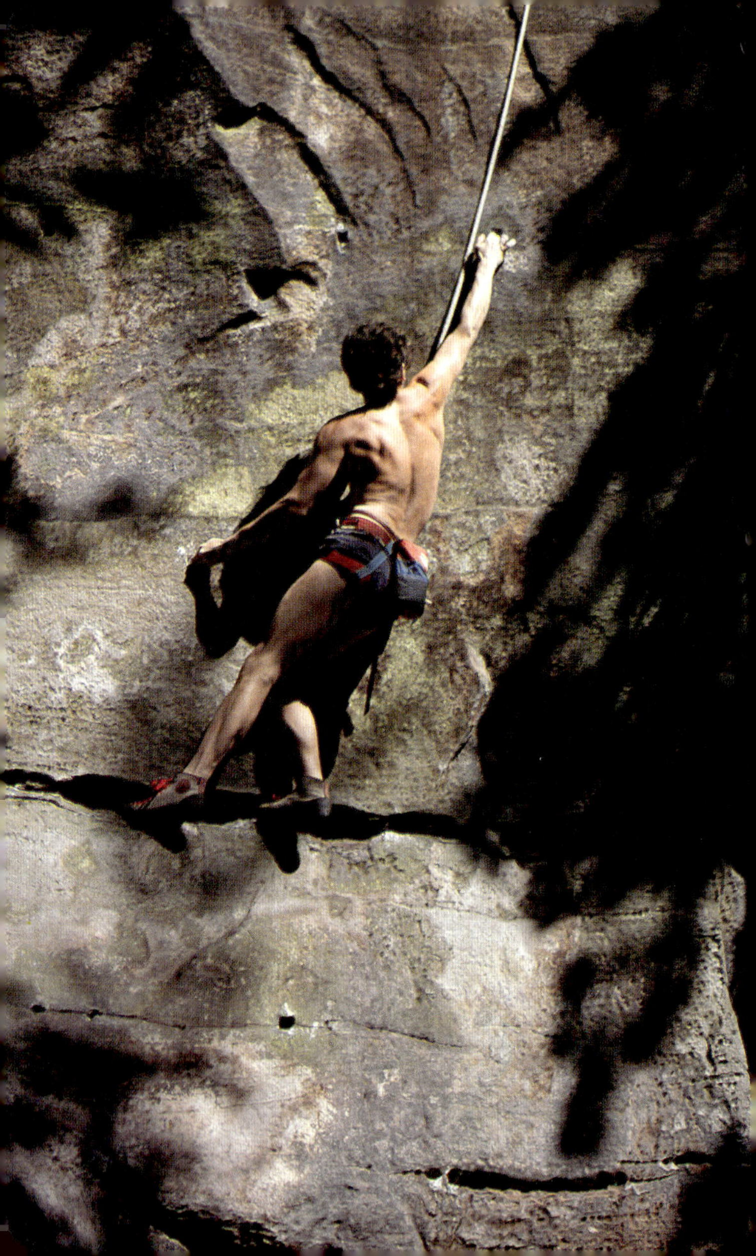

123 **The Gibbet** 5b
The wide (hanging?) crack beneath a silver birch, right of Slant Eyes, can only be recommended.........to masochists.

124 **Cool Bananas 6c(NS)†
The blunt arête and wall right of the bridge gives an intensely technical climb, requiring sustained concentration for success. Start below the arête and gain the break; go up then right to a wide pinch. Layback up the cracks above to a frustrating finish.

125 **Effie 5b
A fine and popular climb taking the split crack just past the bridge. Take the right fork until it is possible to reach across and move left. On the break hand-traverse left to finish near the bridge. Alternatively, traverse right and struggle up the delightful crack in the overhang.

126 **Mamba Crack** 4b
A tedious, tiring tortuous trip, with an earthy finish to top it off nicely. It is best climbed facing left. Not a climb to 'remamba'.

127 **Colorado Crack** 2b
Face right and climb easily up to a ledge on the right wall.

128 **Rattlesnake** 4b
A semi-layback start leads to a rake sloping up left into Colorado Crack. Finish up the wall above the rake.

129 **Bright Eyes** 5b
Climb the short wall right of the last route. Start at the right-hand end of the wall and trend diagonally left to the trees.

130 **Short Chimney** 2a
A worthless non-route up the wide crack with tree roots at the back.

On the opposite side of the Grand Canyon is:

131 **Issingdown** 5a
First climbed in the rain? The first crack from the left is very short and awkward.

132 **Python Crack** 5a
Face right and climb with the left leg in, to an earthy traverse leading left to the top.

133 **Beanstalk** 5b
The wide crack right of Python is a fight.

134 **Peapod** 6b(NS)
The short flared groove immediately right of Beanstalk gives one very hard move. Trend left to finish. An unsatisfying experience.

*135 **Cheetah** 6b(NS)
The arête to the left of Coronation Crack. A sandy undercut hold (the fastest wearing hold on sandstone?) is used to reach the ledge over the bulge; another hard move follows to stand up on this. Finish more easily up the fine arête above.

---

14. Dyno Sore, 6b, High Rocks. *Climber: Dave Turner.* Photo Ben Pritchard.

Back on the main wall is:

136 Coronation Crack 5c(NS)
A classic jamming route following the striking crack-line in the steep wall. The climbing is elegant in concept but rarely so in practice -barring good conditions or a huge pair of fists. Start at the bottom and so to the top.

***137 Krait Arête** 6b(NS)
A wonderful route up the blunt arête left of the old air-raid shelter. Start on the right then make a technical rockover move to get established on the arête, after which elegant friction and layaway moves culminate in a strenuous finale on jugs. Brilliant.

138 Shelter Arête 5c(NS)
Climb the flake crack left of and using the air-raid shelter; move right and pull awkwardly onto the arête(crux). Continue up the front face of the arête and finish over the left wall of the passage. The hardest part is avoiding the opposite side of the chimney.

*139 Shelter Chimney** 2b
Go straight up the chimney starting off the roof of the air-raid shelter.

140 Shelter Passage 4b
Chimney up the passage about halfway to the back. The smooth walls make this very strenuous.

The steep walls round to the right feature a number of good routes, all based on the square-cut holes - the holes were originally cut to enable the attachment of an advertising hoarding visible from the railway below.

141 Shelter Slabs 5b
Go carefully up the middle of the steep slabs right of Shelter Chimney to a ledge on the corner halfway up. Traverse left and finish up the chimney.

142 Advertisement Wall 5b
Start as for Shelter Slabs but instead of traversing left continue up the left edge of the wall using the cut holes to a mantelshelf finish. The cut holes can be avoided totally, giving a nice 5c problem. A harder direct start can be made up the rounded nose to the left of the slabs - also 5c.

143 Engagement Wall 6a(NS)
To the right of Advertisement Wall. Use the third and fourth holes from the left to reach the horizontal break. Finish strenuously slightly to the right.

144 Dyno-Sore 6b(NS)
The right-hand-most pairs of cut holes, with a long reach to get off the first break followed by a massive leap for good holds on the next break. The finish is much easier.

145 Quirkus 4c
The right arête of the Engagement Wall block. Start up the crack on the left, then move right to the arête and go up it. Use the tree if you like.

146 Dirty Dick 4b
A layback crack in the corner.

HIGH ROCKS 131

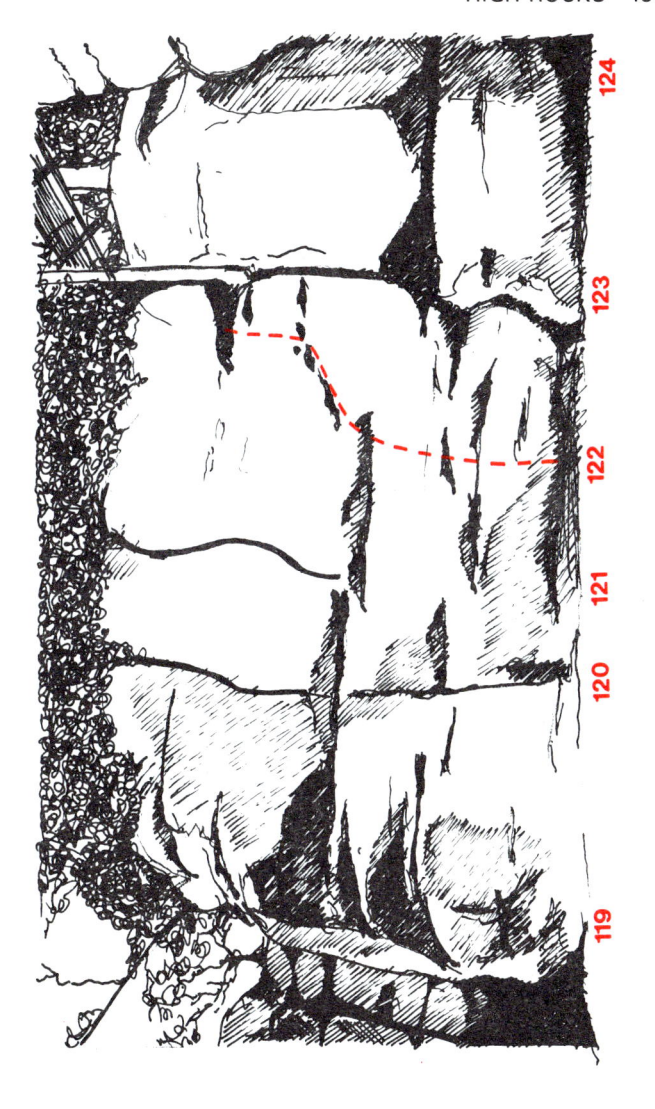

147 Crypt Crack 4a
The short but awkward crack right of the last route is most difficult where it narrows.

148 Look Sharp 6b
A very technical eliminate climb, which involves laybacking the left arête of Short Chimney. This is becoming increasingly difficult as the initial holds wear away.

149 Short Chimney 2a
This can be done facing either way.

150 Mervin Direct 6b(NS)
The right side of the wall right of Short Chimney. Climb the line of square-cut holds, tending slightly right at the top.

***151 Crack and Wall Front** 5a
The short crack formed by the detached block followed by the arête above. The tree gets in the way a bit.

152 Hut Transverse Arête 5a
The greasy arête across the gap from Crack and Wall Front.

153 Hut Transverse Passage - Ordinary Route 2b
Climb straight up close to the entrance to Brushwood Chimney.

154 Brushwood Chimney 2b
Start at the Hut Transverse Passage end and go straight up to finish out of a hole between the top of the left wall and the capstone.

****155 Kinda Lingers** 6c(NS)†
The front left arête of the block. Start on the right with some perverse contortions, requiring not a little forethought. Move left on the break and climb the arête with difficulty on its right side to a climactic finish. The start can be avoided by traversing in from the left - 6b.

156 Celebration Hangover
An old, rarely ascended aid climb. Start as for the previous route and using natural eyelets, bolts and pegs go up for three metres and then traverse right to the next corner. From here bolts lead over the main overhang. Please DO NOT put in any more aid points.

157 Roobarb 5c
Climb the middle of the wall beneath the big roof of Celebration Hangover. Traverse right at the roof and finish up the chimney. It is also possible to use a flake in the roof to bridge out to the oak tree - **All That Meat but only Two Veg** 6a(NS); doing this may increase the pitch of your voice.

158 Brushwood Chimney - Outside Route 3a
The chimney between the two oak trees; finish on the front side of the capstone.

Starting on the left side of the oak tree is:

****158A Boonoonoonoos** 6b(NS)
Go straight up to the main break, without using the tree. Follow the obvious holds rightwards, then back left to the break in the middle of the smooth wall. Make a long powerful move to reach a good hold and finish easily.

HIGH ROCKS 133

134 HIGH ROCKS

*159 Firebird 6a(NS)
The impending wall just right of the tree. Climb straight up on good holds to the horizontal ledge, and continue up the wall above.

**160 Mulligan's Wall 5c
The obvious crack by the steps is climbed on good jams to a ledge below the top. Either move left and finish using the tree or finish direct, very thin and 6a.

*161 Bludgeon 5c(NS)
Follow Mulligan's Wall to the ledge then traverse right and finish up Firefly.

*162 Firefly 6b(NS)
A good route if you like this sort of thing. Gain and desperately climb the short shallow rounded crack three metres right of Mulligan's Wall; continue up the wall trending left to finish up a wider crack.

**163 Celebration 5c
The arête just beyond the top of the steps gives a very pleasant climb. Start at the boundary of smooth and honeycomb rock. Move left and go straight up to finish by some rhododendron bushes.

*164 Hut Transverse Passage - Rufrock Route 3a
A straightforward chimney climb at the entrance near the steps.

165 Hut Transverse Passage - Central Route 3b
At the highest point of the floor. Smooth and strenuous.

The wall right of Hut Transverse Passage has some steep and impressive routes. There is also a good low-level traverse of this wall - **Lord** 6a.

*166 Tilley Lamp Crack 6a(NS)
The crack two metres right of the passage entrance is climbed until it peters out whence a hard move is made (once you've seen the light) to gain the break and an awkward finish.

**167 Nemesis 6b(NS)
The comeuppance for hubris? An excellent route taking the centre of the wall right of Tilley Lamp Crack. Precision pocket-pulling leads to a short diagonal crack and a very tricky move to reach the horizontal break; move a little right to finish with interest.

*168 A Touch Too Much 6b
The pocketed wall just left of Viper Crack is easier than Nemesis but still technically absorbing. Start as for Nemesis or (better) direct. The crux is passing the steep rounded ramp to gain the break and easy ground.

169 Viper Crack 5b
The wide crack bounding the right side of the wall is often green and is harder than it looks.

170 Shattered 6b
The arête immediately right of Viper Crack is a powerful boulder problem.

171 Jug of Flowers 6b(NS)
The square-cut pocket in the wall left of Easy Crack is gained either from the right, by starting just left of Easy Crack and using the obvious

HIGH ROCKS 135

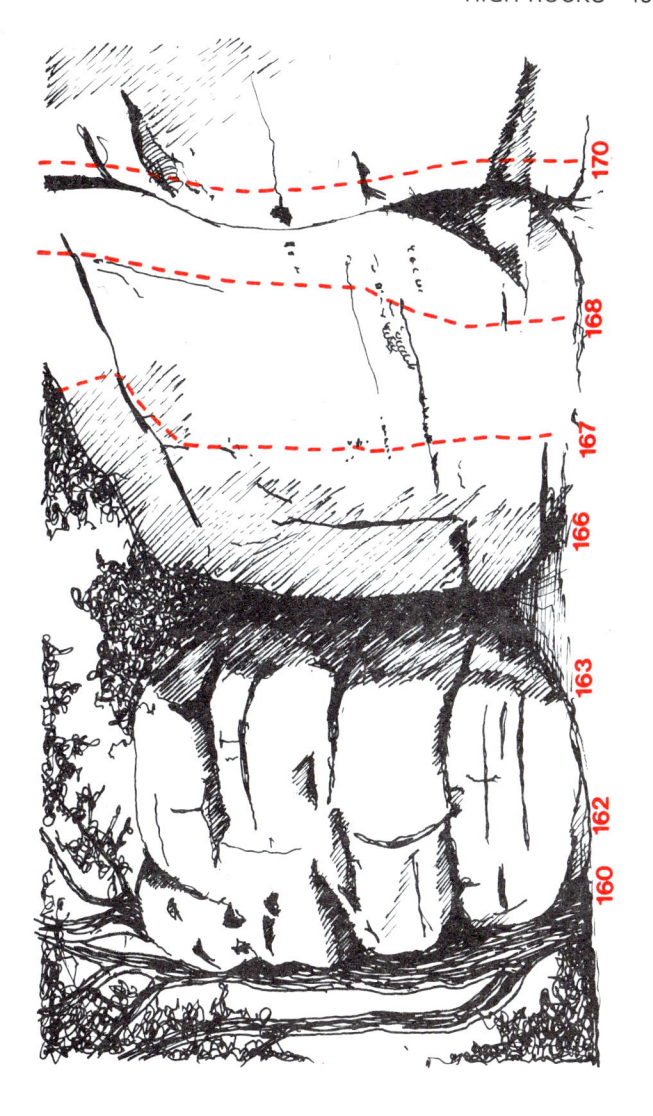

diagonal undercuts, or with more difficulty direct. Either way there is a hard move to get stood up in the pocket.

*172 Easy Crack 2a
The wide crack in the main wall opposite Hut Boulder.

*173 Bold Finish 5a
The rounded arête at the right end of the wall, with a tricky finish especially for a soloist.

The next series of climbs are on the Hut Boulder; between this and the main wall are the brick remains of the Sandstone Club Hut. There is a metal belay point cemented into the top of the boulder. There is no easy access to the top but a rope can be thrown over the front face from the top of the main wall or from the ground. Crack Route can then be top-roped to get to the belay point. This route is described first:

**174 Crack Route 4c
A good climb. The obvious central crack on the front face is climbed on good holds to the ledge. Pull over the top on jugs.

*175 Pinchgrip 5c
Fine technical climbing up the centre of the impending wall two metres right of Crack Route.

*176 Pussyfoot 5b
The right arête of the front face. Start in a small depression on the left; move right to the arête, using a short wide crack, and follow it to the top.

*177 Swing Face 5b
The middle of the end face. Start at the wide cracks on the right, go up a little and move strenuously left to the middle. Continue directly to the top. There is a harder (5c) direct start.

**178 Birthday Arête 5b
The arête right of Swing Face, again starting by the wide cracks.

179 Sequins of Cosmic Turbulence 5c(NS)
Start as for Roof Route and climb the wall right of Birthday Arête without touching adjacent routes. Hard at about two-thirds height.

*180 Roof Route 5a
The obvious left-to-right slanting crack on the back wall is followed strenuously to easier ground. Finish at the tree on the right or, harder, straight up.

181 Rockney 5c
Start a metre right of Roof Route by some square-cut holds and make some hard moves to the break and gain the large pothole. Exit right from this and then go straight up. An easier start can be made from the bricks two metres further right.

*182 Cough Drop 5b
Start at a short flared crack and go up to the ledge, swing left and climb the flakes near the centre of the wall to the tree.

183 Rhino's Eyebrow 5a
Start as for the previous route to the ledge and make an ascending traverse right then back left on sloping mossy holds. Not very inspiring.

HIGH ROCKS

*184 Roofus 6b(NS)
Climb the right-hand edge of the overhanging end of the Boulder. At the obvious break swing left to the centre on jugs and surmount the overhang.

185 Long Stretch 5c
The crack at the extreme left end of the front face of the Boulder, just right of Roofus. The start is the crux.

186 Bludnok Wall 5c
Just before the platform at the base of Long Crack and two metres right of Long Stretch. Gain the ledges at waist level. Stand on the bulge, make a long reach for the next ledge and traverse off - needs a direct finish chaps.

There are several routes on the wall opposite Swing Face and beyond some stone steps. The next four routes are rarely climbed as they are usually in very poor condition.

187 Bush Arête 4b
On the extreme left of this section of the face, opposite Swing Face.

188 Open Groove 5b
An obvious awkward groove three metres right of Bush Arête.

189 Rhododendron Route 3b
On the main wall opposite Swing Face is a wet and unattractive route up the obvious square-cut shallow recess.

190 Seaman's Wall 5c(NS)
A horrible route climbed only by guide-book writers - honest. Climb directly up the green arête just right of the last route, with a series of slippery snatches.

Opposite the hut and round to the right of the last four routes there is a passage divided by a long low block. There are several routes on the blocks to the right of this passage.

191 Solo 5a
The not-so-high but nonetheless strenuous crack around the corner from the extreme left end of the passage.

There is a good pumpy traverse starting round the corner to the left of Solo, crossing it and continuing rightwards to finish under the bridge.

192 Awkward Corner 5b
The extreme left edge of the wall has a hard finish.

193 Bow Crack 5a
Two metres right of the edge a crack begins at head-height, which leads to another hard finish. An eliminate problem takes the wall just right on sharp holds - 6a.

194 Orrer Crack 5c
The thin curved crack in the centre of the wall on sharp holds and an 'orribly painful jam.

195 Rum, Bum and Biscuits 6a
Truly the Navy Way? The wall immediately right of Orrer Crack has good sharp holds.

138   HIGH ROCKS

*196   Navy Way 5c
The wall between Orrer Crack and the right arête of the wall. Start just left of the arête, climb the flakes and finish left of the bulge.

**197   Odin's Wall 5c
Just around the arête from Navy Way, between the arête and the crack. Go straight up the wall on good holds to the top which is very hard.

198   Something Crack 6a(NS)
The obvious S-shaped crack to the right of the arête. It is difficult to keep out of Odin's Wall.

199   Ping Pong A2(2pts)
The vague crack three metres right of Something Crack using two jammed slings for aid. Originally, given A2 but certainly not climbed in any such style recently. Free-climbable?

Continuing rightwards round the corner, and on the front of the comparatively tall, narrow boulder left of the steps is:

200   Profiterole 5c
Start up the right side of the front face of the tall boulder and finish up the centre avoiding degenerate's holds all the way. It can also be started on the left.

*201   Degenerate 5a
Straight up the front right-hand arête of the tall boulder. A nice problem.

On the next wall opposite the Isolated Boulder are a couple of good but short routes:

**202   Honeycomb 6b
Start just left of the centre of the steep pocketed wall. Go straight up for two metres, move two metres right and climb the steep wall with increasing difficulty on friable holds. Sadly, a chipped hold has recently appeared on the top. There is a harder direct start on the right.

An independent route, **Honeycomb Variant** *6b(NS)†, starts just left of the original and climbs the steep wall left of the blunt nose on very friable pocket holds. Unfortunately, again there are some chipped holds at the top - no more, please.*

*203   Craig-y-blanco 6a
The steep arête right of Honeycomb is strenuous with small sharp friable holds.

204   Dagger Crack 6a
The thin curving crack, bearing right at the top to a dirty finish.

205   Greasy Crack 5a
The very unpleasant crack right of Dagger Crack.

206   Wishful Thinking 5b or 6b
The wall with writing on, just right of Greasy Crack. The easiest way to do it is to run at it, whilst a normal approach is very painful.

207   Woofus Wejects 5c(NS)
The doidy cwack just wight of the wall with whiting on it. A twemendous awe-inspiwing woute.

HIGH ROCKS 139

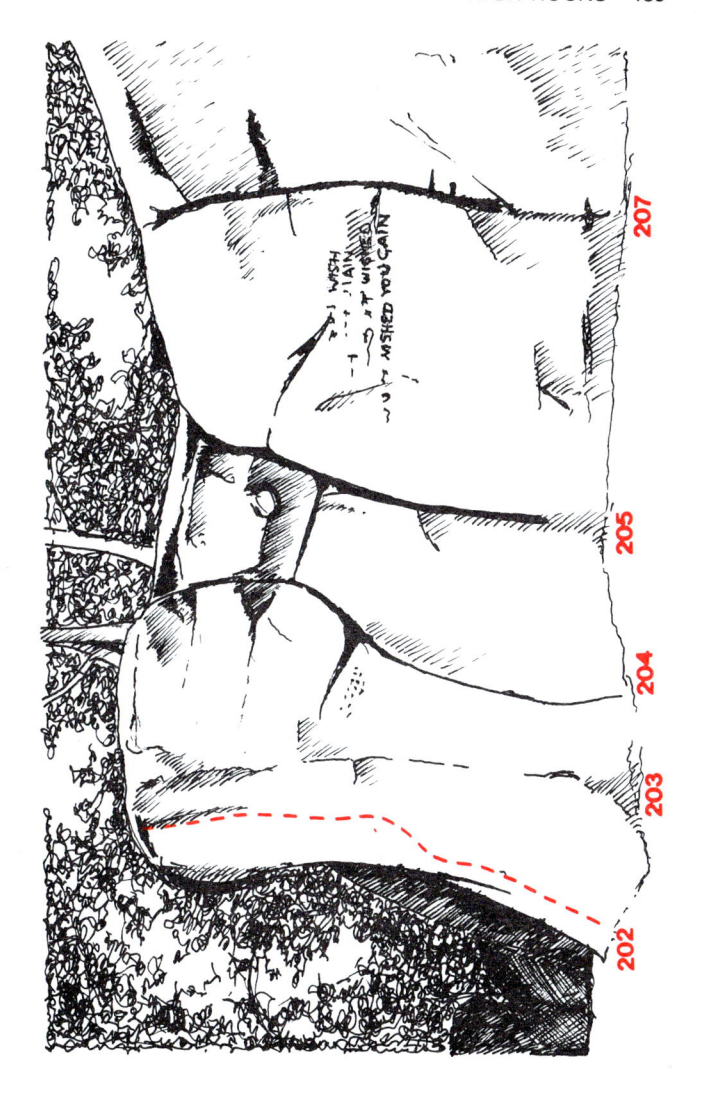

208 Ides of March 6a(NS)
Climb the wall one metre or so right of Woofus Wejects.
209 Lunge'N'Shelf 6a(NS)
A short dynamic problem only just left of Puzzle Corner; finish left of and without using the bridge.
210 Puzzle Corner 4c
Go straight up the rounded arête, at the far right-hand end of the wall, currently obstructed by the bridge.

A worthwhile traverse can be made starting at Honeycomb and finishing at Puzzle Corner. To the right is a low block with stone steps in front of it and a tree.

211 Marathon Man 6a
Start by a square block on the ledge under the overhang. Swing up to the break and move left to an awkward mantelshelf finish. Is it safe?
212 Beer Gut Shuffle 6a(NS)
Go over the small overhang at some weaknesses three metres right of Marathon Man.
213 P.E. Traverse 4a
Traverse awkwardly from right to left under the overhang, finishing round the corner and near the bridge.

Opposite this boulder there is the large Isolated Boulder with many good routes. The top must first be gained by soloing a route; Ordinary Route or Simian Progress are recommended. Descend by climbing, abseil, lowering off, or by accident. There is also the lower Slab Boulder next to the Isolated Boulder.

*214 Ordinary Route 4a
Opposite the easy-angled side of Slab Boulder. Climb up to the overhang and traverse right beneath it. Finish up the awkward wide crack.
215 Devastator 6a
Start just left of the large oak tree. Move up to the first break, traverse sandily left into a recess and go up to the small yew tree. Finish straight above this.
*216 Graveyard Groove 5c
Start as for Devastator but go straight up. A route with varied climbing and thus of some interest. Do not use the tree.

The next three routes right of the tree are all very strenuous, particularly their starts.

*217 Fork 5c
The crack system right of the tree without using it, the tree that is.
***218 Knife 5c
The best of the three. The crack to the right of Fork is slightly easier and has the same finish.
**219 Dinner Plate 5c
An undercut start enables one to gain the crack, which is followed to the ledge. Finish up the wall above on good holds.

HIGH ROCKS 141

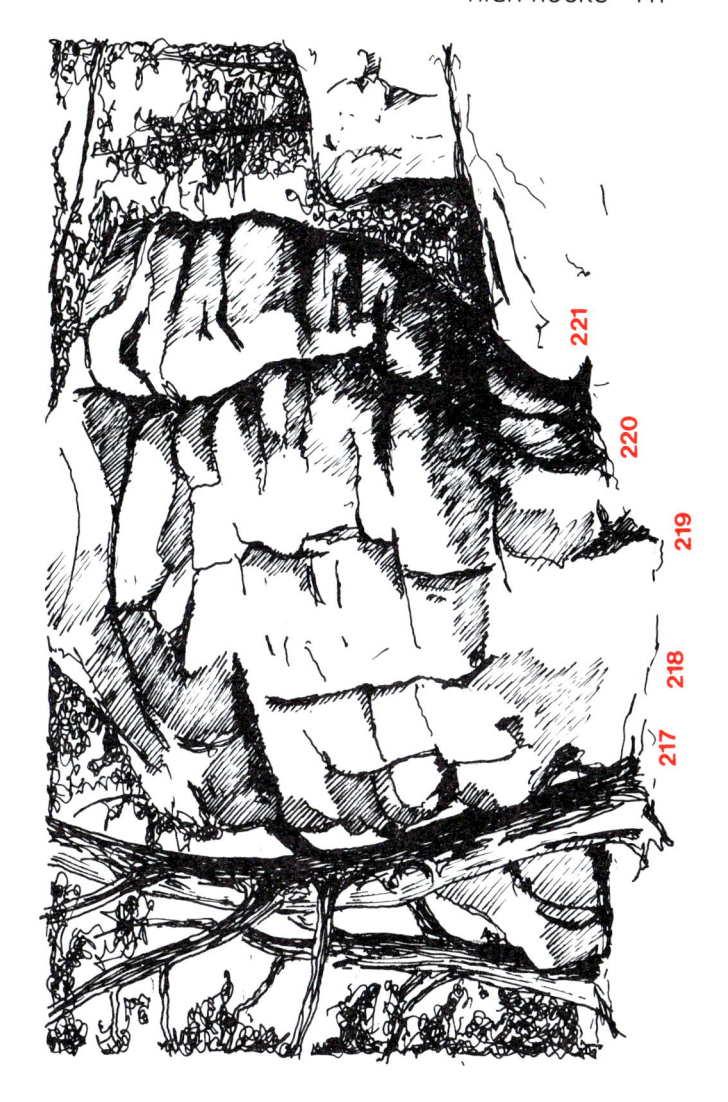

220 Breakfast 6a
Climb the thin overhanging crack in the centre of the undercut face - a direct start to Simian Progress. When possible pull more easily left onto the sandy juggy nose and finish straight up, including the final overhang.

*** 221 Simian Progress 5a
A classic, the start being the hard part. Begin at the right-hand end of the undercut face either with a long stride from the boulder, or with a 5b long reach and pull up from the ground. Monkey strenuously left on big holds to the main crack and finish up this.

* 222 Simian Face 5b
Start as for Simian Progress, but go straight up before the crack is reached staying on the face all the way. More sustained than the Progress. A direct start is 5c.

** 223 Monkey Nut 5b
The overhanging arête to the right of Simian Face is very strenuous. Start on the right of the arête, move left and go straight up it. Finish directly over the bulges at the top.

* 224 The Sphinx 6a
Start as for Simian Mistake but step left and go up the overhanging wall on sharp ironstone holds. Strenuous and technical. An alternative is to move further left almost to the arête on the sharp ironstone holds and then go straight up - **Monkey's Sphincter** 6a(NS).

** 225 Simian Mistake 5c
Follow the large flake in the centre of the wall up rightwards until it peters out. Either finish straight up or, equally difficult, go diagonally right to the usual finish of North Wall. An alternative start is a 6b boulder problem two metres right.

226 Sputnik 6a(NS)
The overhanging arête left of North Wall. Start on the boulder and finish straight up in the same line.

227 North Wall 5a
Climb the sharp layback crack to the overhang, then traverse left to a break and so to the top.

** 228 The Helix 5a
A very worthwhile traverse route over thirty metres long, which starts at the foot of North Wall and winds its way round the block:

1. Go up for two or three metres then pull right to a broad ledge, which is followed to a thread belay at its end.
2. Descend to the recess on Ordinary Route and continue its traverse across to the yew tree and further to belay on the oak.
3. Continue at the same level to the foot of the final crack of Simian Progress, belay.
4. Either finish up Simian Progress or go further right and up Simian Face.

This is the original route, but one can complete the girdle at sustained 5c. Descend the direct finish of Simian Mistake to the top of the flake, then move right onto the finish of North Wall and reverse this to the start.

The following routes are on the Slab Boulder, starting on the easy-angled face with two popular climbs:

*229 Outside Edge Route 3b
Go up the wall behind, and using, the tree on good hand holds, then delicately up the left edge of the slab. If the tree is not used to start the grade is 5a.

*230 Holly Route 2b
Start by a high mantelshelf at the right end of the slab and then go easily up the right edge of the boulder; follow the ridge leftwards to the top. Various other harder starts are possible round to the left.

There is also a 6a boulder problem up the edge to the right of Holly Route.

On the impending front face are a number of routelets:

231 J.P.S. 6a
The left arête of the front face is hard to finish.

232 Miss Embassy 5c
Start as for the next route but finish straight up using a sharp, upright ironstone hold.

*233 Z'Mutt 5a
Short but good. Start with difficulty in the centre of the overhanging wall, move right and do a hard mantelshelf to stand up. Finish easily. A boulder problem direct start is possible at 6b. An easier start is to traverse in from J.P.S. on the first ledge.

**234 Brenva 5b
An excellent little route up the leaning arête right of Z'Mutt. Move a little left towards the top. An alternative is to swing right at half-height and finish up a shallow crack - 5c.

A 6b problem has been done up the steep slab right of Brenva to join Outside Edge Route a little above half-height. Hand-traverse the edge to the top.

Fifty metres toward the road are four large but low boulders with many short problems at various grades - find out for yourself.

High Rocks Annexe OS Ref 562 385

This small outcrop faces the eastern (left-hand) end of High Rocks across the valley, in a wood beside the Tunbridge Wells road. The approaches are as for High Rocks.

These rocks, the true local name being Bristol Jacks, offer a reasonable number of short but good quality routes. Due to the presence of dense top vegetation in some places the rocks can become very greasy. Spring and autumn can offer good climbing conditions when there are few leaves on the trees such that the sun can dry the rock. The rocks are on private land and permission is required from the owner of the bungalow at the rear of the outcrop. Despite the lack of traffic here:

AS WITH ALL SANDSTONE CRAGS PLEASE USE A LONG BELAY SLING AND POSITION THE KARABINER OVER THE EDGE OF THE CRAG SO AS TO MINIMISE DAMAGE TO THE ROCK BY MOVING ROPES.

At the extreme left of the main wall is a face with a wide crack in its left end, which runs up to a yew tree. This appropriately enough is Yew Tree Wall.

The first climb is on the green block some fifteen metres left of Yew Tree Wall.

1 Bluebell 5a
Climb the short block starting on the right and finishing on the left. An exceptionally minor route.

On Yew Tree Wall is, somewhat surprisingly:

2 Yew Tree Wall Climb 3a
Go up the small buttress two metres left of the crack, moving right to follow the rock.

3 Yew Tree Crack 4b
The off-width crack. Possibly a one-boot one-rubber climb.

4 Shidid 5b
Round the corner from Yew Tree Wall on the left side of the slab.

5 Annexe Slab 5b
The right-hand side of the slab is climbed trending rightwards. Better and slightly easier than the last route.

The following three routes are on the small detached boulder right of the slab:

6 Titch Arête 5a
Gymnastic moves up the left edge of the boulder.

7 Meander 5a
Start a metre right of the left edge. Ascend diagonally right to a mantelshelf finish.

8 Twitch 5c
Straight up the blunt arête in the centre - small holds with a dynamic move in the middle.

To the right is a prominent nose, imaginatively called Nose One.

*9 Double Top 6b(NS)
Start beneath an old yew and follow a line of improbable-looking pockets directly to the tree trunk. Very thin and technical climbing.

10 Ones Traverse 3a
Start left of Nose One and traverse across it and Chimney Wall into the chimney. A strange, contrived climb.

*11 Nose One 5b
Climb directly up the nose on sandy holds with a tricky finish. Moving right at mid-height reduces the grade considerably.

12 Chimney Wall 4b
Immediately right of the previous route finish just left of the tree.

13 Chimney One 2a
A straightforward but thrutchy thing.

14 Spleen Slab 5a
Go delicately up the steep slab just a metre right of the last route. The footholds are poor but the handholds good.

15 Brain's Missing 5b
Quite possibly. The crack line two metres left of Nose Two.

16 Nose Two 4a
The outside edge of the short chimney.

17 Chimney Two 2a
An easy but not recommended way down.

18 Thinner 5a
Straight up the wall left of Nose Three, to finish just left of the tree.

*19 Nose Three 3b
Climb straight up the nose using the tree roots to finish.

20 Valkyrie Wall 5c
Three metres right of the last route, just right of a short crack. A technically interesting start leads to easier ground.

21 Chute and Chimney 3b
The chute leads awkwardly to the dirty chimney, which can also be gained more directly by laybacking.

22 Didshi 5b
Climb the wall immediately right of the last route on poor holds.

23 Gorilla Wall 5a
Step off the pedestal and follow the groove left; move back right after a metre or so, and so to the top.

Continuing down the slope is a wall with some flutings in its lower part.

*24 Purgatory 5a
Despite the name, a pleasant route. Climb straight up from the flutings on good holds.

25 Augustus 5b
The arête to the right of the last route is climbed without using holds on the face.

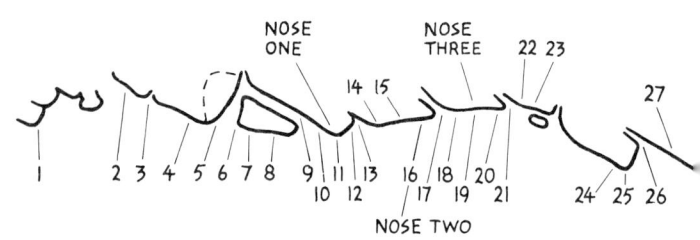

HIGH ROCKS ANNEXE

26 Corner Crack 3a
Without the use of the fallen tree, especially since it's not there any more. Dirty and uninteresting.

On the next wall is:

*27 The Entertainer 6a
The wall left of Valhalla has small holds.

*28 Valhalla Wall 4c
A good climb on small holds up the right edge of the wall.

To the right is a lower bulging wall and isolated block, providing some little problems.

29 Patrick's Wall 5b
Straight up the overhanging front of the block, following the broken holds.

30 Dumpy 5a
The short nose left of the crack, with an earthy finish, is definitely not worthwhile.

31 Flatus Groove 1a
The wide crack between the block and the main wall leads to another earthy finish.

32 Quickset 3b
The nose just right of the crack.

Up the broad slope and on the left-hand side is:

33 The Prow 3a
A short nose - perhaps better than a long one.

On the opposite side of the broad slope is:

*34 Horizontal Wall-Routes 1 and 2 3b
Short face climbs on excellent holds giving brief but enjoyable climbing.

Back down the slope and further right is a large split buttress, upon which there are four climbs.

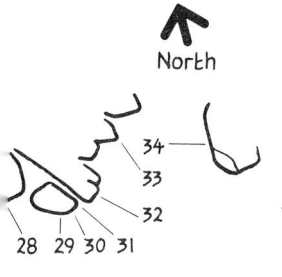

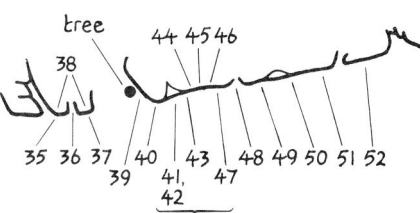

HIGH ROCKS ANNEXE 147

35 **Monolith Left Buttress** 5a
Start immediately left of the crack and go straight up over the nose to finish. The original finish traversed left and up over the letter 'T'. This is 4a.

36 **Monolith Crack** 3a
The wide crack can be climbed outside or, after a tight entry, inside.

37 **Monolith Right Buttress** 4a
Go straight up, with a mantelshelf to finish.

38 **Monolith Girdle** 2b
This route crosses the last three climbs halfway up.

Across the next slope is a sign on a tree pointing out the 'Dangerous Rocks and Trees' (?!). Behind the tree is:

39 **Leg Break** 5a
Ascend the buttress left of Googly. Go up behind the tree, then move right to the top. It is easier if the tree is used.

40 **Nob Nose** 5b
The nose right of Leg Break is climbed direct.

41 **Googly** 3a
Start up the small crack in the left of the wall. Move left at two metres into a wide opening, which leads to the top. It is also possible to start direct - 4a.

Immediately right of Googly is a steep wall called Cricket Pitch Wall, having a crack or break on either side. All its routes are good.

*42 **Run Out** 5a
Traverse the wall at mid-height from Googly to Charon's Staircase or vice versa.

*43 **Off Stump** 4c
Start as for Googly but go straight up. Traverse right near the top to finish left of the yew tree.

HIGH ROCKS ANNEXE

*44 Middle and Off 5a
Start below the yew tree on the left and go straight up.

*45 Middle Stump 5b
If you've had a nasty accident. The centre of the face on small holds is more difficult than it looks.

*46 Leg Stump 5a
Better than losing middle. On the right of the wall. Start in a crack, and go straight up left of the tree.

47 Out 3b
The nose left of Boundary Gully.

48 Boundary Gully 2b
The break right of Cricket Pitch Wall.

The remainder of the rocks is less continuous, lower and very vegetated in places, although they would provide reasonable little problems if their condition ever improved. On the short bulging wall to the right are three routes:

49 IN 4b
The little bulges above the vague carved initials 'I.N', and immediately right of Boundary Gully.

50 Eureka 3b
You'll be so pleased you've discovered this one. A metre further right is a bulging wall, which is climbed to the shelf.

51 Charon's Staircase Hard Very Bellamy
A vegetated route for (bearded) enthusiasts only. Go straight up the right side of the groove avoiding the small tree.

Further right is a mossy undercut boulder, which provides one route:

52 One Move 4b
The overgrown complex of cracks is more awkward than it looks.

Thirty metres further right there is a buttress close to the road.

53 Green Groove 2b
Start on the left of the buttress and go straight up the groove, which is not always green - honest.

54 Seat Climb 2b
Start in the centre and go straight up. The route is easier than it appears.

Stone Farm Rocks OS Ref 382 348

The rocks are situated three and a half km south-south-west of East Grinstead, and just south of a dirt track leading west from Stone Farm on the Saint Hill to Tyes Cross road.

An approach is best determined by reference to the map below or the 1:50 000 OS Landranger map. The track leading west from Stone Farm is a footpath only. Cars may be parked about 100 metres further down the road and should not be left to obstruct the entrance to the Rocks.

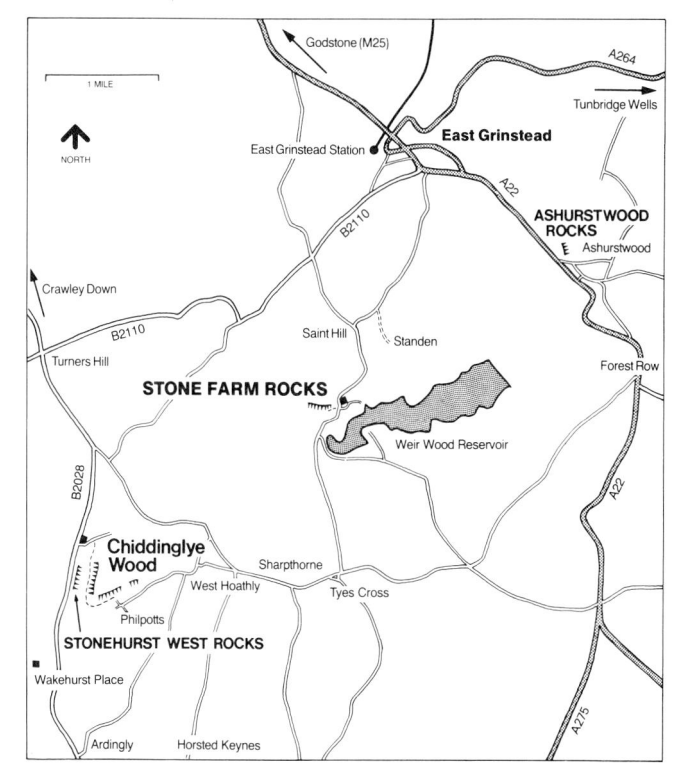

The Rocks comprise a number of isolated boulders and rock faces situated on an open hillside facing south at an altitude of about one hundred and ten metres. In the valley below, the infant Medway feeds

STONE FARM ROCKS

the Weir Wood reservoir which stretches from here to Forest Row; this enhances the scenery considerably. The Forest Ridge rises beyond with Ashdown Forest in the south-east. In the summer birds twitter in the trees, sheep gambol in the fields and a breeze gently caresses the sun-bronzed rock athletes - bliss.

The total length of the outcrop approaches two hundred metres and, in spite of the fact that its height seldom exceeds six metres, is deservedly popular on account of its excellent situation. The southern aspect and comparative absence of overhanging trees mean that the rocks are little vegetated and dry very quickly. The climbing is mostly on good quality rock which, coupled with its low height, makes it a good bouldering venue, particularly on a summer's evening.

Unfortunately, numerous CHIPPED HOLDS have appeared here since the last guide and despite the fact that some good moves have been created this VANDALISM CANNOT BE TOLERATED. The presence of stars on some of these routes is NOT meant as encouragement to chip holds. Give the rock and those able a chance please. Furthermore, many rope grooves have appeared at the tops of the more popular climbs due to the abraison of moving top-ropes.

AS WITH ALL SANDSTONE CRAGS PLEASE USE A LONG BELAY SLING AND POSITION THE KARABINER OVER THE EDGE OF THE CRAG SO AS TO MINIMISE DAMAGE TO THE ROCK BY MOVING ROPES. If this advice is ignored there will eventually be no crag left at all.

The climbs are numbered starting at the far end from the road. Therefore, the entire outcrop is passed before the first listed climbs are reached. There are three small easy-angled buttresses in the trees about forty metres beyond the main wall, the first of which gives:

1 Moss Wall 3b
The centre of the left-hand block. There are 4b problems on each side of this and a route up the centre of each of the other two blocks - both about 2b.

The first part of the main wall has a low block with a boulder on top. The next four routes are here:

2 Pyramid Route 4b
Step onto the ledge at the left end with difficulty, mantelshelf then finish up the left side of the block.

3 Kneeling Boulder 4b
Also difficult to start. Begin on the left and move right to the centre then reach over the overhang to good finishing holds. A direct start with a hard mantelshelf is 5b.

There is a 5b problem 1½ metres right making use of good layaway pockets.

4 One Hold Route 3b
The short wall on the right has many good holds!

5 Obscene Gesture 3a
Go up the right arête of the wall, passing a two-finger undercut.

On the next wall is:

*6 Medway Slab 2a
Follow the narrow ramp which slants across the wall left of Stone Farm Chimney.

*7 Footie 5c
The steep wall immediately left of Stone Farm Chimney can be climbed on smallish layaway/undercut holds. A good sequence of moves but sadly it has been chipped.

The wall below the ramp and left of Footie gives a couple of 6a problems.

*8 Stone Farm Chimney 4a
The obvious chimney behind the buttress. The tight overhanging upper section is awkward.

*9 Girdle Traverse 5c
Commence midway up Stone Farm Chimney. The hardest move is getting round onto the front - feet at half-height. Continue across Cat Wall, Pine Buttress etc., to eventually reach easy ground above the slab. From here Garden Wall Traverse may be reversed and a small but tricky boulder traversed to finish.

*10 Kathmandu 6a
Start at the left end of the front face. Gain the first break, move up to an undercut on the right and pull delicately onto the slab above to finish.

The left edge of Kathmandu has been climbed more directly to the same finish - **Chalk'N'Cheese** *6a.*

**11 Cat Wall 5b
Begin in the centre of the wall and move up the overlap on good holds trending right to finish three metres left of Stone Farm Crack. A good climb.

*11A Top Cat 6a
A direct line through Cat Wall, consisting of a direct start on the left to join the normal route and a direct finish.

An eliminate has been climbed up the wall just left of Stone Farm Crack - **Sweet Carol** *5b or 5c depending on which holds you allow yourself.*

**12 Stone Farm Crack 4b
The crack that runs up just left of the pine tree at the top, with a delicate finish. Another old classic.

*13 Pine Buttress 5b
Between the two cracks. Pull onto the centre of the face either from the left or direct. Finish more easily to the right or, more sustained, straight up.

The right side of the face can be climbed at about 5c, depending on the holds used.

*14 Pine Crack 3b
The crack just right of the last route is harder than it looks.

15 The Face 4a
Go up to the 'face' that is carved in the rock, finish leftwards to tree

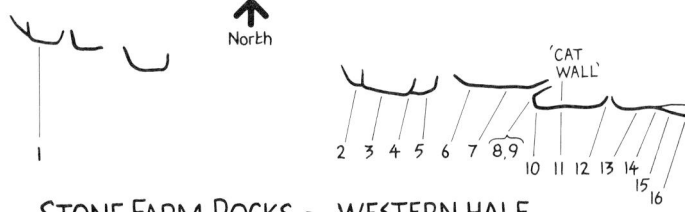

STONE FARM ROCKS ~ WESTERN HALF

roots. Alternatively, finish rightwards to some other small tree roots -4b.

16 The Ramp 2a
Passes up by the 'face', to finish at the top of the chimney.

17 Root Chimney 1a
A very dirty and unpleasant route, climbed mainly on tree roots.

Between Root Chimney and the yew tree is:

18 Slab Buttress 4b
Start at the bottom left-hand corner and step up right. Tricky balance problems then lead to an easy finish. One can go straight up at 5a. The wall round to the left gives an only just independent problem, also 5a.

In front of the yew tree and set forward from the main wall is:

19 Slab Direct 4a
Climb straight up the centre of the slab, starting on the left.

20 Slab Arête 2a
The easy-angled right edge. A tricky eliminate, 5a, climbs up just left of the arête without touching it.

21 Yew Arête 5b
Go up the arête above the slab. Tricky.

22 Garden Wall Crack 3a
The next obvious wide crack.

*23 Remote 4c
A metre right of the last route. Climb the steep slab to the oak tree.

*24 Control 5c
The wall right of Remote, via undercuts at half-height and with some very trusting moves. A good problem despite the chipped holds. Has been done without the offending holds.

25 Garden Wall Traverse 3a
From the foot of the next route traverse left, gradually ascending. Step across to Garden Wall Crack and continue along a narrow ledge to easy ground above the slab. A pleasant little diversion.

26 Holly Leaf Crack 2a
Follow the crack to the ledge and finish up the wall on the left. A number of problems have been done on the right side of this boulder.

STONE FARM ROCKS   153

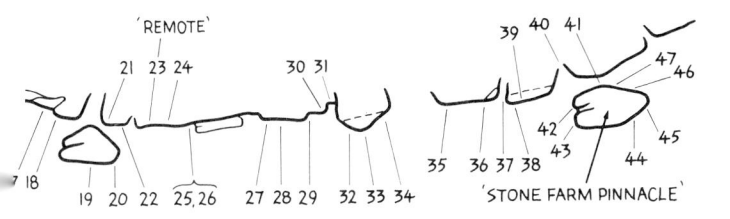

Beyond the boulder is:

27 Thin 5c
Up the blunt nose on the left-hand side of the slab. Delicate climbing. Start on the left or more directly.

28 Chipperydoodah 6a
A technical but again heavily chipped route up the middle of the face, with an awkward move left into Thin near the top. A more direct finish is 6b, avoiding holds on Thin entirely.

**29 Curling Crack 3b
The obvious jamming crack in the centre of the wall is short but good.

30 Illusion 6b
Very thin and technical climbing up the wall right of Curling Crack, again with at least one chipped hold. Frankly, this is not on.

31 Inside or Out? 2b
Between the two walls. Climb up round the jammed boulder; this used to be at the top of the climb and thankfully one is no longer faced by the momentous decision suggested by the name.

On the next block is:

*32 Front Face 5b
Climb the left edge of the block, trending right to the centre to finish. Poor holds.

33 Mania 5c
The undercut face between Front Face and the next route leads to a tricky finish.

34 Undercut Wall 3b
The right-hand side of the block. Pull onto the overhang without using the holly and then go straight to the top.

Beyond the small holly tree is:

35 Pinnacle Buttress Arête 5b
Climb directly up the left edge of the block on its left side without using the tree. It can be climbed totally on the right side at 6a with some very iffy moves - soloists beware.

*36 Pinnacle Buttress 5a
Just to the right of the last route. Climb straight up the wall to the

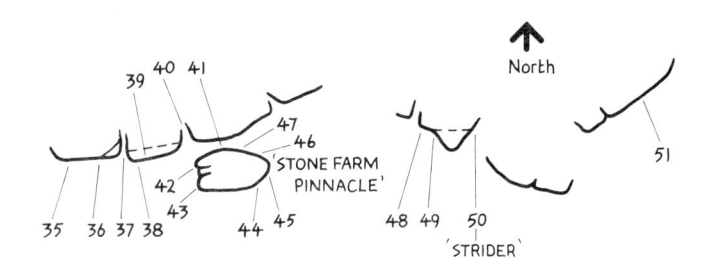

scoop and so to the top. The scoop can be approached more easily from the right at 4a.

An eliminate, **Praying Mantles** *5b, has been climbed straight up about two metres left of Easy Crack.*

37 Easy Crack 1a
Between the two blocks.
38 Bare Necessities 6a
The rounded arête right of Easy Crack is very strenuous and not a little sandy.
39 Bare Essentials 5c
Climb the centre of the block left of Stone Farm Pinnacle, finishing towards the left - despite the hold-cutting a good climb, especially when the topmost rope-grooves are avoided.
40 Pinnacle Chimney 2a
Behind the left end of the pinnacle. Straightforward.

Next is the prominent Stone Farm Pinnacle, which provides seven routes. There is a metal belay stake at the top; the easiest way up is Central Jordan.

41 Central Jordan 2a
The easy route to the top. Step across from the top of the main wall and then up.
**42 Key Wall 4c
The left face of the pinnacle. Climb the wall to the niche then go up the wide crack above. One can also finish to the right of the niche - 5b.
**43 Belle Vue Terrace 5c
Start on the front face just right of the previous route. Go up diagonally right to the centre of the face then trend back left to finish. Delicate balance moves.
44 Quoi Faire 6c
Start two metres left of the right edge. Pull up using a good hold and swing a metre right along the break; then make an extremely powerful move to stand up. Finish by moving back left a little.

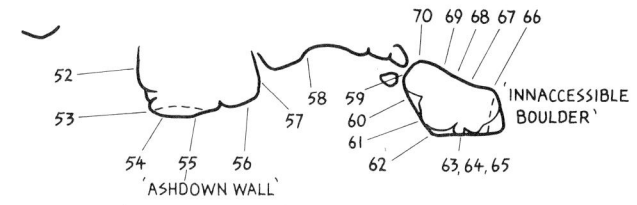

STONE FARM ROCKS ~ EASTERN HALF

45 Nose Direct 5c
High in the grade. Straight up the nose at the right-hand end of the pinnacle. A long reach for small holds to start and an awkward finish. Pick your holds carefully. Starting on the right makes the climb 5b.

46 East Jordan Route 2a
Large sandy holds are followed up the back of the pinnacle, bridging to start with. Without bridging the climb is 4a.

47 Leisure Line 5c
The sandy wall between the Jordan routes.

On the bulging boulder behind and right of Stone Farm Pinnacle is **Arthur's Little Problem** 6b, *which may be little but is quite hard for its entire length.*

The next three routes are on a large boulder ten metres to the right, beyond some broken ground.

48 Milestone Arête 4a
Straight up the rear left-hand arête. Stepping off the small boulder makes the climb much much easier.

49 Milestone Stride 4b
Climb the centre of the left side of the boulder on poor holds. There seems to be little advantage in stepping off the small boulder.

The front arête of the block gives a difficult, 6a, mantelshelf problem.

50 Concentration Cut 5c
Start round the corner from the previous route. Use the large pocket and small crack to gain the top - harder for the short. Yet another chipped route.

More broken ground leads to a boulder. The next problems are on a low wall ten metres further on. The original route here is:

51 Traverse and Crack 2a
Start by traversing in from the right and climb the pocketed depression. A harder direct start is possible.

There is an obvious line at the right end of the boulder (1a), and an undercut crack on the left (3b), which is reached by continuing the traverse of the original route. The small crack just left again is 4c, and there are a couple more boulder problems left again at around 5a.

On the next sizeable block is:

52 Open Chimney 3a
The shallow recess just left of the nose on the blunt arête. There is another very short crack just to the left - 2b.

*53 Bulging Corner 3b
An obvious line of weakness with good holds on the front left side of the block.

A climb straight up the nose from the start of Bulging Corner is Transparent Accelerating Banana 5b; *the name is longer than the route.*

54 Bulging Wall 5b
Strenuous climbing either two or three metres right of Bulging Corner.

*55 Ashdown Wall 4b
Go strenuously up the centre of the front face on good holds.

56 Introductory Climb 2a
From the cleft in the far right of the block, traverse left across the slab and finish up the crack in the centre of the face. This can be started more directly at a shallow scoop 2b, and finished above this at 3a, or further right at 4a.

*57 Dinosaurs Don't Dyno 1a
Walk up the cut holds on the far right of the slab. A good beginner's route.

58 Gap Traverse 4a
Commence on the wall right of the narrow cleft; move left and step across the cleft at low-level. Continue along the easy ledges of the last route, across Ashdown Wall, round to Bulging Corner and then onto easy ground.

The initial wall of Gap Traverse provides a number of pleasant little problems - the central line is 3a.

The remainder of the routes are on the Inaccessible Boulder. This very large boulder gives some good routes over a range of difficulty. The easiest approach to the belay bolt on top is by S.E. Corner Crack - a suitably long sling should be used. Please don't make the rope grooves here worse by simply looping the rope over the buttress to belay. The first route starts by the boulder adjacent to the left face:

*59 Guy's Route 6b(NS)†
The centre of the impending wall left of the triangular niche. Start direct - mind your back! - or step more easily off the top of the boulder. Very strenuous. Alternatively, from the niche of Leaning Crack, pull left onto the wall - 5c.

**60 Leaning Crack 5a
Start left of the crack and climb into the triangular niche. Continue up the crack above. The start can be avoided by stepping off the boulder. The crack can be climbed to the niche at 5a.

61 Ducking Fesperate 6a
A spitty woonerism? Climb the steep wall one metre right of the crack

to a balance move to stand on the ledge. Finish with further interest up the slab.

*62 S.W. Corner Scoop 5a
Start two metres right of Leaning Crack. Some strenuous moves lead to the ledge, after which a move left enables the scoop to be gained.

*63 Primitive Groove 4b
Begin strenuously in the centre of the front face on large holds, then go up the groove on the left.

64 Boulder Wall 5c
Various starts are possible - some of them difficult but all leading to the left of centre of the overhang to finish. The overhang can also be climbed on its right side, again at 5b.

*65 S.E. Corner Crack 4b
Start strenuously as for Primitive Groove but then traverse easily right to finish up the short crack in the bulge.

The lower wall below the S.E. Corner Crack finish gives a number of boulder problems. The left side of the undercut nose is 5c, whilst its right side is 5b. There is a 5c mantelshelf just to the right and right again is:

65A Balham Boot Boys 6a
An awkward mantelshelf onto the ledge left of N.E. Corner. Finish direct.

66 N.E. Corner 4c
Climb directly up the rear right-hand arête from the boulder.

**67 Diagonal Route 5b
Start as for N.E. Corner. Make an ascending rightwards traverse, crossing Green Wall and continuing in the same line to finish on the north-west arête. Difficult just after the start.

68 Simpering Savage 5b
The wall two metres right of the arête using the vandalised incut holds. It is possible to start further left and then move right into the line.

69 Green Wall 5a
A hard pull up the initial wall brings large flat holds to hand, or to foot if you climb upside down - take your pick. Trend left more easily to the top or finish direct - also 5a - while a right-hand finish is 4c.

**70 Birdie Num-Nums 6b(NS)
The rear left-hand arête of the pinnacle is a precarious proposition. Gain a standing position in the obvious pocket and then fall round onto the arête itself. Finish direct. The arête can also be reached by stepping off the large boulder - 5c.

71 Low Level Girdle 6b
A very strenuous and sustained low-level girdle of the Inaccessible Boulder, though not as yet across Birdie Num-Nums.

Under Rockes   OS Ref 555 264

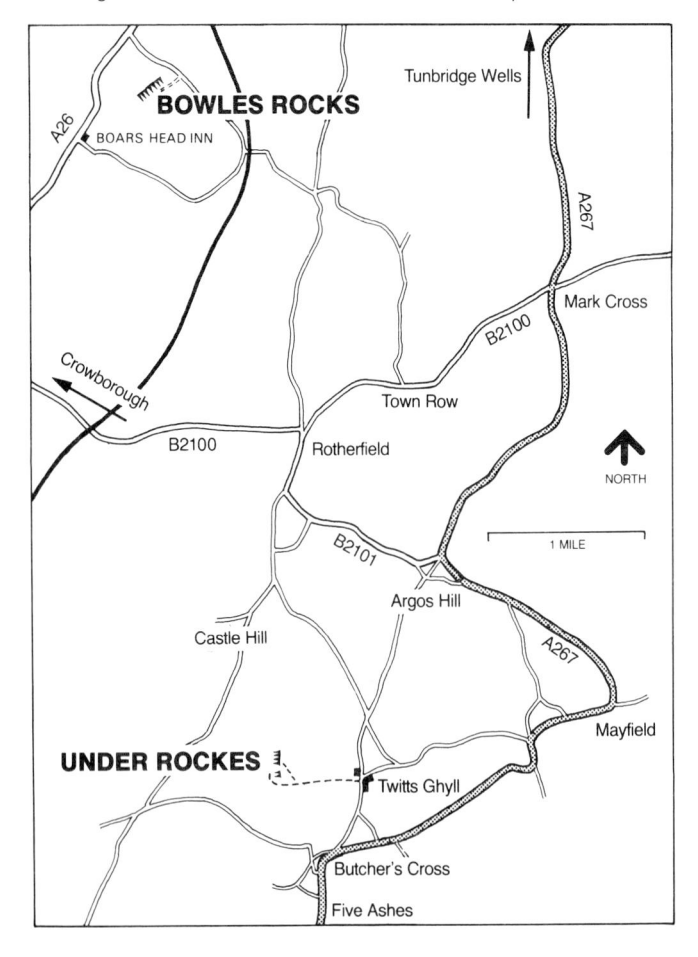

Under Rockes is a pleasant secluded outcrop consisting primarily of a fine steep wall which provides a number of good hard routes, certainly worth the effort of a visit. There are also a few good climbs here in the easier grades. The rock can be in condition all the year round but is probably at its best in spring and autumn when there are few leaves on the trees.

The outcrop is on private land the owners of which are not known. The access situation is therefore vague but no problems have occured thus far in this respect. It is clearly sensible to be discreet when walking across the fields.

Under Rockes lie about three km south of Rotherfield. The maps and diagrams show how to get there - going south from Rotherfield follow the signs to Heathfield and Five Ashes until a house called Twitts Ghyll is reached. There is a small road signposted to Mayfield by the house. To avoid conflict with the residents please DO NOT park in front of the house - there is a layby slightly further down the road.

A footpath starts almost opposite the house and quickly leads to a much wider track. This runs between the fields for about four hundred metres until an old iron gate is reached. The track continues but deteriorates after this, so just before the gate step over the fence into the field on the right. Carry on in the same direction along the edge of the field parallel to the track and go over/through a gate into another field. Diagonally right from this is a line of trees that stops well before the fence on the left is reached. Either walk across to these and follow them for about fifty metres then step over the fence to end up (hopefully) above and behind the crag. Alternatively, drop down into the next field and go over a stile on the right.

AS WITH ALL SANDSTONE CRAGS PLEASE USE A LONG BELAY SLING AND POSITION THE KARABINER OVER THE EDGE OF THE CRAG SO AS TO MINIMISE DAMAGE TO THE ROCK BY MOVING ROPES.

The first route is on a short wall to the left of the main wall:

1 Battery Wall 4a
A direct line two metres left of the wide crack. The angle eases fairly quickly. The wide crack itself is best left alone.

The main wall has five lines of large, square-cut pockets running vertically, all of which form good hard routes.

2 The Thirteenth Light 6a(NS)
The left-hand most set of potholes, reaching left for layaway holds to finish.

*3 Lionheart 6a(NS)
High in the grade. The line of potholes second from left to a still tricky finish.

A climb has been done between Lionheart and Uganda Wall, avoiding the potholes entirely - 6b(NS).

*4 Uganda Wall 5c
Climb the central line of potholes.

A line straight up between the potholes of Uganda Wall and Fireball has been climbed - **Magic Pebble** 6a(NS).

*5 Fireball 5c
Similar to Uganda Wall - the line of pockets second from right.

*6 In One Hole... 6a(NS)
The far right set of potholes on the wall. Exit leftwards from the last hole.

**7 Central Crack 5c
An excellent route up the obvious steep crack bounding the right side of the main wall. The corner has been bridged all the way, without touching the crack itself.

*8 The Touch 5c
A pleasant climb on the wall facing the main wall. Follow a direct line up the centre of the wall to the arête; then go up the arête on its right side as for Evening Arête to the top.

An eliminate with an imaginative(?) name has been climbed up the wall to the right of the lower section of The Touch - **The Alien Succumbs to the Macho Intergalactic Funkativity of the Funkblasters** 5c.

**9 Evening Arête 5a
A pleasant little route. Climb the arête on its right side to the large ledge and continue in the same line up the mossy wall above with a long reach. The route is 4c if one traverses off right, so avoiding the long reach.

10 Hear No Evil 5a
Climb up just left of centre of the slab with a long reach near the bottom. Finish where you like. An eliminate line just to the right is 5b.

11 Speak No Evil 4b
The right-hand end of the slab, passing a big pocket low down.

12 Girdle Traverse 5b
It is possible to make a very worthwhile girdle traverse, from Battery Wall (1) to Speak No Evil (11), while a complete traverse has yet to be done in one push.

The next feature is a rounded bulging wall. The next two routes are on the front where the rock is cleaner but sandy, particularly on the right side:

13 Rapunzel 5c(NS)
Start at the left end of the wall. Climb diagonally rightwards to a problematical finish up to the strange looking tree.

14 Meridian 6b(NS)
The bulging, overhung arête directly below the tree is gained by a traverse in from the right. Pull powerfully onto the right side of the arête where the breaks peter out - friable holds abound. Finish at the tree.

15 Dark Crack 5c
Climb the obvious overhanging crack. A good route with a difficult middle section and which is generally harder than it looks.

16 Peregrine 5b
Start two to three metres right of Dark Crack. Pull onto the ledges and climb the wall diagonally rightwards to the tree stump and holly bush. Finish dirtily here.

Thirty metres further right and over an earth hump there is a smaller easy-angled outcrop.

UNDER ROCKES

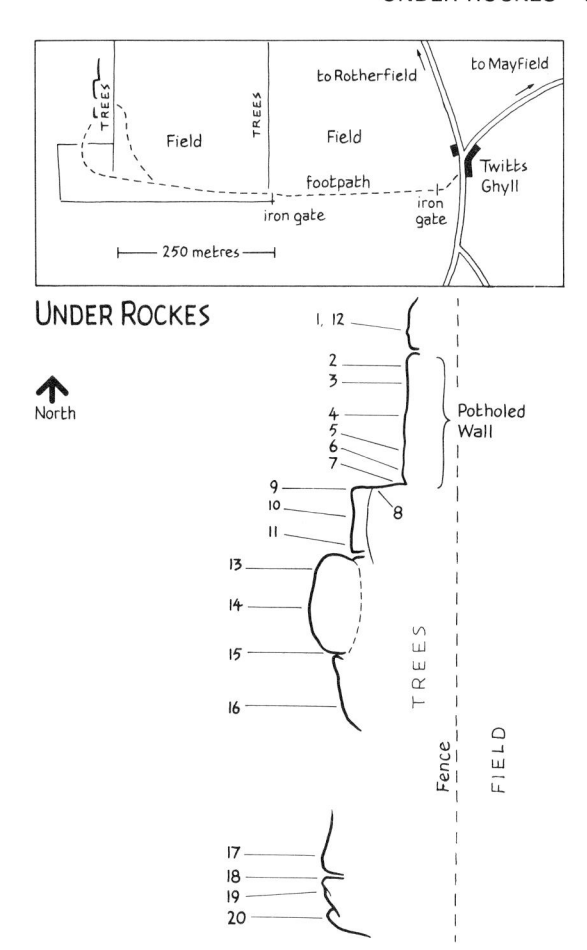

17 Departure Slab 4a
The centre of the slab left of the oak tree.
18 Lamplight 5a
Start just right of the oak tree and climb the left edge of the slab.
19 No Ghosts 5b
Climb straight up the centre of the slab mainly on pockets.
20 Roger's Wall 3a
On the right is a rightwards-slanting crack, which is followed to the top.

Minor Outcrops

CHIDDINGLYE WOOD OS Ref 348 324

The rocks are situated one and a half km west-south-west of West Hoathly church, close to the B2028 between Turner's Hill and Ardingly. They are on strictly private land in their entirety. Notices make prospective climbers aware of this and, despite recent attempts, no climbers have been able to get climbing permission.

The site is a designated SSSI, the idea being an attempt to preserve the rock features and rare mosses and lichens for scientific purposes. The owner of Stonehurst Estate and Nurseries, Mr Derek Straus, with the support of the Nature Conservancy Council (NCC), has banned climbing at the outcrop - access is only permitted to groups with legitimate scientific interests who apply in writing beforehand. The one time dense covering of rhododendrons has been thoroughly cleared at the suggestion of the NCC to allow the mosses and lichens to flourish -rhododendrons are not native to England, having been introduced from abroad in Victorian times. Perhaps ironically, the result of the clearing work means that much virgin rock has been exposed, a high proportion being in excellent climbing condition. The prospect for new climbs is very good, should the access position ever change.

The routes described are all in the westerly valley which is in the grounds of Stonehurst. The rocks in the easterly valley (OS Ref 350 322) extend into the grounds of Philpots and are extensive though discontinuous. These too have recently been cleared of vegetation and are no longer heavily shaded by trees. Consequently, the rock is in much better condition than previously and the possibilities for bouldering and for Stone Farm type routes seem to be excellent.

Where the two outcrops meet there is a large boulder standing on a tiny plinth (accessible by jumping over from the adjacent crag). This is the famous Great-upon-Little. The valley below the boulder is said to be haunted by *Gytrack*, "*a gurt black ghost hound*", though only a ginger tom has been seen lately; and, according to R.T. Hopkins' *Ghosts over England*, 'here the just control of Providence ceases and one comes under the powers of unseen presences which are inimical.' There is an interesting Sacrificial Boulder just to the east of Great-upon-Little of about three metres in height. This has an easy-angled side with steps cut into it and, parallel to these, a narrow channel (for blood) leads down from the flat top. There is also said to be a Druid's Stone nearby.

The following climbs are all in the westerly valley. Park in a layby close to the Whitehart Pub on the B2028 and follow a track into the estate -see the diagram. This eventually leads to some low rock walls. From here a walk of two hundred or so metres to the right leads to a recently exposed rock wall with a cave - 'Cave Adullam' - near the left end. However, the first described climbs are not reached until about a hundred metres right of this, where there is a wide open bay with an

CHIDDINGLYE WOOD

overhanging wall on the front left side. The first route is on the green arête to the left of the overhanging wall:

**1 Amethyst 5c
Climb the blunt arête mainly on stalactite holds, until it is possible to trend right to finish. The rock offers more friction than appearances suggest.

**2 Harlequin 6b(NS)
Go easily up the crack just left of First Visit to a poor bridging rest. Use the right-hand hold to go up and left over the overhang.

*3 First Visit 3b
Take the buttress between the overhanging wall and the left-hand cleft.

4 Gascape 4c
Climb the left end of the central wall, finishing up the short ramp.

5 Warrior 5a
After starting near the centre of the wall move right and finish awkwardly at the right-hand end. The finishing holds may require excavating. A direct finish up the middle of the face has been done at 6a(NS) with a hard finishing move.

The next three routes are on the right-hand buttress.

6 Doina da J'al 5c(NS)
Go straight up the left-hand arête to an interesting finish.

**7 Hounds Wall 4a
Climb the left side of the wall on good holds.

***8 Gytrack 4b
Start just right of the last route and go straight up the pock-marked wall to its highest point. A good climb.

The next routes are on some isolated blocks on the other side of the wide bay, some fifty metres further right. There are no recorded climbs on the low greasy boulders in between. On the first block with the obvious large square-cut roof is:

*9 R-Maker 5b
Start in the left-hand corner of the roof, move up and finger-traverse rightwards to the nose. Finish straight up the thin wall. A direct start can be done which avoids the initial traverse.

The next four routes are on the adjacent isolated block.

10 Spook 5a
Climb directly up the left side of the front arête, passing a small rhododendron.

**11 Sacrifice 4a
At the end of the passage. Climb the easy-angled arête. This route is normally soloed to get to the belay; however, it is not always in condition.

*12 Karen 5b
Start a metre or so right of the front arête and climb the thin wall, finishing up the steep shallow groove.

**13 Stone's Route 5c
The wall right of Karen gives a worthwhile route - the exact line it takes is uncertain.

164 CHIDDINGLYE WOOD

The following impressive buttresses have no routes as yet, except for three recent additions at their right-hand end:

*11 Herbal Abuse 5a
The steep bulging right arête of the last big block has some excellent big holds.

**12 Lord Chumley Pootings 5b(NS)
The fine steep pocketed wall right of the last route and just left of an earth and bush filled gully.

13 Percy Pustule Went to Town 4c
The steep slab right of the gully with an awkward long reach low down.

Working rightwards from here (see diagram) the easterly valley can be found - see crag introduction.

PENNS ROCKS

These rocks comprise two separate outcrops which are situated 1½ km west of Eridge Station and 2¼ km south-south-west of Groombridge Station. Both outcrops are on private land forming parts of the grounds of Penns House. Permission to climb here has not been granted, although a number of new routes have been done discreetly since the last guide. The general route quality is good. It is best to park in a layby on the B2188 just up the road from the drive leading to the rocks. Approaching down the drive leading from the B2188 to Penns House the first outcrop to be encountered is Jockey's Wood Rocks:

JOCKEY'S WOOD ROCKS   OS Ref 516 346

This a rock wall one hundred and fifty metres from and parallel to the drive, on the right when heading into the estate. These rocks are readily visible from the drive in spring and autumn when the leaves are off the trees. The main part of the outcrop consists of two buttresses, the right-hand of which is the most attractive being about eight metres high. The following routes are described from left to right:

1 Rodomontade 5b
The thin crack and shallow groove in the centre of the left-hand buttress, leads to a tree to finish.

*2 Identity Crisis 6b(NS) †
Start just left of Dying... and gain the break, swing left and reach left for some obvious sloping diagonal holds. Somehow pull over the bulge using these to reach easier ground above.

*3 Dying for a Tomtit 5b
The right arête of the block, next to the gully, gives a pleasant climb.

Across the gully is the more impressive right-hand block.

**4 Huntsmans' Wall 5c
Start two metres left of the obvious arête. Climb directly up the steep thin wall, trending right to finish.

**5 Jockey's Wall 5b
Start immediately left of the arête and continue trending right to a large diagonal break, which leads to a large recess on the front.

PENNS ROCKS 165

CHIDDINGLYE WOOD ROCKS

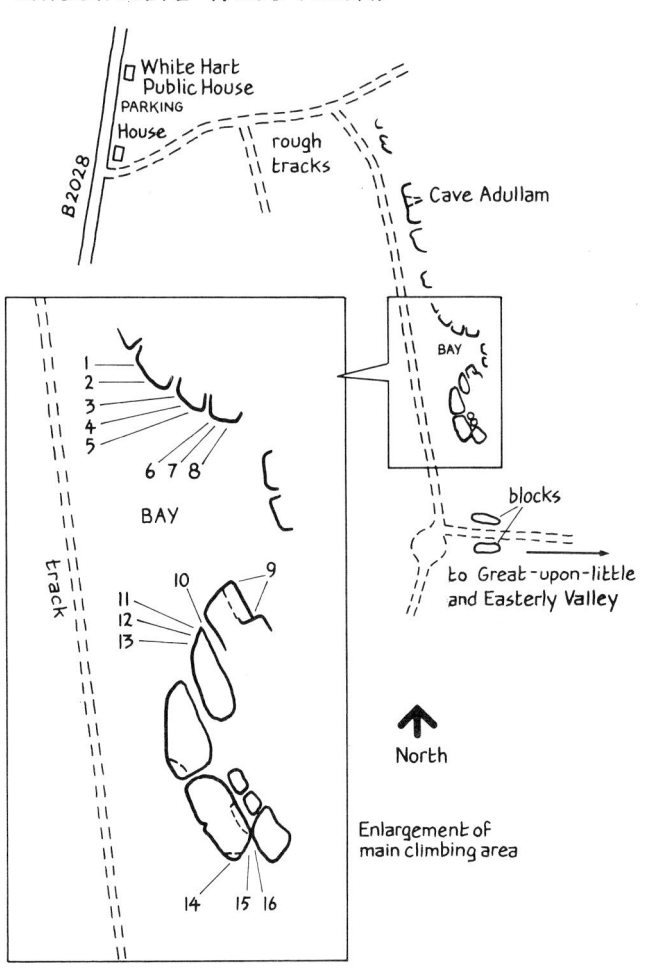

The wall to the right provides some difficult boulder problems. The next route is just to the right:

*6 Woodpecker Crack 5b
The obvious steep crack below the recess.

7 Tartan Custard 5c
Start as for the last route. Move right at the rounded flake and then climb the wall. Finish at the recess. Delicate.

***8 Pie an' Ear-ring 5c
Start three metres right of Woodpecker Crack. Take a direct line up the short crack, the slab and the impending wall above. A very enjoyable climb with surprisingly good holds.

PENNS HOUSE ROCKS   OS Ref 520 346

These are a fine group of large boulders near the House. The easiest way to get to them is to follow the drive until fairly close to the house then head off right (discreetly!) across some fields. The rocks are at the top of a large field and are partially obscured by a line of planted trees. They offer climbs of varying difficulties, some of which are of reasonable length, and in an idyllic setting. The rock is generally in excellent condition as the area has been cleared of bushy vegetation by the landowners.

The climbs are described starting from the left end of the boulders that face the planted trees and fence.

1 One up the Rectum Don't Affect'em 5b
The crack right of the tree. Continue up over the bulges above. Alternatively, step left and avoid half the climb.

2 Crusaders 5c(NS)
Start up a groove just left of Streetlife, move up to the obvious undercut and use this to reach good holds directly above.

**3 Streetlife 5c(NS)
The arête left of Midweek Chimney is very strenuous and awkward.

4 Midweek Chimney 2a
The obvious chimney on the left side of the boulders.

5 Pullover 5a
Start on the bulge right of the previous route; move up and slightly right to the ledge, then thrutch up the wide crack above - the last guide suggested bridging up this crack?

*6 Recess Chimney 2b
Bridge up the big recess and go up through a hole in the back. Entertaining.

7 Cretin 5c(NS)
Start as for Recess Chimney and bridge out backwards in a cretin-like manner.

*8 Going Turbo 6a(NS)
This is the holdless right arête of Recess Chimney; gain a (once rather large) hold a metre right of this and go for the top.

PENNS ROCKS 167

PENNS HOUSE ROCKS

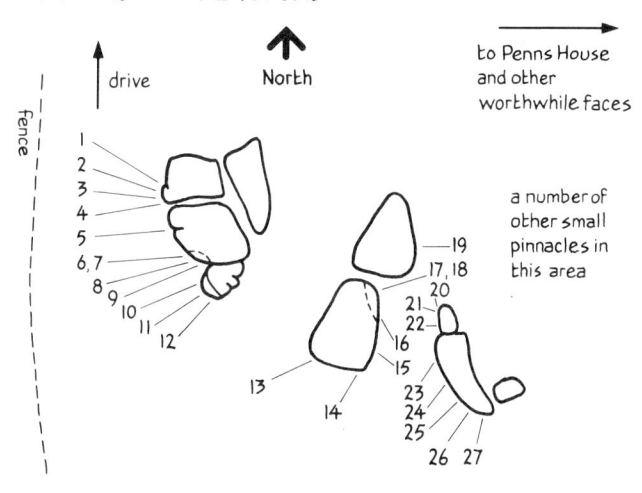

JOCKEY'S WOOD ROCKS

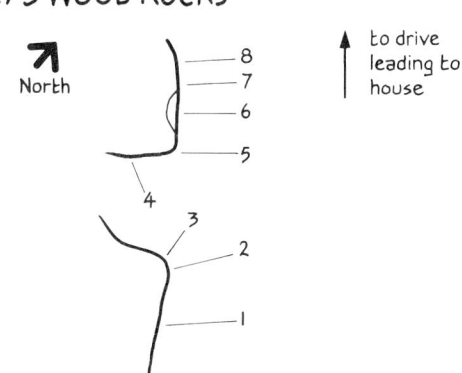

168 PENNS ROCKS

*9 Cowgirl In The Sand 5c(NS)
Climb the wall 1½ metres right of the chimney using an obvious broken undercut.

*10 Split's Groove 4b
The left-hand groove.

11 Spook's Groove 4c
The right-hand groove.

12 Rocket Man 5a
The arête right of Spook's Groove.

Further right and up the slope a bit is the largest boulder:

***13 Upwards Scoop 5a
The fine open groove on the left edge. Go straight up delicately on good holds to finish slightly to the right.

**14 The Juggler 4a
The right-hand corner. Climb the short crack and then pull into the large scoop.

15 Déjà Vu 6a
Climb the wall left of the overhanging crack and finish straight up.

*16 Trapeze Crack 5b
Climb the overhanging crack and trend slightly right to finish with a hard mantelshelf.

17 The Contortionist 5c
A hand-traverse from the right-hand side of the overhang enables one to pull over the second overhang at a point just right of the last route.

*18 Electric Rainbow 5c(NS)
The obvious mid-height traverse from right to left constitutes the continuation of The Contortionist. Finish up a groove just left of The Juggler.

On the low block just to right is:

19 The Lion Tamer 4a
Near the corner of the block is a scoop which is climbed on big layaways.

On the opposite wall, with the big yew tree in it, there are eight routes:

20 Parba Nangbat 5b
The wag bill left of The Clown.

21 The Clown 3b
The left-hand side of the short wall left of the tree.

22 The Acrobat 3b
A problem just right of the last route.

23 The Fire-Eater 5c
Climb the series of layaway holds just right of the tree.

24 Dynamo Deltoid 6a
Layback the grooves a metre or so right of The Fire-Eater.

24 The Ring Master 5b
Climb the large layback crack four metres right of the tree. Very strenuous.

26 Lunar Music Suite 5b
Pull into the next short groove from the left.
27 Station Master Leroy Winston 5a
The small arête right again and behind the tree.

Round to the right is a short arête, which is about 4a.

In the area immediately behind this wall and further up the slope are a number of low boulders and isolated pinnacles, which give many short easy boulder problems. Much nearer Penns House, and across a wide clear area, are some low, but steep and clean, walls with some potential for good new routes. The 1969 guide reported that a few routes have been done here but details have never been available.

RAMSLYE FARM ROCKS   OS Ref 568 379

These rocks are situated two km south-west of Tunbridge Wells and half a kilometre north-west of Strawberry Hill. The quickest approach is from Strawberry Hill on the A26 but the rocks can also be (approached by a ten minute walk along a footpath leading from High Rocks eastwards to the Farm. The path starts from the main gravelled car-park at the right-hand end of High Rocks and runs next to the new fence -continue straight on into the wood where the fence turns.

The slightly better, right-hand, part of the outcrop lies behind farm buildings; the remainder though strictly on private land is readily accessible from the public footpath. There is no formal permission to climb here and the five new routes are the result of discreet visits by a few people. The outcrop is about five metres high at the left-hand end and somewhat higher in the region of Headhumter. The climbs themselves are generally not steep but have small holds. The rock is sound and in reasonable condition despite the fact that it is shaded by trees.

The routes described first are all on the clean slabby wall adjacent to the large oak tree. A good place to bring novices. Starting just to the left of the tree is:

1 Tumble 4b
Go straight up the blunt arête after an awkward start.
2 Tequila Mockingbird 6a
The boulder problem arête right of Tumble.
3 Thin Wall 5b
Start slightly right of the centre of the wall and go straight up the obvious line of holds.
4 Cut Holds 3b
Start on cut holds just left of the big overlap. Finish up the slab almost anywhere.
5 Overlap Centre 5a
The easiest line is to start as for Undercut then move left onto the arête. A harder direct line can be done by starting at the centre of the overlap.
6 Undercut 3b
An obvious diagonal line beneath the big overlap.

7 Short Wall 4a
Take a direct line just right of the end of the overlap.

8 Jamber 2a
The extremely short crack at the right-hand end of the wall.

9 Grandad Goes Bird Watching 1a
One of the best and most impressive routes on sandstone, an experience not to be missed. The two metre crack right of Jamber.

Seventy metres right is, you guessed it, the right-hand section, immediately behind the farmyard. The base is currently very overgrown with head-high nettles, so bring a scythe. All the routes are short and steep.

10 Squirter 5b(NS)
Towards the left end of the wall; climb up via two small trees to finish on grass. Delightful.

*11 Doing the Dirty 5c(NS)
A climb up left of Headhunter, passing two square potholes.

*12 Headhunter 5c(NS)
Behind the remains of the cowshed is a crack two metres in from the end of the shed.

*13 Equinox 5c(NS)
Start two metres right of Headhunter. Go up to the pothole then move right to the centre of the wall to finish straight up.

*14 Phoenix 6b(NS)
A direct start to Equinox. Start two metres right of Equinox and go up to the break and the final headwall above.

*15 Hanging Crack 5c(NS)
The second crack. Climb Headhunter for three metres then traverse right into the crack.

*16 Chez Moi 5c(NS)
Start at the far right end of Headhunter Buttress. Traverse left past the first crack. Go up a little, and move left to finish as for Equinox.

Other Outcrops

The purpose of this section is to record all known (or even hinted at) rock in the south-east and to give some indication of that worth visiting, that best left alone and that about which little is known. This is a different approach to that of Daniells's 1981 guide, which listed only those outcrops considered to be worth visiting. Such outcrops have been denoted by a single star. Most of Daniells's comments are still pertinent and have largely not been altered. This also applies to information gleaned from Holliwell's 1969 guide - denoted by quotes.

The list is certainly not comprehensive, as can be seen by scouring the 1:25000 OS Maps of the area, and it is hoped that further details and outcrops will be added in the future. The writer has certainly not visited all the outcrops mentioned.

The authors referred to include:
(1) *Highways and Byeways in Sussex*, by E.V. Lucas - 1904, 1950.
(2) *Rock Climbs Round London*, by H.C. Bryson - 1936.
(3) *The Fossils of the South Downs*, by Mantell - 1822.

For further sources of information see the bibliography in the 1969 guide.

* ASHURSTWOOD ROCKS   OS Ref 415 370

This outcrop is to be found about two km south east of East Grinstead, running roughly parallel to the A22 Forest Row road. It can be approached by taking the left-hand of two roads immediately opposite the car-park of The Three Crowns public house. Follow the road past some new houses keeping left along a track which leads to the rocks.

The outcrop is apparently quite extensive and would be of some interest to climbers if access were permitted. However, it lies on private land and furthermore the area is a designated Site of Special Scientific Interest (SSSI) and climbing is not allowed. An outlying outcrop of interest to climbers lies to the north where the waste-land borders a field, though this is also on private ground. There is a clean buttress here, about five metres high upon which two easy climbs were done a long time ago.

* BALCOMBE MILL ROCKS   OS Ref 317 370

These rocks lie about one km east-north-east of Balcombe station, beside the road west of a small lake. The interesting outcrop is above the sharp bend in the road where it passes the mill. Its total length is about 25 metres and its height about five metres. The rock is apparently usually dry in summer.

The crag is on strictly private land and is sign-posted as such. Should access be possible there would appear to be four or five routes on two reasonably clean buttresses, although they are overgrown at the top. Elsewhere the rock tends to be lichenous.

BLOOMER'S VALLEY ROCKS   OS Ref 33 31

'A quarter mile west of the Turner's Hill-Ardingly road. An extensive natural outcrop, but too low and carrying too much vegetation for the climber.' Close to Wakehurst Place Rocks. Also known as LONG WOOD ROCKS.

BLUNDS HOLE ROCKS   OS Ref 412 368

'On the opposite side of the A22 from Ashurstwood Rocks. Follow the public footpath from the road junction. A few small buttresses on private land. The rock is comparatively clean and free from vegetation. A pinnacle and adjacent buttress facing the field appear to offer the best chance of a route or two.'

BOARSHEAD ROCKS   OS Ref 53 32

'There are several isolated blocks, one of which is close to 25 feet high; some of them would be of climbing interest if they were accessible. There are numerous low rock walls.' A 'Loaf of Bread Rock' is noted, situated in the grounds of Rocklands and visible from the road but with apparently little climbing potential.

BUDLETT'S GREEN ROCKS   OS Ref 47 23

'Three-quarters of a mile S.S.E. of Maresfield Church. Bryson draws attention to rocks here but they are very elusive.'

BUXTED ROCKS   OS Ref 48 32 and 49 23

'Lucas speaks of rocks beside the road to Maresfield and Uckfield, but they seem to be rather elusive.'

THE CHIDDING STONE   OS Ref 501 451

'In Chiddingstone Park behind the half-timbered houses in Chiddingstone village street. A small boulder some ten feet high, a walk on one side, rather tricky on the other.'

CLAY'S WOOD ROCKS   OS Ref 583 280

'Three quarters of a mile N.N.W. of Mayfield Church. A super Bulls Hollow, being also an ex-quarry, but lower, dirtier, and more(!) quaggy. Some slight possibility and much room for improvement.'

CLIFF END

See Hastings, in Sea Cliff Climbing section.

CODMORE HILL FARM ROCKS   OS Ref 04 20

'South of the yellow road, one mile north of Pulborough. This little practice crag, an ex-quarry which was unearthed by local school

COOPER'S GREEN ROCKS

See Warren Rocks.

CULVER FARM ROCKS   OS Ref 425 375

This little outcrop is next to the road to Ashurstwood from the A264, and lies just north of the town. It is obvious from the road as one drives by. There are a couple of buttresses of extremely soft sandstone, best left alone.

*DENNY BOTTOM ROCKS   OS Ref 568 395

These rocks are on Rusthall Common, 1 ½ km west of Tunbridge Wells and very close to Bulls Hollow.

Numerous boulders and short rock walls adjoin the village, providing many scrambles. Notable are the isolated rock called Denny Bottom Pinnacle, which is situated in someone's front garden (the East Face is 4b, the South Crack 5c), and the famous Toad Rock, which is fenced-off.

EAST GRINSTEAD ROCKS

'This title serves to introduce a quotation from Lucas. The rocks in question have not been identified: "The most beautiful rocks in Sussex and perhaps in England are those near East Grinstead which Mr. Hanbury has converted into a garden and made colourful... In this precipitous paradise pious horticulturists scramble like goats, expressing as they pass recognition and emotion in long Latin names."!

Though probably of little use to the climber, the scenic attractions of this outcrop, wherever it maybe, would appear to be considerable.'

EAST HILL

See Hastings, in Sea Cliff Climbing section.

ECCLESBOURNE GLEN

See Hastings, in Sea Cliff Climbing section.

FAIRLIGHT GLEN

See Hastings, in Sea Cliff Climbing section.

GLEN ANDRED ROCKS   OS Ref 530 356

'Nearly a mile S.S.W. of Groombridge Station. These rocks, which are strictly on private land, face Harrison's Rocks across the valley and are conspicuous therefrom. Here the early OS maps show an Eagle's Rock and a Ward's Rock. Sandstone is also exposed in the railway cutting nearby.'

174 OTHER OUTCROPS

*HAPPY VALLEY ROCKS   OS Ref 565 392

These rocks are to be found immediately west of St. Paul's Church on Rusthall Common, and 1 km west of Tunbridge Wells. A finger-post on the main Tunbridge Wells to East Grinstead road (A264) indicates a footpath to Happy Valley, which is in fact only ten minutes walk from Bulls Hollow.

There are several routes on the main wall, the majority of which are in the lower and middle grades and which never exceed five metres in height. An isolated pinnacle with a masonry plinth is the principal attraction. The three cracks on the front face have been climbed. The less distinct left-hand line is **Eckpfeiler** 6a; the central line is 5b; and the right-hand line is friable 5c. There is a route on each end face. The quality of the rock is variable but much of it is soft and very sandy.

*HERMITAGE ROCKS   OS Ref 496 251

These rocks are located 1½ km north of Buxted Station and immediately south of the junction of two footpaths.

This outcrop remains in good condition, having negligible tree cover, so that the rock is light-coloured and lichen-free. The rock itself is reasonably sound. It has an unusual character in that the tops of the buttresses form large domes, somewhat reminiscent of the sandstone boulders of Fontainebleau.

The rocks are on private land, in fact in some paddocks, and overlooked by stables.

The climbs are all about six metres long, and range from wide middle grade cracks to steep technical walls with thin slab finishes. There are about ten routes in all.

*HOATH HOUSE ROCKS   OS Ref 492 427

Hoath House Rocks lie about 1½ km north-east of Cowden Station, on the north side of the road and opposite Hoath House, which is an extremely unusual building well worth a quick look itself.

A five metre high vertical wall right next to the road-edge sports a steep crack in the centre of the left-hand portion, which is 5a. There is potential for a couple more routes here but the rock is of poor quality, though it is often quite dry.

HOMESTALL HOUSE QUARRY   OS Ref 424 374

'One and a half miles E.S.E. of East Grinstead. On the west side of the yellow road. A small rock exposure perhaps 30 feet high. rotten and in need of gardening, might offer a rock-starved climber a route or two.'

JOCKEY'S WOOD ROCKS

See Penn's Rocks, in Minor Outcrops section.

LAKE WOOD ROCKS

See Uckfield Rocks.

LAMPOOL FARM ROCKS   OS Ref 46 25

'Bryson mentions one or two rocks in a garden east of the B2026, also a man-made rock cave beside the track leading through the nearby Maresfield Park.'

LANGTON GREEN ROCKS   OS Ref 541 392

'At the west end of the village, north of the Groombridge road. A sandy wall of no climbing interest.'

LEYSWOOD HOUSE ROCKS   OS Ref 528 350

'One mile W.N.W. of Eridge Station. There are said to be some rock walls in the grounds; the current 1:25000 OS map certainly shows many rock faces to be present, but they are strictly on private land. Rocks Wood is nearby and maybe part of the same outcrop - this has yet to be investigated.'

LONG WOOD ROCKS

See Bloomer's Valley Rocks.

MARESFIELD ROCKS

See Warren Rocks.

ORE ROCKS   OS Ref 84 41

'On the north side of the Ore to Fairlight road, half a mile from Ore. A small rock wall below the road might give a short climb or two.'

PHILPOTS ROCKS

See Chiddingly Wood Rocks, in Minor Outcrops section.

*REDLEAF HOUSE   OS Ref 523 456

Nearly one km south-south-east of Penshurst Station, on the south edge of a wood facing Redleaf House, is a crag on private land. The outcrop is about fifteen metres in length and five metres in height. It is mainly overhanging and very undercut at its base. If access were possible a couple of short uninteresting routes may be climbable on horizontal features. This outcrop is probably best left to the sheep that shelter under it.

*ROCKROBIN QUARRY   OS Ref 626 333

The quarry can be found half a km north-east of Wadhurst Station. This sandstone exposure would be a veritable climbing area if it was not on strictly private land. The walls themselves are rather overgrown and between five and ten metres high. There are no signs of recent quarrying but the top three metres appears to be very friable.

OTHER OUTCROPS

If the access situation should ever change and when the rock has weathered properly this quarry would probably provide about twenty steep wall climbs.

ROCKS ESTATE

See Uckfield Rocks.

*ROCKS INN   OS Ref 497 431

These rocks lie two km north-east of Cowden Station and are marked Hoath Corner on the OS map. The rocks are immediately seen on the right-hand side, after forking left from the Rocks Inn when heading south. Access to the rocks is improbable as they are at the far side of some allotments. A steep wall can be seen clearly from the road. Although slightly green, the rock is in fairly good condition and dry. Appearances would suggest that several crack and chimney type climbs of about five metres in length and of varying quality might be possible if ever there was access.

ROCKS LANE-BUXTED   OS Ref 48/9 25

'One and an eighth miles N.N.W. of Buxted Station. The only rocks actually discovered so far are the very miniature samples on the south side of the road at its east end - only suitable for very young aspirants. However, suggestive names like 'Rocks Wood,' 'the Rocks,' etc, are found on the 1:25000 OS map, which also shows some rock lines on private ground. In Topley (1875) there is a woodcut of an outcrop said to be near Rocks Farm, Buxted. Rocks Farm was the name formerly given to the house near the east end of the lane, now called 'The Rocks,' and it is most likely that he was referring to Hermitage Rocks which are close by. If not, there is an outcrop here awaiting rediscovery.'

ROCKS WOOD   OS Ref 524 351

'There are a few low rock walls scattered about in this wood, some of which exceed 15 feet in height but are not very interesting. Also, a fine detached pinnacle has been climbed - Penns Approach Pinnacle. The bridle paths are open to the public, but climbing is not permitted.

ROCK WOOD-MARESFIELD   OS Ref 470 259

'One and an eighth miles N.N.E. of Maresfield. A low natural outcrop of no climbing interest.'

ROCKY WOOD   OS Ref 445 204

'One and three-quarter miles W.S.W. of Uckfield Church. On the west side of a wood, above the River Ouse, below Buckham Hill House. Difficult access but apparently 15-20 feet high and in need of gardening.'

---

15. Honeycombe, 6b, High Rocks. *Climber: Gary Wickham.* Photo Dave Turner.

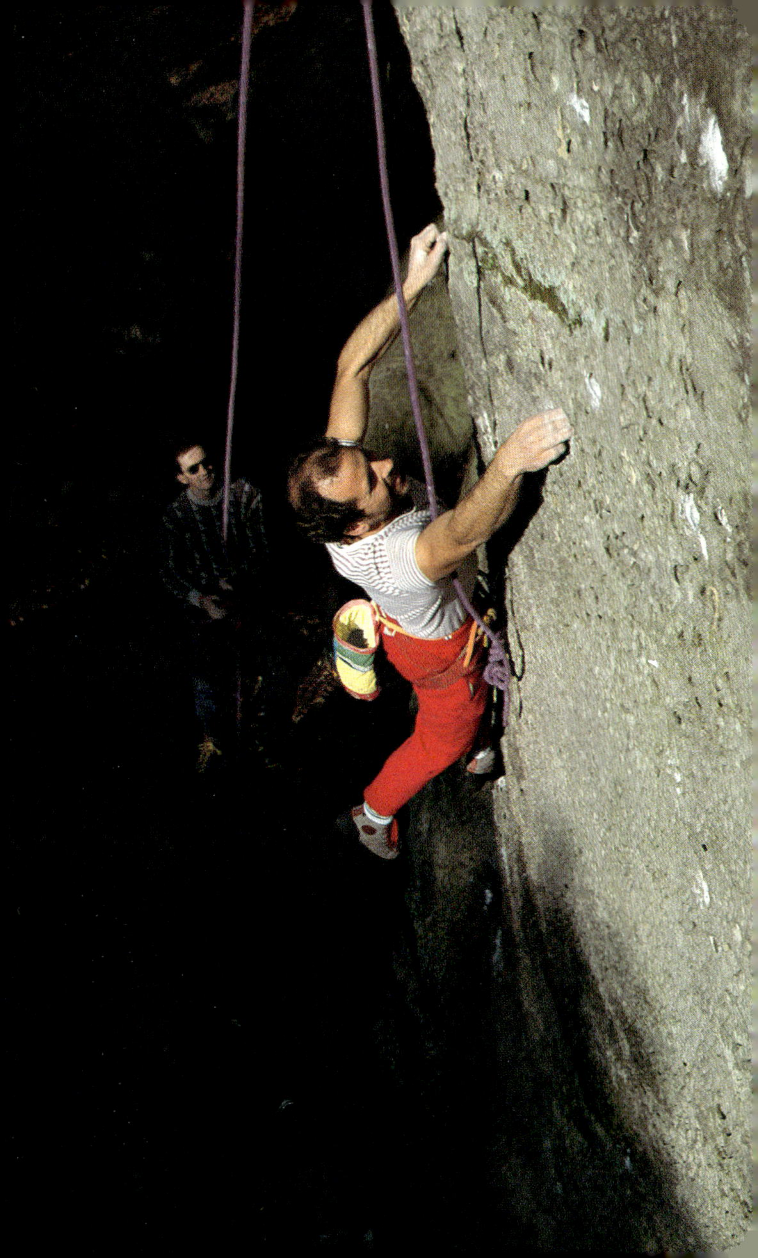

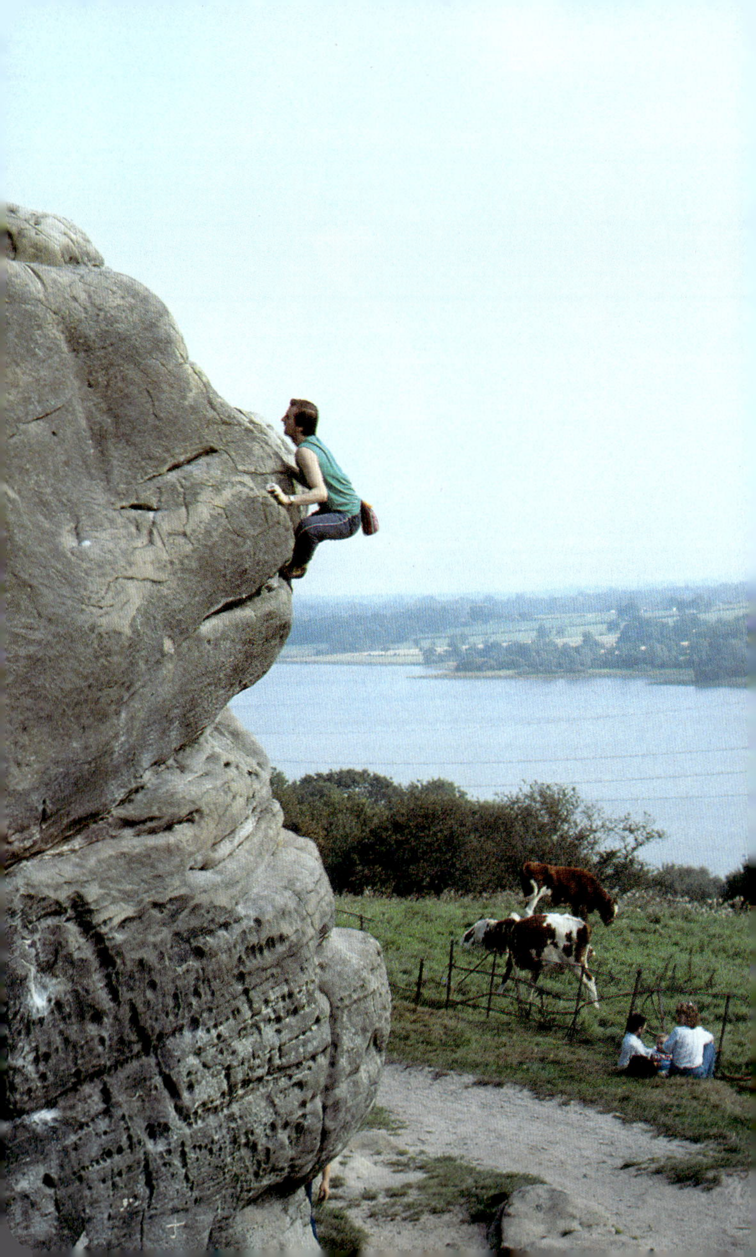

ROWHILL WOOD ROCKS   OS Ref 303 293

'Half a mile S.S.W. of Balcombe Station. There are a few small buttresses in the wood immediately below the road on the east side. Very lichenous at present, but a few routes possible.'

RYE   OS Ref 91/2 20

'One or two short climbs are reported on small rock walls in and around the town. All are strictly private.'

*SANDFIELD HOUSE QUARRY   OS Ref 485 413

This quarry is located about ¾ km south-east of Cowden Station, on private farm land overlooking the railway line. The quarry is well weathered and therefore of sound quality. The rock is in reasonable condition but has very earthy summits which reach a maximum height of six metres. The possibilities are two good crack lines, if someone bothers to clean them up, and one face climb on small holds.

SANDHOLE WOOD QUARRY   OS Ref 336 298

'A quarter mile west of Ardingly on the north side of the Balcombe road. Provides the passing motorist with a few climbs of 12-15 feet, one of which is known to have been done.'

SANDSTONE QUARRIES

A number of sandstone quarries are listed in the 1969 guide, none of which were considered suitable for climbing for various reasons; principally, insufficient weathering. This is unlikely to have changed much since then, but the list is included for completeness: (1) near Rotherfield (567 294) now a garden; (2) Selsfield House (1½ miles north-west of West Hoathly church) also a garden; (3) Rock Cottage (372 226) on the west side of the road; (4) Rocks Farm (517 284) marked on the 1-inch OS map; (5) (356 312) opposite Hook Farm Quarry; (6) near Pennybridge Farm (599 281) on the east side of the road; (7) near Calkin's Mill Farm (602 281) on the east side of the road; (8) on the east side of the road between Eridge Station and Park Corner; (9) in Hawksden Park Wood (611 262); (10) at Bestbeech Hill (619 315) north-east of the cross road; (11) immediately north of Balcombe Station; (12) near Saint Hill (383 360) north of the road.

SHEFFIELD FOREST ROCKS   OS Ref 41 25/6

'Mantell writes of "A fine lake overhung with sandstone rock near the seat of the Earl of Sheffield in the parish of Fletching". A local inhabitant we consulted said that the rocks there are "as high as that house" indicating one of size that would make them the highest rocks in this part of the country. Those we did find were only some ten feet high, so that all the indications point to a magnificent outcrop here awaiting discovery.'

---

16. Primative Groove, 4b, Stone Farm Rocks. *Climber: Gary Wickham.* Photo Dave Turner.

'Recently, a 25 foot buttress has materialised on the valley slope east of the lake, with a couple of possibilities for the climber, but the lofty outcrop referred to above remains as elusive as ever.'

STANDEN HOUSE ROCKS   OS Ref 389 357

'One and a quarter miles S.S.W. of East Grinstead near Saint Hill. The OS map shows rock here, but whatever its nature it is close to the House and completely inaccessible.'

STONEHURST

See Chiddinglye Wood Rocks, in Minor Outcrops section.

*STONEHURST WEST ROCKS   OS Ref 345 324

This is a rock wall just below the Turners Hill to Haywards Heath road (B2028) running north from Stonehurst and facing Chiddinglye Wood Rocks across the valley. A public footpath leading to Philpots House from the B2028 crosses the outcrop at an unimpressive part, while finer rock outcrops to the south of this point, with a private path along the base. A few unrecorded routes have been done on this latter section by discreet visitors.

*STONEWALL PARK ROCKS   OS Ref 499 424

A fine outcrop just below the road on the north side, and two km east-north-east of Cowden Station. This outcrop is on strictly private land and is sign-posted as such. Although shaded by trees the rock is in good condition being very dry, despite a certain deceptive greenness. The rocks vary between five and six metres in height but tend to be rather friable at their bases.

If access to the rocks were possible the outcrop would provide up to twenty routes of reasonable quality, the climbing being mainly on buttresses with few cracks.

STRAWBERRY HILL ROCKS

Name sometimes given to Ramslye Farm Rocks, see Minor Outcrops section.

STRIDEWOOD SHAW ROCKS   OS Ref 490 417

'Nearly a mile west of Cowden Station. In the wood alongside the footpath (near to Bassett's Farm). A low natural outcrop. No climbing.'

TILGATE WOOD ROCKS   OS Ref 33 30/31

'One mile N.W. of Ardingly. Here one might justifiably quote "If their climbing facilities equalled their beauty, this spot would be paradise." A place for picnics and scrambles which is apparently not too seriously private. One or two short climbs have already been made.'

TOAD ROCK

See Denny Bottom Rocks.

TOOT ROCK

See Hastings, in Sea Cliff Climbing Section.

UCKFIELD ROCKS   OS Ref 465 216

This collection of outcrops lie on either side of the Uckfield to Haywards Heath road (A272), about one km from the former. There are three groups of rocks situated in different estates, but apparently all part of the same outcrop. The first is Lake Wood Rocks (OS Ref 464 216), a low sandy wall of no interest to the climber; the second is White Cottage Rocks (OS Ref 468 216), again of little climbing interest. The third outcrop - Rocks Estate (OS Ref 465 216) - is very scenic, rising as it does out of a lake, and is of a reasonable height. Much of it, however, is vegetated, though a reasonably good 5b route has been done at the left end of the main buttress.

WAKEHURST PLACE ROCKS   OS Ref 337 318

These rocks lie just to the north of Wakehurst Place, which itself lies to the west of the Turners Hill to Haywards Heath road (B2028), within National Trust land. The outcrop, though about five hundred metres long, is very green and unpleasant, nowhere exceeds five metres and is typically very much lower. It is best ignored. See also Bloomer's Valley Rocks.

WARREN ROCKS   OS Ref 475 232

'One km S.E. of Maresfield church. Bryson mentions these rocks (Cooper's Green Rocks) and the 1:25000 OS map shows plenty of rock hereabouts. They seem to be very much mixed up with private gardens, etc, and are completely inaccessible.'

WELLINGTON ROCKS   OS Ref 57 39

'Close to Wellington Hotel on the north side of Tunbridge Wells Common. A children's playground suitable for the initiation of beginners of the youngest age group. There are one or two odd rock walls also along the top edge of the Common, but no real climbing prospects.'

WEST HILL

See Hastings, in Sea Cliff Climbing Section.

WEST HOATHLY NORTH ROCKS   OS Ref 363 307

'Half a mile N.N.W. of West Hoathly church. A small outcrop immediately below the road from West Hoathly to Turner's Hill on its north side. The rocks are out in the open. Mentioned optimistically at one time, the outcrop has only yielded one route so far, **Icicle Crack**

3a, just right of the big overhang. Prospects for further development are very limited.'

WHITE COTTAGE ROCKS

See Uckfield Rocks.

WHITESTONE HOUSE ROCKS   OS Ref 363 307

'Quarter mile north of Highbrook church. A low wall faces east across the road, a higher one faces west across the fields behind the first. A climb or two just possible.'

WICKEN'S FARM QUARRY   OS Ref 48 41

'Half a mile E.S.E. of Cowden Station. This is mentioned by Bryson as having one climb.'

Other Rock

CHALK QUARRIES

The North and South Downs and the other lesser chalk ridges are gashed at intervals by quarry workings - great and small, some active and some disused. A certain amount of climbing has been done in some of these on chalk of varying quality, requiring various specialised techniques as per the Chalk Sea Cliffs. In all cases the rock is extremely unstable and great care is required. Warlingham Quarry has provided a 25 metre climb, **Sandinista**, up the obvious crack in the back right-hand side of the quarry (S Shimitzu, D Cook).

WHITE ROCKS OS Ref 560 530

Some development is recorded at White Rocks, One Tree Hill, east of Sevenoaks. This 8 metre outcrop lies on National Trust property and as a bird-nesting site is best avoided during Spring and Summer. The 'rock' is "rag with a small proportion of interbedded sand and hassock." It is very loose in places, of similar unreliability as chalk, and thus requires a great deal of care. A number of lines, up to about 5a standard, have been climbed - due to loss of holds, the climbs tend to change after each ascent.

The Seven Outcrops Walk, in fact, starts at One Tree Hill and is worth doing as a scrambling/walking trip. It passes some tiny outcrops on the NW side of Oldbury Hill; goes across to some apparently excellent rock by the paleolithic shelters on the NE side; passes some unexpectedly interesting caves which can be entered; and eventually returns to One Tree Hill via the disintegrating outcrop on Wilmot Hill, which provides some steep scrambles.

AND
NOW FOR
SOMETHING
COMPLETELY DIFFERENT

The Sea Cliffs of South East England

INTRODUCTION

The chalk ridges of th Weald are terminated abruptly by the sea, giving the characteristic white cliffs of England, by far the highest and steepest in South East England. The South Downs end in the line of chalk cliffs stretching from Brighton past the Seven Sisters and Beachy Head to Eastbourne, whilst the North Downs give the chalk cliff-line which runs through Dover to St. Margaret's Bay and beyond. Further north, a subsidiary ridge provides some lower less interesting cliffs around Birchington.

Long ignored as a potential climbing ground the use of specialised equipment and the acceptance of increasingly loose rock has enabled great progress to be made. This coastline now boasts without doubt the longest and most spectacular climbs in South East England. Nevertheless, it must be emphasised that both chalk and sandstone sea cliffs can be extremely serious and caution is necessary. The consistency of the cliffs varies considerably as does the approach required to tackle them. In the St Margaret's Bay area the chalk cliffs are soft enough to allow effective use of pure front-pointing ice techniques, with drive-in ice-screws providing reliable belays and protection - the climbs in this area have, therefore, been given ice grades. At Beachy Head, however, a more blocky chalk structure prevails and conventional rock climbing equipment need only be supplemented by a selection of rock and ice-pegs. Needless to say, on all chalk small nuts and wires prove useless and are not worth carrying.

The Hastings area provides a unique climbing ground. The eastern cliffs demand ice climbing equipment whereas the western cliffs above the town are more conventional and protectable largely by big nuts, although it is advisable to carry some rock pegs as well.

The chalk cliffs in particular have endless possibilities for very technical sea-level traverses but great care should be taken to avoid getting cut off by incoming tides. There are frequently long sections of steep high cliffs with absolutely no easy way up, and close proximity to the busy shipping lanes of the English channel means that any apparently stuck climber stands a very good chance of being reported to the Coastguard - with a consequent rescue alert. For the same reasons it is always wise to inform the Coastguard of any proposed climb as failure to do so could well result in an enjoyable days climbing degenerating into an involuntary rescue of the type which undoubtedly prejudices the authorities against climbers. It is in climbers' own interests that good relations are maintained along this unique section of coastline so please: .... INFORM THE COASTGUARD PRIOR TO ATTEMPTING ANY CLIMBING ACTIVITY. The Dover area Coastguard telephone number is (Dover) 210 008 and the Beachy Head number (Eastbourne) 20 634. These coastguards are now used to climbers.

THE SEA CLIFFS OF SOUTH EAST ENGLAND

HISTORICAL

Perhaps surprisingly, the chalk cliffs were amongst the first in Britain to receive attention from the climber. The late 19th century Alpinists were well aware of the challenges available and regarded these cliffs as a training ground for their Alpine exploits. Mummery was active in the St Margaret's Bay area producing problems "amongst the hardest mauvais pas with which I am acquainted" and Edward Whymper, perhaps the best known Alpinist of the period, also climbed occasionally on the cliffs. However, all of these early explorations kept to the steep grass and chalk slopes or the more reliable chalk below the high tide-mark. It is unfortunate that no records remain of the exact achievements of the era.

A tremendous change in attitude came in the 1890s in the form of Aleister Crowley. Crowley was a leading Alpinist of the day but was shunned by the Alpine Club and took a positive delight in the bizarre. Supposedly indulgent of some notoriously perverse activities, his climbs on chalk were generally considered as just a further example of his eccentricity. On reflection his achievements are now seen to be truly remarkable for their time. As early as 1893 he climbed *Etheldreda's Pinnacle* and the even more spectacular *Devil's Chimney*, which unfortunately collapsed in the 1950s.. Etheldreda's Pinnacle still retains a Very Severe grading. Still more impressive was his attempt on the soaring crack (now named after him) in the main face adjacent to the pinnacle. Although unsuccessful in his efforts, which resulted in him being rescued by the coastguard from two-thirds height, the standard of climbing to reach his high point was probably the most difficult then achieved in Britain. Crowley's enthusiasm was not daunted by the derision of the Alpine Club and he undoubtedly thrived on the criticism, producing many unreported and sadly untraceable routes.

No activity following Crowley's efforts was reported until the 1950s, when Tom Patey and John Cleare proved famously unsuccessful in their attempt to reach the base of Etheldreda's Pinnacle. This event undoubtedly consolidated the opinions of most climbers who considered the cliffs to be too loose and dangerous to provide any worthwhile climbing. It was nearly 90 years after Crowley's example that a small group of climbers began a more enthusiastic appraisal of this exciting area.

1979 saw Arnis Strapcans re-ascend Etheldreda's Pinnacle by a new route and in 1980 the crack which provided the scene of Crowley's epic rescue was finally climbed by Mick Fowler, Mike Morrison and Brian Wyvill.

1981 was to prove a crucial year for South Coast climbing. In January of that year a revolutionary precedent was set when Fowler, Chris Watts and Andy Meyers made the first true ascent of the white cliffs of Dover. Their ascent of *Dry Ice* was noteworthy not because of extreme difficulty but because it was the first clear demonstration that ice axes and crampons could be used effectively on steep pure chalk. Unfortunately, the ascent was plagued by a determined rescue effort mounted by the coastguard and the police, which culminated in the

THE SEA CLIFFS OF SOUTH EAST ENGLAND

appearance of a BBC photographic crew and a feature on the national news. This publicity had a detrimental affect on further development for nearly two years, as climbers became reluctant to risk the wrath of the coastguard.

Throughout the rest of 1981 and 1982 Fowler transferred his attentions to the many fine lines at Beachy Head. *Albino* and *Vaginoff* became the first extremes on the coast and in December 1982 with Morrison and Watts he succeeded on the stupendous *Monster Crack* in the sheer wall of Beachy Head itself.

1982 also saw the first appearance of a future key figure on the South Coast scene. Over the next few years Phil Thornhill was to amaze his contemporaries and become renowned for his remarkable persistence and daunting solo exploits. Frequently enduring solitary winter weekends alone and enjoying numerous night-time epics (both on and off the crag) he managed a coastguard-free ascent of *Dover Patrol* in December 1982 and thereby rekindled interest in the area. The following four months saw Thornhill spearheading frantic activity on the cliffs between St Margaret's Bay and Dover Harbour, culminating in his ascent of *The Ferryman* with Crag Jones and *The Great White Fright* with Fowler and Watts.

The latter part of 1983 saw his attention move to other cliffs in the south-east. Almost always climbing roped-solo he produced two routes at Brighton and several horrors on the sandstone cliffs at Hastings; the highlight being the 4100 feet six-day traverse of *Reasons to be Fearful*, climbed with Anthony Saunders and completed in January 1984.

Thereafter Thornhill's interest waned somewhat and the flood of new routes slowed to a trickle in 1985 and 1986. This was really a period of consolidation with interest spreading and several new faces acquainting themselves with the cliffs by repeating the existing lines.

By 1987 a brief interim guide had been written and the time was ripe for another new route boom. Mark Lynden accompanied Fowler on *The Fog* before adding several fine lines of his own - *The Fortress* with Noel Craine and *The South Face of Kent* with John Sylvester being particularly fine. Duncan Tunstall added several lines and Simon Ballantine teamed up with Andy Perkins to climb the horrifically overhanging *Dukes of Hazard* - the first route on the cliffs between Dover and Folkestone.

The chalk cliffs are now increasing in popularity and, although many of the best lines in the popular areas have now been climbed, vast potential still exists which will no doubt provide exploratory excitement for many years to come.

The abbreviations after the first ascentionists names are: (AL) -alternate leads; (VL) - varied leads. Most (all?) pitch lengths have not been measured accurately and should therefore be treated with caution.

MARGATE AREA

The cliffs here are too small to give any important routes but two short climbs have been recorded.

Between Birchington and Westgate is a stretch of low cliff without a concrete walkway at its base. At low tide an obvious deep chimney can be seen with a distinctive overhang formed by a horizontal layer of chalk.

Margate Chimney 50 feet Difficult/Very Difficult

1 50 feet Climb the aforementioned chimney direct.

First recorded ascent 1983

Tiny White Tremble 50 feet IV†

1 50 feet Just to the left of the above route between it and an inset bay with a concrete walkway is an identifiable groove-line, which gives the line of the route.

P.Thornhill 1983

DOVER

The first and most easterly route lies on the Kingsdown-to-St Margaret's Bay cliffs. Approaching via the firing range at Kingsdown, after approximately 700 yards, an obvious feature is a very smooth east-facing brown slabby wall. About 250 yards east of this is a distinctive small cave at 30 feet.

French Tickler 160 feet V/VI†

Start directly below the small cave. A deceptively difficult route.

1 30 feet Climb to the cave with no special difficulty.

2 60 feet Move left for 20 feet and surmount the overhanging wall at its weakest point. Continue steeply diagonally right to belay at a foothold in a scoop.

3 70 feet A serious pitch. Ascend steeply right to reach grass tufts and proceed direct on precarious ground to the top. A hawthorn bush provides a convenient belay.

M.Fowler, C.Watts(AL) 8 January 1984

On the cliff half a mile east of St Margaret's Bay is a route of little merit, which takes a line up the most easterly of two grass slopes capped by a 30 foot rock wall.

Oily Bird 280 feet IV†

Start at the bottom left-hand corner of the grass slope.

1 230 feet Ascend chalk for 25 feet to gain the grass, which is followed diagonally rightwards, choosing the easiest line, to its highest point.

2 50 feet Move up left on tufty grass for 25 feet, then climb directly to the top just right of a line of disintegrating flakes.

M.Fowler, P.Thornhill 13 January 1983

Continuing west along the beach a prominent feature is a very fine groove in the arête 700 yards east of St Margaret's Bay. It is unusual in that the upper section sports an obvious crack. The following route starts 20 yards east of the groove-line, just to the left of a big rockfall.

***The Time Warp** 250 feet V†

1 110 feet Climb for 40 feet to beneath a clean-cut roof, traverse right round the roof and ascend to a good stance.

2 140 feet Climb easily up the scoop, trending slightly left. After 70 feet the wall steepens to vertical and becomes loose. Climb up into the corner for 10 feet and then traverse left out of the corner to finish up the face.

S.Ballantine, P.Murphy(AL) 1 November 1987

****Into The Groove** 250 feet V†

Start directly beneath the groove. A fine route.

1 120 feet Ascend rightwards on conglomerate rock and vegetation and then back left on a fine clean chalk ramp to belay at the base of the groove.

2 100 feet Climb the steep (overhanging in places) groove to an easing of the angle at 70 feet. A further 30 feet of looser ground leads to a surprisingly good ledge on the right arête.

3 30 feet Move back in to the groove which is climbed first on the left wall then on the right to the top.

M.Fowler, M.Lynden(AL) 21 December 1986

Approximately 100 yards further towards St Margaret's Bay is an arête bounded on its right-hand side by a grey slab in the lower third. The slab is bounded on the right by an obvious corner which also peters out at one-third height. Start in the centre of the grey slab.

*****More Neck Than Simon Ballantine** 220 feet IV/V

1 70 feet Climb directly up the slab to belay at 70ft.

2 160 feet Move up leftwards and follow the increasingly loose right-hand side of the arête to the top. It is possible to split the pitch by belaying some 30 feet from the top at the point where the loose material ends.

S.Ballantine, M. Nicholson 4-11-84 (Final moves top-roped in the dark)
D.Tunstall, A.Wood 21 September 1986 (Without top-rope)

From the Coastguard pub at St Margaret's Bay walk 200 yards west along the beach to reach the first section of cliff. Located here is the obvious man-made cave of The Birds at 50 feet with the prominent grey ramp-line of Dry Ice above and to the left.

*****The Birds** 150 feet IV/V

Start at the foot of a slight groove just right of a point directly below the cave.

1 70 feet Climb the shallow groove, moving left at its top to a small ledge. Move up steeply and cross the wall to enter the cave.

2 Explore the interesting tunnels (head-torch recommended): great ornithological interest and a possible escape point (when the exit by the promenade is not fully bricked up).

3 80 feet Step down from the cave and ascend leftwards beneath an overhang to gain a small ledge. Climb diagonally right up through the overhangs above to reach steep grass and the finish of Dry Ice.

M.Fowler, P.Thornhill(AL), A.Meyers 8 January 1983

Dry Ice 180 feet III

The original route of the cliffs is justifiably popular and provides an excellent introduction to the area. Start at the foot of the prominent grey ramp-line slanting from left-to-right just left of the previous route.

1 80 feet Pull over a short bulge and gain the ramp. Climb the left-bounding corner for 50 feet before traversing 10 feet right to belay on grass tufts.

2 100 feet Follow a slightly rising line up to the right to gain easier grass-tuft climbing after 70 feet. Fence-post belay well back.

M.Fowler, C.Watts(AL), A.Meyers 4 January 1981

Sound Effects 140 feet IV/VI

The obvious ramp-line just left of Dry Ice with a loose exit.

1 140 feet Climb the ramp easily to a desperate finish direct up the short headwall.

An alternative easier finish - The Inevitable Plastic Inflatable Finish - takes a line just to the right of the original on the final wall and reduces the overall grade to IV.

M.Lynden, K.Slevin, D.McDonald, M.Moss 8 March 1987

Alternative finish - Leeds University Group 1987

The next line of weakness lies about 250 yards westwards up a twisting grassy groove-cum-gully. Thirty yards east of this are two prominent disjointed grooves; the first groove starts from a small cave on the beach and initially has a pocketed crack in the back:

Old Red Eyes 180 feet V†

There has been much "rock" fall in this area since the first ascent of this route, leaving some loose overhanging remnants.

1 80 feet Climb the left wall of the groove until it fades away in steeper rock.

2 100 feet Traverse left and move up into the second groove. Follow this to loose vertical walls and move 15 feet right before ascending these to the top.

M.Fowler, J.Lincoln 18 October 1987

Lunchtime Gully 200 feet IV

This is the prominent groove-cum-gully mentioned above. The line is variable following the easiest line to the top.

M.Fowler, P.Thornhill(Solo) 27 February 1983

The Kiss 200 feet V†

Start 30 yards west of Lunchtime Gully below the obvious grey left trending ramp.

1 140 feet Follow the ramp leftwards to the centre of the 'X' formed by a less obvious ramp rising from left to right to this point. Ascend 20 feet on the right-hand ramp above to belay.

2 60 feet Climb the loose ramp above (the top right-hand part of the 'X') to an absorbing cornice finish.

D.Tunstall, M. Fowler(AL), J.Lincoln 11 December 1988

Three hundred and fifty yards west of Lunchtime Gully is a prominent rightward-trending crack-line ending in a series of caves near the top of the cliff. Stepping back from the foot of the cliff it is apparent that the crack forks at about 200 feet and forms the letter 'Y'. Channel Holes takes the right-hand fork and provides an excellent route.

*** Channel Holes   260 feet VI†

Start 30 feet right of the base of the fault-line in a leftward leaning corner.

1 100 feet Climb the left wall of the corner for 30 feet and move diagonally left between small bulges to gain the fault-line after 65 feet. Continue up the fault-line to belay on a small grass ledge.

2 40 feet Climb the slabby ramp to a small overhang and continue to a belay in a constricted cave.

3 80 feet Continue in the same line to a large cave at 70 feet. Pull over the overhang above to a smaller cave.

4 40 feet Surmount the overhang above to gain a ledge. Move right for 6 feet before taking a direct line up the loose material forming the final wall.

M.Fowler, C.Watts(AL), N.Bankhead 25 September 1983

About 400 yards west of Channel Holes is a very smooth wall easily identified by a prominent shallow depression (the "Navel") at 100 feet. The next route starts by a short groove, with an overhang low down, below the grass slopes right of the wall.

*** The South Face of Kent   270 feet VI

An excellent and very sustained route, which climbs the shallow groove snaking its way up one of Dover's most impressive walls.

1 90 feet Climb to the left of the overhang onto a grass ramp then straight up to the cave. It is advisable to carry a 2 foot stake to belay in the cave.

2 110 feet Exit from the cave on the left then trend up and left to gain the shallow groove. Follow this until it is possible to take a hanging stance on good well spaced screws.

3 70 feet Climb up the groove, trending generally leftwards and then straight up to finish.

M.Lynden, J.Silvester, D.Tunstall(VL - D.Tunstall not present on Day 3) 7-9 November 1987

About 100 yards west of The South Face of Kent is an obvious groove ending just above an overhang at 60 feet. This gives the start of The Fog.

**The Fog 250 ft VI†

A very fine route with a serious finish.

1 90 feet Climb the groove to the overhang; this is passed by moving onto the arête on the left. Move back right across the overhung ledge forming the top of the overhang and belay at the foot of a steep smooth right-trending ramp/slab.

2 80 feet Climb the ramp to overhangs and move right to belay on the arête, which is actually the left edge of an area of tufty ground stretching rightwards to a prominent corner with a crack at the back which cleaves the upper third of the cliff.

3 80 feet Ascend the wall with projecting flints, trending slightly left until it is possible to step left onto very loose ground, which leads in 20 feet to the final overhangs. Traverse horizontally left for 20 feet, the last 10 feet being overhanging (and overhanging the base of the cliff), until it is possible to pull over onto a short slab leading to the top.

M.Fowler, M.Lynden(AL) 8 February 1987

About 250 yards west of The Fog is a grass slope protected by a 50 foot wall. The following route has little merit and was first climbed as an escape from an incoming tide.

Escape Hatch 320 feet IV

1 75 feet Move up easily for a few feet until it is necessary to traverse steeply right to a resting place. Climb back up left to gain the left edge of the vegetated slope.

2 245 feet Hack rightwards through the jungle, then up the grassy slope to where a steepening on worrying tufty vegetation leads to a final easy exit-chimney.

P.Thornhill(Solo) 18 December 1982

No Surrender 355 feet IV†

1 75 feet As for Escape Hatch.

2 60 feet Climb a short wall and follow easier-angled vegetated ground into a shallow depresssion.

3 90 feet Traverse delicately rightwards to a steep rib. Climb the rib and move left to belay at the foot of a corner.

4 130 feet Climb the corner and follow a ramp to finish.

D.Tunstall, S.Brookes 8 February 1987

***Dover Patrol 350 feet V

One of the best routes in the area. This climbs the very fine groove sporting grassy tufts and angling rightwards up the full height of the cliff. Start beneath the obvious groove 150 yards west of Escape Hatch and 250 yards east of The Fortress.

1 140 feet Climb the prominent ramp, past a narrowing at 40 feet and follow the groove above easily for 30 feet (possible belay). Move out right and continue up trending right until eventually a stance is reached on the right-hand edge of the groove, below where it steepens and becomes very smooth.

2 150 feet Climb up and left into the corner and follow it for 70 feet to gain a ledge below a short steep wall. Surmount this wall on loose material and continue for 50 feet to belay. A fine pitch. Note: it is safer to belay just before the loose material as the climb is consistently very loose from there to the top.

3 60 feet Continue up the loose earthy corner above (or the steep wall on the right) and follow an obvious flake chimney leading to the top of a pinnacle. From here step across onto the cliff top.

P.Thornhill(Roped solo) 27 December 1982

Dover Patrol provides a useful midway marker to help decide from which end of the cliffs one should approach the routes. Continuing past Dover Patrol towards Dover Harbour is the most unmistakeable feature on the cliffs - a 5 foot-wide parallel-sided chimney, which is deeply cut in its upper reaches. This is climbed by The Tube.

*** The Fortress 340 feet VI

Approximately 80 yards east of The Tube are two chalk buttresses with a shallow depression between them which is more prominent in the upper section of the cliff. Start from the beach directly beneath the depression, just west of an old grass/chalk slide. A small letter 'F' is carved in the rock. An extremely fine and varied climb.

1 140 feet Climb straight up for 40 feet before trending left to enter the obvious depression-line. Follow this steeply and continue delicately on more unstable ground to a ledge on the left beneath obviously solid chalk.

2 80 feet Traverse 10 feet right and climb up for 60 feet (just left of poorer quality chalk) before traversing 10 feet right to belay.

3 120 feet Move back left and climb up very steeply on flakey chalk to gain a depression beneath a disjointed crack-line. Step right and continue to the top. A hard pitch.

M.Lynden, N.Craine 8 March 1987

The Cormorant 340 feet IV/V

Start 50 yards east of The Tube in a small cave at the foot of a rightward-trending ramp leading to the bottom right-hand corner of a large grassy depression.

1 140 feet Climb the ramp to an obvious narrowing, which gives the crux. Above this move left to a large ledge.

2 140 feet Climb up left, then trend right into a vague gully-line leading to a niche beneath a steepening.

3 60 feet Make a detour to the right to avoid "dinner-plating" chalk and regain the gully above, which is followed to the top - or climb the "dinner-plating" chalk direct at a higher standard. P.Thornhill(Roped solo) 6 March 1983

** The Tube 310 feet IV

A good route up a prominent interesting feature. Start by scrambling up landslide debris to a point below and left of the start of the chimney.

1 130 feet Ascend diagonally rightwards and move up into the foot of the chimney. Continue for 60 feet and belay up and to the left on a ledge. Alternatively, ascend diagonally leftwards continuing in the same line until forced to belay. Then move some 60 feet right into the chimney.

2 180 feet Continue up the chimney using a wide variety of techniques and passing a wedged metal plate (invisible from below).

P.Thornhill, M.Fowler(AL), A.Meyers 8 January 1983

A hundred yards west of The Tube is a striking and highly impressive prow of chalk which is climbed by one of the most spectacular routes in the area - The Great White Fright.

*** The Great White Fright   290 feet VI

A magnificent route on very steep ground. Start 15 feet left of the arête.

1 100 feet Climb to a small ledge at 15 feet. Ascend diagonally rightwards and swing round the arête to gain a shallow depression. Follow this trending slightly right and surmount a gently overhanging bulge on the left to gain a good stance on the arête itself.

2 70 feet Follow the leftward-trending ramp with increasing difficulty to a superb stance on a dubious pillar.

3 120 feet Climb the white overhanging wall above, trending slightly rightwards to beneath large square-cut overhangs. Cross the thin crack on the right and climb the grey shield of rock for 20 feet until it is possible to move out left onto the wall above the main overhangs. Continue directly to the top. A phenomenal pitch.

P.Thornhill, M.Fowler, C.Watts(VL) 23/24 April 1983 (C.Watts did not climb P3)

*** The Ferryman   240 feet VI

This excellent route climbs the shallow depression immediately left of Great White Fright. Start 50 feet left of that route.

1 110 feet Climb to a ledge at 10 feet then continue to the right-hand end of a grassy ledge above. From the left end of this climb steeply left then back right to follow a vague groove on dubious rock to the foot of a shattered pillar.

2 60 feet Traverse round the base of the pillar and ascend its right-hand side to a rubble-covered ledge.

3 70 feet The vertical wall above is climbed trending slightly leftwards to the top.

P.Thornhill, C.Jones(AL) 12/13 March 1983

The Furious Tax Collector   200 feet V†

Start 50 yards east of Fisherman's Friend, below an area of very steep rock with a narrow ramp-line running up from right to left towards an upper amphitheatre.

1 60 feet Follow the ramp to a ledge.

2 50 feet Descend from the overhanging wall on the left (in an uncontrolled fashion on the first ascent) to gain a lower traverse-line, from which it is possible to climb up the steep wall above to the prominent amphitheatre.

---

17. Great White Fright, VI, Dover. *Climber: Phil Thornhill*. Photo Mick Fowler.

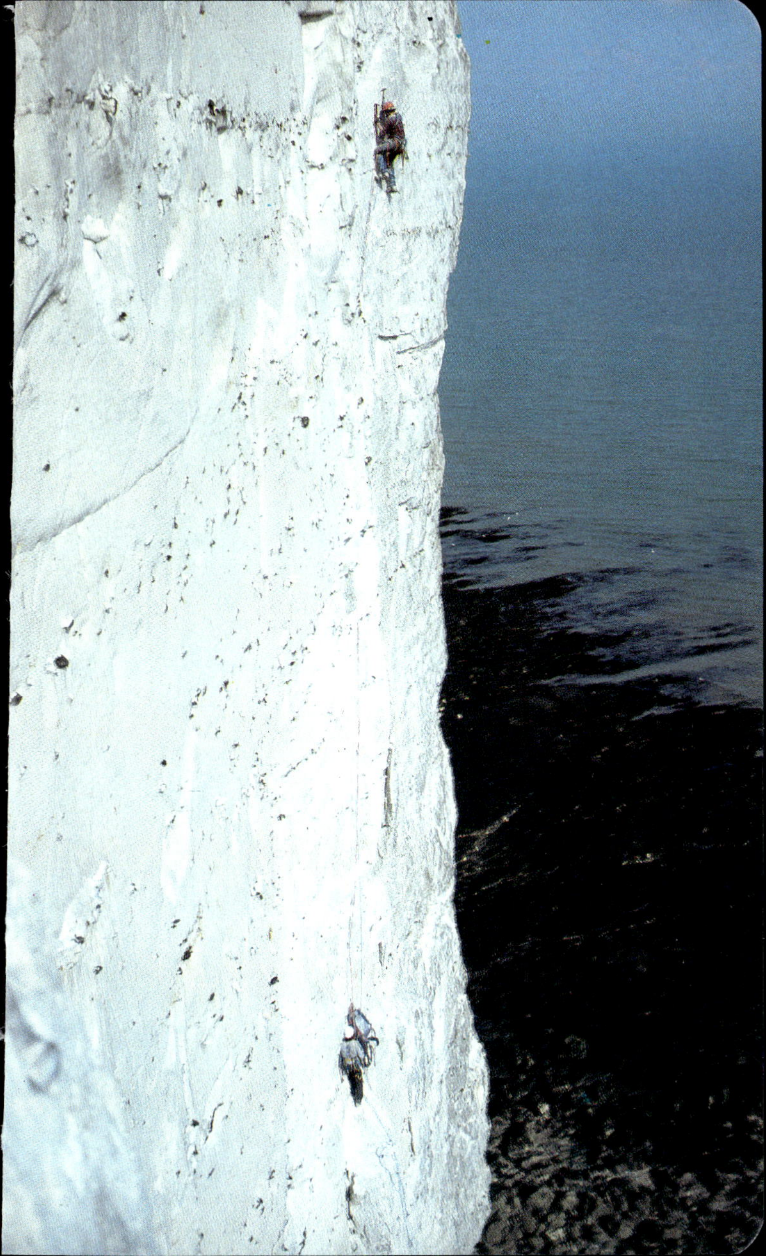

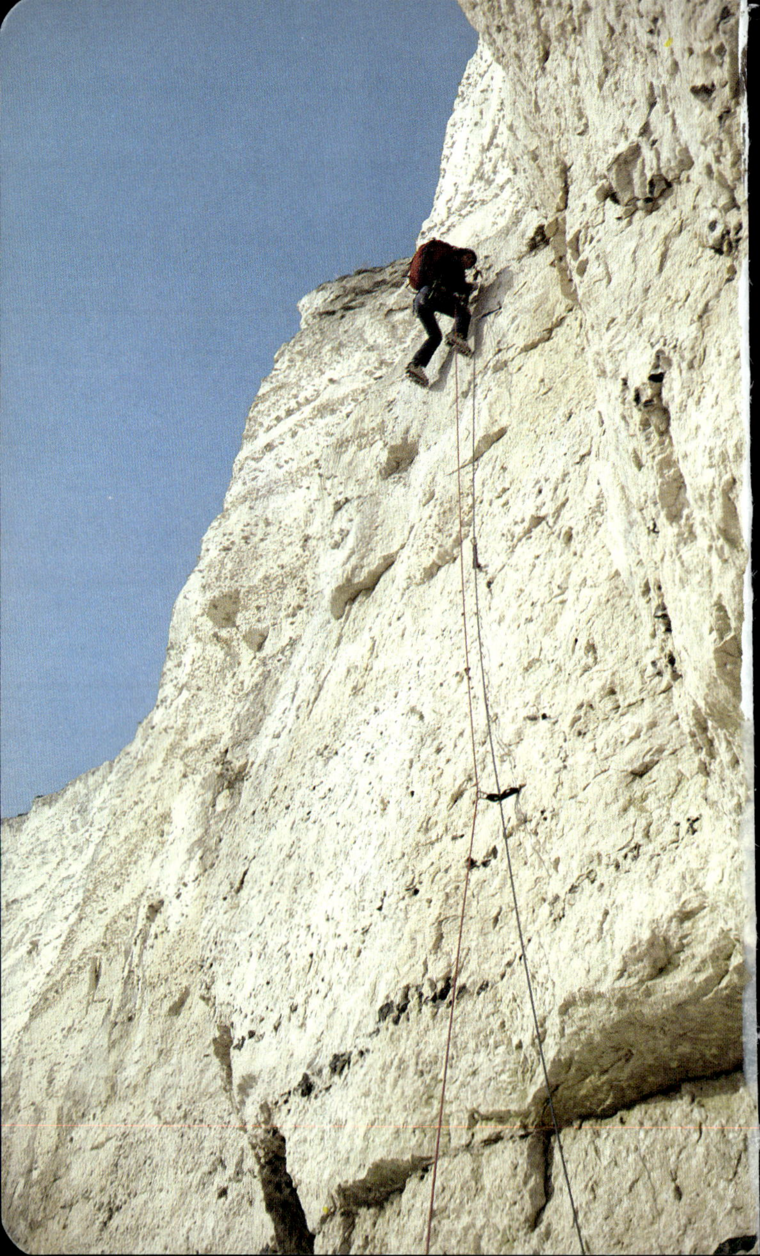

3 90 feet Climb rightwards up vegetation, then steeper chalk leads to the top.

P.Thornhill, N.Craine(AL) 8 February 1987

Fisherman's Friend 200 feet V†

A prominent feature of this part of the cliff is a steel plated door inset 15 feet above the high tide-mark. This route takes a right-to-left slanting line above the door. Start 15 feet right of the door.

1 60 feet Climb the deceptively steep left wall of the groove until the angle eases slightly - 10 feet higher traverse 10 feet left to a belay ledge.

2 120 feet Continue diagonally left on dubious chalk to cross a small loose overhang and gain the toe of a prominent grass-tufted ramp, which leads more easily to a belay below the final wall.

3 20 feet The final wall - a convenient bush provides a belay well back.

M.Lynden, M.Fowler(AL) 1 February 1987

The next route was Dry Throat VI, which began twenty five yards west of the steel door and climbed a steep left-to-right trending ramp-line. This recently collapsed completely, so be warned. Approaching from the west the foreshore walk passes beneath a series of towers high up the cliff and separated by gullies. Further on, a slight projection results in a reduced period of access due to the tides. Immediately after this the cliff is set back in a shallow bay with long strands of cable hanging over the edge on the west side. To the right of of these cables the cliff consists of a short rock step at sea-level, a long intermediate grassy slope, and a grey headwall approximately 150 feet high. This headwall has two prominent rightwards-slanting grooves in its centre. Dover Soul takes the right-hand groove, having approached it from the lower wall and grass.

§ Dover Soul 400 feet V

The start is some 400 yards west of Fisherman's Friend.

1 150 feet Climb anywhere to reach the vegetated slope, which is ascended via a shallow leftward-leaning depression.

2 100 feet Traverse right and move up a vague groove to the foot of the upper wall.

3 50 feet Follow the ramp, passing a cave on the left, and take a hanging belay on ice-screws.

4 100 feet Continue steeply up the ramp to the top.

P.Thornhill, J.Tinker 22/23 January 1983

The following route is currently the only climb on the cliffs west of Dover Harbour. The chalk here is considerably harder than on the other Dover cliffs; the angle of the one climb is such that on the two ascents so far etriers or foot-slings have been used attached to ice axes. This makes the climbing feel more like artificial work, hence the unusual grading for the area.

---

18. Fisherman's Friend, V, Dover. *Climber: Mark Lyden.* Photo Mick Fowler.

194   THE SEA CLIFFS OF SOUTH EAST ENGLAND

*Dukes of Hazard   260 feet V/A3

The climb is on the first cliffs to the west of the harbour. At the point where the cliff-top footpath leaves the road cross the railway by means of a foot-bridge and walk west along the beach for 200 yards to a very overhanging 120 feet high wall, which leads up to a mixed rock and grass arête. Start directly beneath the wall.

1   120 feet Trend diagonally rightwards to the bottom right-hand side of the overhanging wall. Ascend this (foot-slings on ice axes used) to gain a shallow niche where the angle relents to vertical (possible belay). Continue up the gently overhanging wall above to the highest point of the overhanging wall. Good screw belays on the left.

2   140 feet Climb the mixed arête above direct to the top.

S.Ballantine, A.Perkins(VL) 21/22 November 1987

HASTINGS

Unlike the rest of the South East Coast the cliffs at Hastings are not the characteristic steep chalk that one is used to seeing. On the seafront at the eastern end of Hastings old town lies an outcrop of sandstone sculptured by numerous caves and giving a more conventional style of climbing. These routes have a unique appeal and will no doubt prove of particular interest to any climber beleaguered with their family on holiday.

The vein of sandstone continues eastwards to tempt the adventurous climber again. About half-a-mile to the east of Hastings, and just east of Ecclesbourne Glen, the cliffs consist of bands of sandstone and clay interspersed with various indeterminate materials. The clay tends to fill any corners and pile up on ledges thereby making progress difficult and proving ice gear especially useful. A slightly different approach is required here. Whereas at Dover the chalk gives climbing akin to steep water ice, at Hastings the climbing is analagous to "mixed" climbing -less steep and spectacular but more delicate. The most useful form of protection here seems to be the warthog type drive-in ice-screws but great care should be taken not to test them as any protection on this cliff is highly suspect. All in all a serious place.

At the eastern end of the seafront at Hastings is a car-parking area. Fifty yards along a no-through road is a prominent rack railway going about 50 yards up the hillside. This is the scene of a clandestine route -Railway Crack:

Railway Crack   130 feet Hard Very Severe

1   130 feet 5a In the west wall of the rack railway is an obvious crack splitting a smooth wall. This route climbs the crack and proves more difficult than it looks. Fully open to public gaze, a discreet approach is absolutely essential.

M.Fowler, M.Morrison 1983

The road continues for a short distance beneath the cave-riddled outcrops to a second car-parking area in front of the Hastings Yacht Club. On the hillside above the dry yacht enclosure is an obvious deep chimney with a bottle-neck just over one-third of the way up. This is

One in the Eye for Harold. Approach from the toilet blocks up easy paths to the caves and traverse across the vegetated hillside.

One in the Eye for Harold   80 feet Hard Very Severe

Start at the foot of the chimney in the outcrop east of the caves.

1   80 feet 4c/5a Climb the chimney direct.

P.Thornhill, L.Cole 12 June 1983

The Yacht Club car-park terminates at a concrete breakwater, where a small but pertinent sign reading "Dangerous Cliffs" is attached to metal bars. Up the grassy hillside behind is a leftward-slanting crack-line giving The Battle of Hastings, whilst to the right is the striking corner-line of Norman Corner.

The Battle of Hastings   100 feet Very Severe

1   100 feet 4a Follow the leftward-slanting crack-line to finish in a vague gully. Climb this and the vegetated corner in the short upper tier to finish.

P.Thornhill(Roped solo) 30 May 1983

Norman Corner   80 feet E1

1   80 feet 5a/5b Climb the prominent corner-line.

P.Thornhill(Second did not follow) 11 June 1983

Walking eastwards along the beach one comes to where Ecclesbourne Glen meets the sea. Here the cliff dips to only 20 feet high and sports a small waterfall. To the east again stretching for approximately one mile the cliff has two bands of soft sandstone which outcrop along its entire length. The lower band is about 80 feet thick and the upper band about 40 feet. Steep mud and clay intersperse the outcrops and form the finish to most routes.

Monster Raving Loony   200 feet IV/V

The route takes a direct but not particularly obvious line up steep clay and very broken rock. Start about halfway between Ecclesbourne Glen and a large grassy mound at the base of the cliff, below three well-defined corners in the upper band. Note - the right-hand corner provides the finish of Reasons to be Fearful.

1   200 feet Climb up through the smooth band at the base of the cliff, striking out from a pile of rocks in a short shallow corner. Move left onto easier ground then find a way up the muddy shattered rocks above, with a short steepish clay slope giving access to easy grass slopes. From beneath the upper tier of cleaner sandstone trend left to a prominent corner capped by a final "cornice". Finish up a short clay slope.

P.Thornhill(Roped Solo) 6 August 1983

The Green Ghastly   200 feet IV/A1

Start midway between the Glen and The Prow at what appears to be the easiest way up this area, a series of vegetated corners between terraces about 1500 feet east of the Glen.

1   200 feet From the shore move easily up right a little then left, via a clay slope, to easy ground. On the left is an obvious vegetated corner

with a rock step at the top; follow this to a ledge. Move left a bit and up a very short rock step to easy ground. Continue with aid up a rightward-slanting corner to a broad ledge beneath the upper tier. Traverse about 35 feet right to a grass-filled corner/groove and follow this, using some aid towards the top.
P.Thornhill(Roped Solo) 10 September 1983

On the Western side of The Prow, the distinct clay ridge that is clearly seen from Hastings, is an obvious gully - Gully of the Godless. Further west the cliff juts out slightly before becoming slightly recessed. Screaming Lord Sutch finds a devious way up this recessed area.

Screaming Lord Sutch   210 feet V
Start at the foot of a clay-cone-filled corner situated at the base of the cliff about 300 feet west of Gully of the Godless.

1   150 feet Go up the corner and follow a vague depression above to a steepening. Traverse right to another (deeper) clay-filled corner which gives access to a broad ledge beneath the upper tier. Move right and belay beneath a corner.

2   60 feet Climb broken ground to the foot of the corner. Climb the corner for 3 feet, then traverse right for a few feet to gain a crack/groove leading to the top.
P.Thornhill, A.Saunders(AL) 30 August 1983

Duffyman's Dusk   200 feet IV
The route takes the easiest-looking line between Screaming Lord Sutch and Gully of the Godless.

1   200 feet Ascend the lower tier by a series of rightward-trending grassy corners to gain the Reasons to be Fearful traverse-line. From here challenging tufting leads into a corner and the top.
P.Thornhill(Roped solo) July 1984

Gully of the Godless   200 feet III
Climb the obvious gully 200 feet west of the Prow, avoiding any difficulties by making excursions to the left.
P.Thornhill(Roped solo) 20 August 1983

The Prow   250 feet III
The distinct clay ridge that is clearly seen from Hastings. The ridge is followed, passing a short rock step halfway, to reach the foot of a steep sandstone upper tier giving the crux of the route. At the bottom of this 40 feet rock pitch is a very large in situ peg belay placed by an unknown party.
First recorded ascent: P.Thornhill(Roped solo)

From Ecclesbourne Glen to below the Prow there is an obvious and continuous horizontal band of soft clay just beneath the steep, "solid" upper tier. This band of clay has been followed in its entirety and gives a mammoth outing of over 4000 feet. The first 9 pitches (1350 feet) finishing up the Gully of the Godless makes a logical route in its own right, at grade III.

Reasons to be Fearful 4100 feet (33 pitches) IV

Start to the east of the Prow where the cliff runs out into vegetation. Scramble up and left to gain the line where the first pitch (III) is soon encountered. Easier ground follows then more III to gain The Prow, which is reversed a short way to just above the rock step. Traverse a wide clay band into Gully of the Godless. Climb this to regain the horizontal band and follow this for about 1000 feet (pitches of II and III) to the first crux section. A few hundred feet further on is a second crux area, which is followed by mainly easier ground to reach two blunt prows just before Monster Raving Looney. Here the band loses definition somewhat. Nevertheless, continue at roughly the same level until the second prow is reached; ascend this close to its arête to belay at the foot of the upper tier beneath a prominent crack-line. Move left 3 feet and climb a gully/chimney round the corner to finish. A.Saunders, P.Thornhill(AL) between 26 October 1983 and 8 January 1984 in 6 parts
The following is a rough breakdown of the route:- (1)100 feet I/II; (2)100 feet III; (3)150 feet II; (4)400 feet I; (5)200 feet III; (6)100 feet II; (7)100 feet III; (8)100 feet III; (9)100 feet II; (10)180 feet III; (11)150 feet III); (12)100 feet II; (13)150 feet II/III; (14)100 feet III; (15)150 feet II/III; (16)150 feet IV; (17)100 feet IV; (18)75 feet IV; (18)50 feet I/II; (19)100 feet II/III; (20)100 feet IV; (21)150 feet I/II); (22)150 feet I/II; (23)150 feet III; (24)550 feet I; (25)50 feet II/III; (26)140 feet IV; (27)100 feet IV; (28)60 feet III/IV.

Further outcrops not described above are recorded at:

TOOT HILL/TOOT ROCK   OS Ref 892 135

An ancient cliff line, now inland, occurs at Pett Level. This is of the height of the ordinary inland outcrops and some climbing is reported here. Pett Level itself is apparently as flat as the name suggests.

CLIFF END   OS Ref 886 137

Apparently, sixty foot cliffs capped by clay and dense undergrowth, making the finishes extremely difficult. There is a lower tier with a few possible crack-lines.

LOVER'S SEAT   OS Ref 855 105

This is a small outcrop at the seaward end of Fairlight Glen, which has given one or two short climbs. There are some other low outcrops higher up the Glen. The routes on the cliffs stretching east from here to Ecclesbourne Glen and beyond to Hastings are described above.

WEST HILL   OS Ref 822 095

On the east side of the Castle is a rocky area providing easy scrambles. The crags below the Castle are inaccessible, rising right out of the gardens of houses, and have loose material and vegetation at the top. Some climbs have been reported. Further climbs are described above in the main Hastings Section.

THE SEA CLIFFS OF SOUTH EAST ENGLAND

BEACHY HEAD

Beachy Head is the highest and most spectacular precipice on the entire southern coast of England and presents a most impressive sight for anyone looking over its edge down the 100 yard drop below. Between Beachy Head itself and Birling Gap four miles to the west, the cliffs form a continuously perpendicular wall easily viewed from the beach below, although care should be taken with the tides as there is no easy way whatsoever up this section of cliff. To the west of Birling Gap are the Seven Sisters with the only route here so far (Yorkie) on the most westerly sister.

To the east of the lighthouse the cliffs ease to high-angled grass and chalk leading to a steep headwall. Here lies the famous Etheldreda's Pinnacle, with Crowley's Crack prominent in the main wall behind. Albino follows the smooth groove 100 yards to the west of the pinnacle, whilst Monster Crack takes the mind-blowing face crack directly opposite the lighthouse.

The base of the cliffs is best reached by descending down grass slopes east of the Pub at Beachy Head (this is the name of the cliff-top pub) and then walking along the beach. When one is familiar with the area it is actually quicker to abseil from a fence-post above Vaginoff.

It is particularly important that the coastguard is informed of any climbing activity here as all the routes are clearly visible from the lighthouse - Tel. (Eastbourne 20634).

***Monster Crack**   355 feet Hard Extremely Severe

Piercing the centre of the eastern face of Beachy Head itself is an extremely impressive crack-line giving the best route in the area by far. Protection throughout is by ice-screws and nuts. From the beach opposite the lighthouse ascend grass slopes to the foot of the crack.

1 80 feet 5a Follow a line of discontinuous grass tufts diagonally leftwards and climb the left-hand 'side of a grassy depression to gain a grass-ledge 10 feet to the left of the start of the crack proper.

2 100 feet 5b Move up diagonally right to the foot of the crack. Climb the crack for 15ft, then use two Friends for aid to reach good holds and a small cave. Continue directly up the crack above to reach a stance and ice-screw belays beneath a large roof.

3 75 feet 5b Cross a slab on the left and move up to gain a niche in the crack-line. Continue straight up, passing some dubious flakes, to belay at the foot of a surprisingly large niche.

4 80 feet 5c Ascend rubble in the floor of the niche to gain a narrow foot-ledge in the right wall. Traverse this to the arête (ice-screw runner in situ to the right) and climb with difficulty on flints, passing a second ice-screw, to reach a ledge at the foot of the upper crack. Follow this crack, which leads steeply to the top.

M.Fowler, M.Morrison, C.Watts (Pitches 1-3 20 November 1982, Pitch 4 1 December 1982)

To the right of Monster Crack the steep section of cliff is lower. A prominent feature at the highest point of the grass slopes leading up right from that route is the deep, vertical chimney of Vaginoff with the elegant slim groove-line of Albino 20 feet to the right.

*Vaginoff 150 feet Extremely Severe

Scramble up rightwards to below the obvious chimney.

1 130 feet 5b Climb up past several loose chock-stones until it is possible to move deep inside and on up to the bottle-neck at 80 feet. Bridge and jam up the outside (crux) to gain the easier upper section, which is followed to a belay where the chimney becomes mud-choked and overhanging.

2 20 feet 4c Start by back-and-footing and continue by wide bridging on very loose rock.

M.Fowler (Second did not follow) 20 November 1982 (P2 was soloed with a back rope)

*Albino 150 feet Extremely Severe

The attractive groove to the right of the chimney gives an excellent main pitch protected with nuts and ice-screws. Start 20 feet right of Vaginoff.

1 130 feet 5b Follow the deceptively steep groove, using mostly hand jams. Surmount an overhanging bulge at 70 feet (crux) and enter the easier-angled upper groove above. This provides further interest until a short slab is crossed to gain the upper chimney of Vaginoff.

2 20 feet 4c As for pitch 2 of Vaginoff.

M.Fowler, L.Cole 6 March 1983

Jutting well out from the main cliff, the stubby thumb of Etheldreda's Pinnacle can be clearly seen from above and below. Separating the wall behind the pinnacle from Albino is a left-to-right trending grassy ramp, which provides the exit from Chalk Farm Toad. On the right of the pinnacle the wall sports an historic route, the steep and daunting line of Crowley's Crack.

Chalk Farm Toad 120 feet Hard Very Severe

Immediately west of the pinnacle is a gully-line below a left-to-right trending ramp, giving a route of dubious worth.

1 120 feet 5a Climb the gully to gain a ledge at 70 feet with difficulty. Continue up to a large block-belay on the left at the head of the gully. Scrambling remains up the grassy ramp.

S.Lewis, J.Deakin(AL), P.Thornhill 20 November 1982.

West Chimney 70 feet Very Severe

The best method of access to the neck of the pinnacle.

1 70 feet 4b Climb the prominent chimney facing the lighthouse on the western side of the pinnacle.

M.Fowler, M.Morrison 13 April 1980

Etheldreda's Pinnacle Route 1 25 feet Very Severe

Crowley's original route on the pinnacle.

1 25 feet 4a From the neck climb straight up for 6 feet, then trend right to the right arête of the pinnacle, which is followed to the top.

A. Crowley 1893

Etheldreda's Pinnacle Route 2 30 feet Very Severe
Start lower down the West Chimney than Route 1.
1 30 feet 4b Climb up and out onto the block wedged across the West Chimney. From this gain the right arête of the pinnacle and follow it to the top.
A.Strapcans, G.Forward 1979

*Crowley's Crack 200 feet Mild Extremely Severe
Start below a groove on the east side of Etheldreda's Pinnacle, beneath the impressive crack from which Crowley was rescued.
1 60 feet Climb the groove on loose rock (The East Chimney) until it is possible to move right and belay on ice-screws below the crack.
2 140 feet 5a Follow the crack to the top. The crux is at about two-thirds height.
Pitch 1 A.Crowley c1893
Pitch 2 M.Fowler, M.Morrison, B.Wyvill 13 April 1980

To the right of the Etheldreda's Pinnacle area is an obvious gully running the full height of the cliff. This gives:

Aunt Ethel's Gully 400 feet Hard Very Severe
1 150 feet From the beach climb up easily to a point where it is possible to make an easy escape leftwards onto grass.
2 120 feet Continue more easily up the gully to where the difficulty increases.
3 130 feet 5a Go up to the crux where the climber is forced out onto the right-hand wall, which is climbed on flints. After this an overhang is climbed / turned with care and easy ground leads to the top.
P. Thornhill(Roped Solo) 4 January 1984

About 200 yards east of Etheldreda's Pinnacle a partially hidden wall facing south-east, which is bounded on its right-hand side by a long grassy ridge. This wall has two striking crack/gully-lines and is best approached by scrambling down steep grass from the right.

Croydon Club Route 160 feet Severe
This climbs the obvious left-hand fault-line, to finish in some interesting deep passages. These passages can easily be found from above by looking in the first fenced-off area east of the prow that juts out above Etheldreda's Pinnacle.
R.Gookey and party 1981

Demolition Man 160 feet Hard Very Severe
This takes the fault to the right of Croydon Club Route.
1 100 feet Scramble up into the grassy bay.
2 60 feet 4b Follow the crack-line above, which is full of rubble and very loose.
P.Thornhill(Roped Solo) 25 September 1983

CUCKMERE HAVEN — THE SEVEN SISTERS

***Yorkie** 300 feet VII†

Walking along the beach eastwards from Cuckmere (i.e. towards Beachy Head) the cliffs of the first Sister increase gradually in height and a series of buttresses project onto the beach. After approximately 300 yards (just before the highest point) a buttress projects further than the others. Directly above this are two left-to-right-slanting ramps separated by a vertical wall and capped by a short overhanging wall. Start at the toe of the buttress which forms the right edge of the lower ramp. Hard, serious and very fine climbing.

1 80 feet Climb onto the buttress crest from the right and follow it to belay where it steepens.

2 70 feet Pass the steepening above by climbing the slab on the left and return to the crest, which leads to ledges below very loose shattered rock. Traverse 10 feet left into a vertical groove and ascend this for about 30 feet until it is possible to move right to a good ice-screw belay (in place) above the shattered rock.

3 70 feet Step back left and continue up the groove to gain the foot of the upper ramp. Ascend diagonally up the ramp to belay on the far side.

4 80 feet Climb the ramp to the capping overhangs. Traverse to the right edge and climb a short wall to the top.

M.Fowler, C.Watts(AL), A.Chaudry 25 January 1987

BRIGHTON

In the vicinity of Brighton the chalk cliffs lose the majesty and grandeur so clearly displayed on Beachy Head and at the Seven Sisters. Here they are featureless landscaped banks above a concrete promenade and stretching from Brighton to Saltdean. Where the under-cliff walk terminates at Saltdean the cliff resumes its natural state and provides the climber with some interest. Easily identifiable by lime-green colouring at its left end, the area has been investigated by only two exploratory routes to date and, although unlikely to receive much attention, a few good looking lines await an ascent.

The cliff is approached along the beach eastwards from the promenade at Saltdean.

Saltdean Slab 100 feet IV

Just around the corner from where the under-cliff walk ends at Saltdean is a slabby area of cliff sloping from left to right. This route finds a diagonal line across the slabs starting about 25 yards east of the promenade.

P. Thornhill(Solo) 4 November 1983

Brighton Rock 200 feet IV

Walking eastwards from Saltdean Slab for some 300 yards passing a lime-green coloured area is another slabby area of cliff, also sloping from left to right.

1 140 feet Follow the slab and move across to a niche on its left-hand side to belay.

2 60 feet Traverse out right and slightly up to find the easiest way through the short but steep "barrier" at the top of the cliff, giving the crux of the route.

P. Thornhill(Solo) 14 November 1983

Commandments

This list of 'Commandments' is unashamedly cliquey for the most part, in a similar vein to the one in the Yorkshire 'MESTO' guide from which the idea came. The opinions contained herein do not necessarily reflect those of the management.

1. Climbing with a tight rope makes you go blind.
2. Don't use chalk ($MgCO_3$) at Harrison's otherwise Terry "The Chainsaw" Tullis will nick your rope and keep it for ever and ever.
3. Drinking from the Old Bumblie's "BOTTI" is not recommended.
4. Don't claim any new low-level traverses - the Fat Man has done them ALL before.
5. Bowles is for poseurs, Harrison's is for traditionalists, High Rocks is for reticent bumpy boys, Eridge Green is for botanists and Bulls Hollow is for perverts - take your pick.
6. Belaying Dave Turner on new routes is not advised unless you have the odd week to spare.
7. Waders and a small sailing craft are recommended when climbing at Bulls Hollow and, remember, don't feed the crocodiles.
8. Chalk ($MgCO_3$) is now generally accepted NOT to "develop different muscles."
9. Claiming new routes at Harrison's is bound to elicit such comments as; "Done in 1932 by J.Menlove Edwards' dog."
10. Don't be persuaded to climb on the chalk ($CaCO_3$), it's very very frightening. Stick to $MgCO_3$, it's far safer.
11. Chippers will be made to drink from the Old Bumblie's "BOTTI".
12. Vacate the area if Matt "I'm definitely giving up soloing" Saunders is soloing, or you may be the one who has to pick up the bits.
13. There is no thirteen.
14. Aid climbing also makes you go blind, but worse than that it also makes a nasty mess of the rock.
15. Beware of The Crash Man and Boy Wimper 'cos they're DEATH on four wheels (usually less) and on a road near you.
16. Don't let Gary Wickham recommend routes to you - his idea of a three star route is well twisted.
17. For a long, rich and fulfilled life don't be a hold anywhere near Barry 'Brenva' Knight.
18. "We were there so we just HAD to go for it" - Mick Fowler.
19. Use a long sling so the krab hangs clear of the edge; if not, before you know it you won't have a crag to climb on. A long sling does not cost much and means a lot less damage to the rock.
20. Do plagiarize ideas from other guide-book writers.

Graded List of Selected Routes

This graded list is very much more comprehensive than previously, and consists largely but not solely of starred climbs. The number of listed climbs in each grade is a rough reflection of the relative numbers of good routes at that standard, hence the large number of 5c routes. However, most of the climbs in the top two grades have been listed as those who climb at such a standard often have a greater interest in such things - competitive as they tend to be. The list is in descending order of difficulty and the following abbreviations have been used to help locate the climbs:

BF-Bassett's Farm	Bo-Bowles	BH-Bulls Hollow
CW-Chiddinglye Wood	EG-Eridge Green	Ha-Harrison's
HR(A)-High Rocks (Annexe)	Pe-Penns Rocks	SF-Stone Farm
UR-Under Rockes.		

The dagger symbol ( ) indicates unrepeated climbs, while the letters (NS) indicate that the climb has not been soloed.

6c
Cool Bananas(HR) NS †
Them Monkey Things(Bo) NS †
Carbide Finger(Bo)
Lager Frenzy(Ha) NS †
One Nighter(Bo) NS†
Kinda Lingers(HR) NS †
Woolly Bear(Ha) NS
Judy(HR) NS
Killing Joke(Ha)
Quoi Faire(SF) NS †
What Crisis?(Ha) NS

6b
Guy's Route(SF) NS †
Nutella(Bo) NS
Dyno-Sore(HR) NS
The Crunch(EG) NS
Birdie Num-Nums(SF) NS †
Limpet(Ha) NS
The Beguiled(EG) NS
Time Waits For No One(BH) NS
Snail Trail(EG) NS
Nemesis (HR) NS
Krait Arête(HR) NS
Judy(aid start)(HR) NS
Cheetah(HR) NS
Karate Liz(BF) NS †
Temptation(Bo)
Shattered(HR)
First Crack(HR) NS
Identity Crisis(Pe) NS †
Boonoonoonoos(HR) NS
Diagonal(EG)
Double Top(HRA) NS †
Meridian(UR) NS
Roofus(HR) NS
Salad Days(HR) NS

6b continued
Moving Staircase(HR) NS
The Thing(Bo) NS
A Touch Too Much(HR)
Cardboard Box(Bo)
Sandman(Bo)
Higher Purchase(EG) NS †
Mervin Direct(HR) NS
Harlequin(CW) NS
Kinnard(Bo) NS
Honeycomb(HR)
Smile of the Beyond(EG)
The Republic(Ha) NS
Waffer Thin(EG) NS
Illusion(SF) NS
Patella(Bo)
Karen's Kondom(Ha) NS
Peapod(HR) NS

6a
Dislocator(BF) NS †
Lionheart(UR) NS
Serenade Arête(Bo)
Coronation Crack(Ha)
Going Turbo(Pe) NS †
Infidel(HR)
Robin's Route(HR)
Forgotten Crack(EG) NS
The Shield(BH) NS
Lobster(HR) NS
Firebird(HR) NS
South-West Corner(Ha)
Sandstorm(EG) NS
Sossblitz(Ha)
Craig-y-blanco(HR)
Tilley Lamp Crack(HR) NS
Top Cat(SF)
Blue Murder(Ha)
Hangover III(Ha)
Flakes Direct(Ha)

6a continued
Philippa(Ha)
Boysen's Crack(HR)
Right Unclimbed(Ha)
Steelmill(EG) NS
The Dragon(HR)
The Knam(Ha)
Fly By Knight(EG) NS
Digitalis(Bo)
Dan's Wall(BF) NS
In One Hole…(UR) NS
Kathmandhu(SF)
Nightmare(Bo) NS
Boysen's Arête(Ha)
Monkeys Bow(Ha) NS
Grant's Groove(Ha)
The Mank(Ha)
Forester's Wall Direct(Ha)
Hate(Bo)
Crucifix(Ha)
The Sphinx(HR)
Stirling Moss(EG) NS
Fandango Right Hand(Bo)
Edwards's Effort(Ha)
The Flakes(Ha)
Engagement Wall(HR) NS

5c
Finale(Bo) NS
Pseudonym(BH)
Wailing Wall(Ha)
Target(Bo)
Fork(HR)
Slanting Crack(Ha)
Crowborough Corner(Ha)
Nose Direct(SF)
Streetlife(Pe) NS
Counterfeit(Ha)
Fandango(Bo)
Obelisk(EG) NS
Girdle Traverse(SF)
Banana(Bo)
The Touch(UR)
Knife(HR)
Diversion(Ha)
Orangutang(Ha)
Cowgirl in the Sand(Pe) NS
Control(SF)
Dinner Plate(HR)
The Wall(BH) NS
Concentration Cut(SF)
Belle Vue Terrace(SF)
Coathanger(Bo)
The Pillar(EG) NS
Coronation Crack(HR) NS
Excavator(BF) NS
Toxophiiite(Ha)
The Knott(BH)
Uganda Wall(UR)
Fireball(UR)
Fandango(EG)
Baskerville(Ha)
Blackeye Wall(Ha)
North-West Corner(Ha)
Pie an' Ear-ring(Pe)
Inspiration(Bo)
Portcullis(EG)
Touch Down(EG) NS

5c continued
Quiver(Ha)
Juanita(Bo)
Odin's Wall(HR)
Demon Wall(EG)
Central Crack(UR) NS
Bludgeon(HR) NS
Bonanza(Ha)
Green Fingers(Ha)
Huntsmans' Wall(Pe)
Branchdown(EG) NS
Pig's Ear(Bo)
Bare Essentials(SF)
Lucita(HR)
Celebration(HR)
Good Route…Poor Line(EG) NS
Navy Way(HR)
Bulging Wall/Zig Nose(Ha)
Simian Mistake(HR)
Marquita(HR)
Vulture Crack(Ha)
Rift(Ha)
Slimfinger(Ha)
Jaws(HR)
Mulligans Wall(HR)
West Wall(Ha)
Cut Steps Crack(HR)
Footie(SF)
Far Left(Ha)
Luncheon Shelf(Ha)
Perspiration(Bo)
Elementary(Ha)
Birchden Corner(Ha)
Thin(SF)
Piecemeal Wall(Ha)
Blue Peter(Ha)

5b
Henry the Ninth(HR)
Lord Chumley Pootings(CW) NS
Birchden Wall(Ha)
Advertisement Wall(HR)
Drunkards Dilemma(HR)
Brenva(HR)
Cave Wall(Ha)
The Niblick(Ha)
Unclimbed Wall(Ha)
Amphitheatre Crack(EG)
Lady of the Lake(HR)
Pelmet(Ha)
Steps Crack(HR)
Spider Wall(Ha)
Pinnacle Buttress Arête(SF)
Biceps Buttress(Ha)
Swastika(Bo)
Mammoth Wall(EG)
Monkey Nut(HR)
Three Hands Route(EG)
Jackie(Bo)
Pine Buttress(SF)
Forester's Wall(Ha)
Asterix(EG)
Ken's Wall(BF) NS
Effie(HR)
Drosophila(Bo)
Scooped Slab(EG)
Monkey's Necklace(Ha)

GRADED LIST OF SELECTED CLIMBS

5b continued
Jockey's Wall(Pe)
Mick's Wall(Bo)
Hennesey Heights(Bo)
Burlap(Bo)
Swing Face(HR)
Seltzer(Bo)
Broken Nose(BH)
Woodpecker Crack(Pe)
Cat Wall(SF)
Krankenkopf(HR)
Cough Drop(HR)
Birthday Arête(HR)
Battleship Nose(HR)
Pullthrough(Bo)
Pussy Foot(HR)
Left Edge(HR)
Diagonal Route(SF)
Simian Face(HR)
Hadrian's Wall(EG)
Half-Crown Corner(Ha)
Concorde(EG)
Devaluation(Bo)

5a
Abracadabra(Bo)
ES Cadet Nose(Bo)
Simian Progress(HR)
Herbal Abuse(CW)
Larchant(Bo)
Twin Slabs(EG)
Pinnacle Buttress(SF)
Pig's Nose(Bo)
Chalet Slab Right(Bo)
S.W. Corner Scoop(SF)
Roof Route(HR)
Crack and Wall Front(HR)
Girdle Traverse(Ha)(204)
Two-Toed Sloth(Ha)
Z'Mutt(HR)
Escalator(Bo)
Middle and Off(HRA)
Sagittarius(Ha)
Four-by-Two(Bo)
Garden Slab Right(Ha)
North Wall(HR)
Stupid Effort(Ha)
Long Layback(Ha)
Leaning Crack(SF)
Bell Rock T. P. Route 1 (HR)
Eric(EG)
Zig-Zag(Ha)
Hanging Crack(EG)
Degenerate(HR)
Giant's Ear(Ha)
Purgatory(HRA)
Waistline(BH)
Grant's Crack(Ha)
Garden Slab Left(Ha)
Siesta Wall(EG)
Fragile Arête(Bo)
Battlement Crack(EG)
Nelson's Column(Bo)
Senarra(Ha)
Evening Arête(UR)
Upwards Scoop(Pe)
Bold Finish(HR)
Pince Nez(Ha)

4c
Deadwood Crack(Ha)
Hell Wall(Ha)
High Traverse(Bo)
Nealons(Bo)
Key Wall(SF)
Isolated Buttress Climb(Ha)
Valhalla Wall(HRA)
Sapper(Bo)
Slab Direct(Ha)
Starlight(Ha)
Percy Pustule Went to Town(CW)
October(Bo)
Sunshine Crack(Ha)
Slab Variant(BH)
Remus(EG)
The Vice(Ha)
Off Stump(HRA)
Wander at Leisure(Ha)
Dusk Crack(EG)
Corner Layback(Bo)
Alka(Bo)
Centurion's Groove(BH)
Crack Route(HR)
Chalet Slab Direct(Bo)
Birch Tree Wall(Ha)

4b
Lee Enfield(Bo)
Turret Face(HR)
Babylon(Bo)
Murph's Mount(Bo)
Kemp's Delight(Bo)
Long Crack(Ha)
Pegasus(Bo)
Barbican Buttress(EG)
Pop's Chimney(Bo)
Dival's Diversion(Bo)
Primitive Groove(SF)
S.E. Corner Crack(SF)
Bovril(Bo)
Port Crack(HR)
Moonlight Arête(Ha)
Tiger Wall(HR)
Conway's Crack(BH)
Kenian Crack(BF)
Possibility Wall(BH)
Long Man's Neighbour(EG)
Pothole Crack(HR)
Peter's Perseverance(Bo)
Ashdown Wall(SF)
Ricochet(Bo)
Stone Farm Crack(SF)

4a
Lawson Traverse(Bo)
Bramble Corner(BH)
Limpet Crack(HR)
Orion Crack(HR)
St. Gotthard(Ha)
Sashcord Crack(Ha)
P.E.Traverse(HR)
The Juggler(Pe)
Crack and Cave(Ha)
Sylvie's Slab(Bo)
Anaconda Chimney(HR)
Signal Box Arête(Ha)
Central Groove(Ha)

GRADED LIST OF SELECTED CLIMBS 207

4a continued
Rota(EG)
Simplon Route(Ha)
Netwall(Bo)
Right Circle(Ha)
Yoyo(Bo)
Kennard's Climb(Bo)
Funnel(Bo)
Eyelet(Ha)
Ordinary Route(HR)
Stone Farm Chimney(SF)

3b
Bow Window(Ha)
Birch Tree Crack(Ha)
Snout Crack(Ha)
The Sandpipe(Ha)
Stalactite Wall(HR)
Bulging Corner(SF)
Chalet Slab Left(Bo)
Outside Edge Route(HR)
Hut Transverse Passage Central Route(HR)
Curling Crack(SF)
Root Route 1 (Ha)
Dib(Bo)
Wellington's Nose(Ha)
Warning Rock Buttress(HR)
Pine Crack(SF)
Conway's Variation(BH)
Reclamation Slab Left(Bo)
Fragile Wall(Bo)

3a
Gangway Wall(BH)
Horizontal Birch(Ha)
Sabre Crack(Ha)
Flotsam(Ha)
Hut Transverse Passage - Rufrock Route(HR)
Sing Sing(Bo)
Charlie's Chimney(Bo)
Charon's Chimney(Ha)

3a continued
Well's Reach(Bo)
Chimney and Traverse(Ha)
Skiffle(Bo)

2b
Garden Wall Crack(SF)
Chelsea Traverse(Bo)
Grotto Chimney(Bo)
Boulder Bridge Route(Ha)
Small Chimney(Ha)
Recess Chimney(Pe)
Tame Variant(Ha)
Big Cave Route 2 (Ha)
Holly Route(HR)
The Scouter(Bo)
The Chimney(Ha)
Reclamation Slab Right(Bo)
Shelter Chimney(HR)
Brushwood Chimney(HR)

2a
Dark Chimney(Ha)
Smith's Traverse(Ha)
Medway Slab(SF)
Junend Arête(Ha)
Original Route(Ha)
Easy Crack(HR)
Giant's Staircase(Ha)
Easy Cleft Right(Ha)
Short Chimney(HR)
Windowside Spout(Ha)
Introductory Climb(SF)
Big Cave Route 1 (Ha)
Harden Gully(Ha)

1a
Yew Break(BH)
Scout Chimney(Ha)
Isometric Chimney(Ha)
Birch Crack(Bo)
Reclamation Gully(Bo)
Dinosaurs Don't Dyno(SF)
November(Bo)
Scotland Slab(HR)

Rescue — Sandstone Area

In the event of an accident where an ambulance is required either phone Terry Tullis on Groombridge 238 or dial 999. It is advisable for one member of the party to wait on the nearest road for the ambulance to direct the ambulancemen/women to the site of the accident.

At Harrison's Rocks the nearest phone is at Forge Farm (in the valley beneath the Isolated Boulder(190) to Unclimbed Wall(260) area); wait at the level crossing by Forge Farm.

At High Rocks the nearest phone is obviously in the Hotel.

At Bowles there is a phone in the administrative office near the entrance, and at the house right by the road.

At Stone Farm there is a private house on the opposite side of the road to the start of the footpath to the rocks.

APPENDIX OF NEW ROUTES

HARRISON'S ROCKS

133 Sewar Wall. From the upper ledge, the crack right of that climbed on Sewar Wall is an awkward 6a(NS).

HIGH ROCKS

214A Oven Ready Freddy 6a(NS). Start easily as for Ordinary Route but move round left on the long wide ledge. Climb with difficulty up to the two small trees.

219A The Full Monty 6b(NS). The undercut bulge just left of Breakfast Ledge, with a very difficult start. Finish direct much more easily.

M1
A1(M)
M11
M40
M25
M25
LONDON
M4
Croydon
Reigate
M25
Sevenc
M3
Guildford
A25
M23
Gatwick Airport
Crawley
East Grinstead
A31
A3
Southampton
A23
A22
M27
Portsmouth
A27
Brighton
Newhaven
Seaford
Seven Sister
ISLE OF WIGHT